what we will become

what we will become

A MOTHER, A SON,
AND A JOURNEY OF
TRANSFORMATION

mimi lemay

HOUGHTON MIFFLIN HARCOURT
Boston   New York   2019

For information about permission to reproduce selections from this book,
write to trade.permissions@hmhco.com or to Permissions,
Houghton Mifflin Harcourt Publishing Company,
3 Park Avenue, 19th Floor, New York, New York 10016.

hmhbooks.com

Library of Congress Cataloging-in-Publication Data
Names: Lemay, Mimi, author.
Title: What we will become : a mother, a son, and a journey of
transformation / Mimi Lemay.
Description: Boston : Houghton Mifflin Harcourt Publishing, [2019]
Identifiers: LCCN 2019013136 (print) | LCCN 2019980982 (ebook) |
ISBN 9780544965836 (hardcover) | ISBN 9780544965867 (ebook)
Subjects: LCSH: Parents of transsexuals. | Mother and child.
Classification: LCC HQ77.9 .L446 2019 (print) | LCC HQ77.9 (ebook) |
DDC 306.874 — DC23
LC record available at https://lccn.loc.gov/2019013136
LC ebook record available at https://lccn.loc.gov/2019980982

Book design by Kelly Dubeau Smydra

Printed in the United States of America
DOC 10 9 8 7 6 5 4 3 2 1

All photographs have been provided courtesy of the author unless otherwise credited.

Excerpt from "Ghost Story" by Nikita Gill from *Wild Embers: Poems of Rebellion,
Fire, and Beauty.* Copyright © 2017 by Nikita Gill. Used by permission of Little, Brown
and Company, a division of the Hachette Book Group. All rights reserved. "Now That I
Am Forever with Child" from *The Collected Poems of Audre Lorde.* Copyright © 1968,
1976 by Audre Lorde. Used by permission of W. W. Norton & Company, Inc. All rights
reserved. Poem by Jalal ad-Din Muhammad ar-Rumi from *Love: The Joy That Wounds:
The Love Poems of Rumi.* English translation by Elfreda Powell used by permission
of Souvenir Press, an imprint of Profile Books. "Has Anyone Seen My Chameleon?"
by Kenn Nesbitt from *The Tighty Whitey Spider.* Copyright © 2010 by Kenn Nesbitt.
Reprinted by permission of Sourcebooks, Inc. All rights reserved.

For my loves, Joe, Ella, Jacob, and Lucia

Each entered the forest at a point that he himself had chosen, where it was darkest and there was no path. If there is a path it is someone else's path and you are not on the adventure.

— JOSEPH CAMPBELL, *The Hero's Journey*

Preface

Ask me my favorite ghost story
and I will tell you the one
about your haunted house heart
still housing all the people you used to be.

— NIKITA GILL, "Ghost Story"

*H*OW DID WE GET HERE?
I set out to answer this question in March of 2015, "here" being where my family and I found ourselves a month after my essay "A Letter to My Son Jacob on His 5th Birthday" had gone viral — as inexperienced but determined advocates for transgender children. "Here" was also the climax of a remarkable five-year journey that had brought us our son, Jacob. Finally, here was the rare opportunity to write a full-length memoir about our experiences and, I hoped, to further shape public discourse on gender identity in young children.

However, sitting down to write, I discovered that the answer to the question "How did we get here?" was anything but straightforward.

When our son, Jacob, transitioned in 2014, shortly after his fourth birthday, there were few examples for us to follow and no guidebook for parents of very young transgender children. There were only a handful of therapists experienced enough to help families with transgender children Jacob's age deal with the seismic changes, at home and in the community, that a social transition entailed. At the time, "watchful waiting" was considered the best course of action for a young child who claimed a disparity between his or her gender identity and the one assigned at birth.

Relinquishing to Jacob the choice to transition was an outsize act of faith — in Jacob, in ourselves as parents, and, ultimately, in the world that would need to accept him. How I was able to come to this decision cannot be explained without reaching back to my own early years.

Shortly after her second birthday, when "Em" (a pseudonym Jacob and I chose to avoid using his birth name) started to show signs of emotional decline, the experience had an air of *familiarity* for me, a sense of déjà vu that I could not account for at the time. As I watched my vibrant toddler fade into a shell of a child, angry, distant, almost unrecognizable, bones and shards of my memories began to surface, demanding examination and claiming relevance to this new and confounding moment. Attempting to record the experience for this memoir unfolded in much the same way.

"It's like a . . . ghost story," I tried to explain to my husband, Joe, "but without the ghost." I began to suspect that the specter was *me* or, rather, a former iteration of myself, one that crooked her finger and whispered: "We're not *quite* done here yet."

As I dug up decades of correspondence and journal entries, these "ghosts," no longer content in their interment, began to whisper their own stories, shifting the narrative I had long held of my life until eventually it buckled under the weight of their truths.

The book that I set out to write is not the book I have written; neither is my answer for what sequence of events led us to the moment of Jacob's resurrection. Once I allowed myself the freedom to reexamine the narrative of my life, it began to reshape itself, past lapping at the heels of present, offering insight and interpretation until the two collided in a moment of startling redemption. What emerged was indeed a memoir but, equally, a mystery, a ghost story, and a love story.

As the author, I feel I have had a surprisingly spare role in all this, yet I have emerged from the telling of this story irrevocably changed and with a new perspective on my own history and a greater hope for my son's future.

How did we get here?

It started with a birth. A girl born in 1976 in a hospital overlooking the foothills of Mount Scopus, in Jerusalem. Her mother was her entire world, and that world, one of rarefied ultra-Orthodox Judaism, began to collapse in on her when she discovered the price she would have to pay to live an authentic life.

How did we get here?

It started with a birth. A boy born in 2010 who was his mother's world, a world that began to collapse in on itself when she discovered the price her child would have to pay to live an authentic life.

Memory, degraded by time and human subjectivity, can never claim absolute accuracy. The people mentioned in this book may recall conversations or events differently than I do. I have been fully faithful to memory to the extent that my memory has been faithful to me. Thankfully, I am assisted by a quarter century of diaries, correspondence, photographs, audiotapes, and mementos (what my husband, Joe, wryly refers to as my "hoarder's paradise"). Where memory has failed, such as in accessing the very first moment when Em planted a stake in the ground and declared herself a boy, I have stated so.

It is my fervent wish that no one will be hurt or angered by the things I reveal in this book. There are no villains here, only flawed human beings. We are all a unique composition of our desires, beliefs, greatnesses, and limitations. I say, without prevarication or exaggeration, that, given the chance, I would not trade a minute on my journey for a different one. Every moment of joy or suffering has led me to where I am today, and where I am is where I need to be. For that, I am grateful to everyone, without exception in these pages. The following are pseudonyms in order of their appearance in the book: Em, the Bialik family, Mrs. Blum, and Robbie Gold.

The deepest gratitude I offer to my husband, Joe, who has permitted, even encouraged, me to lay bare intimate details of our life and relationship in as candid a manner as possible. "If it's true, write it," he has told me often during this process. This is a testament to his strength of character and the visionary perspective that has pulled us through the dark moments. He continues to pilot us skillfully through turbulent times, encouraging me and our children to chart a course in life founded on the not-yet-possible.

I am grateful for my daughter Ella, Jacob's older sister and protector, who firmly maintains that her little brother is not the main character of this book. Revealing a characteristic precociousness, she has stated that its main characters are "love and kindness." In this, I believe she is correct. The love and compassion she has displayed throughout what was undoubtedly a time of great turmoil for herself has been and continues to be a fount of blessing for our family. She is Jacob's best friend and fiercest advocate, and I suspect, will be so for the remainder of their lives.

I am grateful for my youngest daughter, Lucia, a source of unconditional love and uncomplicated acceptance, particularly toward her older brother during his most tumultuous months. She is our vision of a world where a generation of children may simply grow up organically accepting one another's differences, whatever they may be, without attempting to define or confine them.

I am grateful for my mother-in-law, Kathy. She has, in her faith and in her strength, provided, during critical junctures, the hard-won wisdom that defines her. She has been fully supportive of Jacob, every step of the way. Shortly after his transition she pulled me aside to tell me that she had started a savings account for him "just in case" in the future he would wish to access costly gender-confirmation treatments. It takes a special woman to plan this far ahead with compassion and open-mindedness. Kathy is that woman.

I am grateful to my brother, Uriyah, for allowing me to reveal sensitive moments in our shared past and for providing invaluable insight and perspective stemming from his singular wisdom. My father, in his last years, had maintained that my brother was a *tzaddik,* a holy man. When I witness in him the unending well of kindness and almost preternatural ability to forgive, I realize that my father was right.

I am grateful for my mother, Judith. Ours is a complex love built on a complicated past, but I have no doubt that every choice she has made for her children has been true to her strong moral compass and deep, abiding faith. She has lived extraordinarily, a life founded on virtues I cannot hope to meet. I admire her. I remain wounded by her. She is a mystery I may never solve.

It is with profound gratitude that I dedicate this book to my son, Jacob.

This story is a tribute to his courage and remarkable will, of which I continue to stand in awe. He is a most precious gift to our family, opening us up to a world we never knew existed, testing our mettle and strengthening us immeasurably. He has also brought me the redemption from my past that I had long denied needing, delivering me back my faith in many things, including myself.

Children like Jacob have much to teach us about authenticity — about who we *truly* are, beneath and beyond our skin and bone. Until they are no longer punished for their nature, I will continue to speak out in the hopes that I can leave them a worthier, more accepting world.

My son, in his daily life, is not an eager sharer. Yet he continues to grant me permission to share our story, which he knows will reflect a moment in time before most people were aware of the existence of transgender children. He has done so with the understanding that not all parents accept their children's identities, and not all schools and public spaces are welcoming and safe for transgender youth and adults. I am awed by the depth of empathy and courage he displays. It is my hope that the reward for his heroism is a society where individual fulfillment need never be sacrificed for safety and acceptance.

Finally, there are those many individuals whose stories cannot be told — they do not share the privileges that have been serendipitously granted us: an accepting community, loving friends and family, physical and financial security. They are never far from my thoughts. They are not forgotten. This book is also dedicated to them. It is a prayer for their future as well as my son's. May we inherit a world that values and embraces their uniqueness. It will be a better world for us all.

Prologue

Into the Woods We Go

It's a lot easier to say when something ended rather than when it began. Most of us can recognize the end from a mile away, but the beginning always slips up on us, lulling us into thinking what we're living through is yet another moment, in yet another day.

— STEVE YARBROUGH, *Safe from the Neighbors*

THAT PARENTING WOULD TRANSFORM ME WAS EXPECTED. I wore those changes on my skin and felt them course in the marrow of my bones.

I was thirty-two when my first child, Ella, was born. My outline metamorphosed into something rounder and softer, my eyes became rimmed with the dusky purple of sleepless nights, and my previously stick-straight dark hair sprang into unruly waves, as if to mirror the onset of entropy in my life.

The internal changes, however, were far more vast — what might best be described as a benign case of possession.

I found that the heart that beat inside my chest was no longer my own. The organ had been all but replaced by that of one, two, finally three little beings whose joys and sorrows would forever steer my emotions in a way I'd be helpless to resist. In a word, I'd been *hacked.*

But even this loss of self, to an extent, I saw coming.

The unexpected changes happened in the realm of my senses. I noticed it when Ella was about nine months old and had taken to scuttling about our hardwood floors like a hybrid lightning bug/vacuum cleaner looking for objects to place in her mouth.

Joe was in the kitchen assembling the last of our new kitchen cabinets, while I was clear across the house in the sunroom stacking blocks and shelving books. Ambient noises of traffic and nature wafted through the open window, mixing with the drone of the electric drill.

Suddenly, my ears pricked, and my spine tingled. I called out to Joe: "Honey, you dropped a screw on the floor." One quick pass turned up nothing. "You dropped a screw," I insisted. "Check again!" Sure enough, there it was, a one-inch screw that had rolled under the cabinet, just within reach of a tiny pincer grasp. "How the hell did you hear that?" Joe asked. "I don't know," I answered truthfully.

On reflection I decided it was only natural that the body that had prepared me so comprehensively to give birth had equipped me to keep the product of that birth alive. From now on, formerly ignorable, undifferentiated sounds would trigger messages in my inflamed amygdala. *Danger! Danger!* synapses would fire.

Therefore, it never fails to amaze me that with my new sensory upgrade, I missed *the* moment itself.

I cannot tell you precisely when everything changed for my middle child, Em, and therefore for us.

I do not have a journal entry labeled *The Day of Great Revelation* or *The Afternoon I Began to Lose Her.*

While I can recall several of those early moments, the very first one eludes me. It has blended, shuffled into the deck with all the others, because, unlike the case of a choking hazard, my early warning system failed me.

I can only offer a vignette, one of a subsequent many, that could have been this watershed moment, but I cannot time-stamp it.

Because, even though I must have heard it happen, I don't think I was listening.

The moment I hear the cascade of Cheerios hit the hardwood of our dining-room floor, there is little doubt in my mind exactly what has been done and, furthermore, whodunnit.

The rapid-fire *pttt-pttt-pttt* reminds me of a sudden Amazonian rainstorm, pellets the size of dimes hitting wide lush leaves. I close my eyes, lingering in a crouch over Ella's school bag that I'm packing, unwilling to confront the cleanup ahead.

"Mama?" Em's gravelly voice wavers. "Mama?"

Big sister Ella, in the role of both defense and prosecution, cuts in. Accusatory: "Em knocked over the cereal, Mama!" Softening: "But she didn't mean it."

"I dudin't mean it." Em takes the cue from her three-foot-tall advocate in pigtails and overalls.

The baby gurgles, delighted, straining against the pricey Swedish bouncer, a shower gift, that rocks wildly as she kicks her feet. She nearly spills out in her efforts to reach the migrating rings that are settling into the far reaches of the room.

"I know you didn't mean it." I'm weary, and frustration creeps into my voice: "But like I told you *many times*, Em, when you wiggle around in your seat so much, you are going to knock things off the table!"

Like a well-timed punch line, Em tips off her chair and into a pile of Cheerios.

Crunch.

"I'm sorry, Mama!" Her voice sounds panicky and I instantly regret the sharpness of my tone.

Em starts to walk around, bending to pick up fistfuls of the cereal that is by now turning to powder under her feet — baby Godzilla wreaking havoc on downtown Tokyo.

Crunch, crunch.

"Em, *Mama* will clean up. Girls, *please* get your coats on!" She ignores me as she stubbornly continues to pick up cereal, her little brown Mary Janes now covered in a fine dusting of oat. *Crunch.*

"Go!" I bark, and Em jumps. "Get your coats and sit on the couch *now!*" They scramble, and I follow with my eyes as spectral Cheerio footprints make their way across the living-room rug. "You don't need to yell, Mama," says Ella and her voice sounds teary. Even baby Lucia, the youngest of the three sisters Lemay, looks at me agape, momentarily still.

I change the subject. "Why don't I put a show on for you while I clean? *Sofia the First*? Which one were you watching last night? We can finish it."

Ella's face brightens. These days, this new-breed Disney show about a spunky princess and her enchanted amulet is everyone's favorite. The episode resolves just as I toss the last Cheerios from under the radiator and lean on my broom handle to rest. The credits are rolling, and Ella and Em begin to waltz to the music. Despite the November chill, the bright morning sun pours in through the large living-room windows, dappling their dancing bodies with flecks of light. Lucia pauses in her exertions again, this time to watch her sisters, transfixed. I feel a penitent tug on my heart. These inconveniences are just that, minor blemishes in a world that is just as it should be.

Ella, ever in charge, says, "Look, Mama! I am Pwincess Sofia and Em is Pwincess Amber and Woozy is . . . what are you, Woozy?" Lucia, owner of the nickname, grunts. "You can be the bunny Clover," Ella decides.

"Ella," I caution her automatically. "Take turns being Sofia with your sister, okay?"

Em cuts into the exchange: "I not be Sofia," she announces. "I not be Amb'a. I be James."

"You can't be James," Ella declares. "James is *a boy.*"

"Ella," I say wearily, heading off this skirmish at the pass, "let

Em make her own choices, love." Thankfully, Ella seems ready to move on. "Mama, who do you want to be?"

"Let's see . . . hmm . . . not Sofia's mom — too obvious." I hoist Ella's backpack onto my left arm; the baby, now strapped into her bucket seat, I grab with the right. My keys and cell phone are tucked under my armpit. I am a morning mom, battle-ready.

"But *I* a *boy*." Em speaks softly but clearly.

"Ooh! I know!" I clap my hands. "I'm Minimus! The unicorn!"

"He is *not* a unicorn, Mama." Ella is scornful. "Unicorns have *horns*. Minimus does *not* have a horn. He is a flying *horse*."

"Okay! Okay! Don't hurt me!" I raise my hands in a pretense of fear. Our eyes meet, and we giggle. I love that she is at the age where she can laugh at herself. I love this age entirely. With four-year-olds, every day brings something new.

We tumble out the door and into our day. Sunshine bleaches memories of spilled cereal, castles of our imaginings, and things, once out of the package, that cannot be so easily squeezed back in.

1

The Interpreter of Dreams

A dream which is not interpreted is like a letter which is not read.
— BABYLONIAN TALMUD

I WAS FOUR WHEN THE WOODEN RAFT I WAS PLAYING ON became unmoored from its dock and began to float down the canal, taking me with it.

The canals that snaked their way behind the trim ranch-style homes in my grandparents' Long Island neighborhood of East Quogue, where we were spending the summer, were murky and deep. My raft was constructed of rough-hewn logs bound together with rotting rope. Alerted by my terrified shrieks and my older brother's hollers, Grandma and Grandpa's friends, our hosts for the afternoon, and my mother came pelting from the kitchen, where they had been sipping their afternoon tea.

I did not get far downstream before our host prostrated himself, half on dry land, half in the water, grabbed the mossy rope, and pulled me to safety.

I was lifted off the raft and collapsed, sobbing, into my mother's embrace. After nearly squeezing the breath from me, she held me at arm's length, and her voice, when she found it, emerged as a curious mix of fury and fear: "I could have *lost* you!"

All the adults present — my mother, the old man, and his wife — were angry at Uriyah and me. These canals were not for playing in.

On the way back to Grandma and Grandpa's home, though the hot August sun beat down on us, I felt a strange chill. My mother walked beside me, a little too fast, her lips tugged into a frown, my arm clasped in her tight grip.

"I could have swum to shore," I muttered.

"Don't be a fool!"

She squeezed my arm harder and I winced.

"Had you jumped in the water, you most certainly would have drowned or . . . *worse.*"

Despite myself, I wondered what could possibly have been worse than drowning. She soon supplied the answer.

"These canals have . . . *quicksand* underneath, Miriam. If you had touched the bottom with your feet, you would have been dragged down into it."

Quicksand? I shivered again. What was that?

"And," she continued, "if Uriyah had jumped in after you, we would never have known what had become of either of you."

That there was a substance on this earth that could disappear a kid seemed horrible enough, but even worse was the thought of my family never knowing what had happened to us. Would they imagine that we had run away? Or been kidnapped by pirates passing through on their way out to sea? Would they wait every day for our return, sitting by the large bay windows, crying as they held our things? What would my father say when my mother called to tell him we were lost? The bleakness of this image tugged at my heart.

It would be decades before I questioned whether the canals in Long Island were home to beds of quicksand, but that day was my first acquaintance with mortality, and to my four-year-old mind, evidence of it seemed to lurk everywhere.

Death even appeared on the roadside on our walk home, in the form of a matted ball of blood, fur, and viscera — a hapless squirrel insufficiently nimble to avoid the crushing wheels of one of the Olds or Buicks that occasionally rumbled down the sleepy streets of this neighborhood of retirees.

"Look!" Uriyah whispered viciously, pointing to the creature, whose guts, on display, baked on the hot asphalt. He wiggled his fingers in front of my face: "*Deeaad* like *that!*"

I kicked at his legs, but he danced just out of reach. My mother, deep in thought, ignored our exchange.

"We will not tell Grandma and Grandpa about this," she concluded. "Grandpa's heart could not take the shock. It would kill him."

More death.

As I saw my grandparents' house ahead, I broke free from my mother's grip, ran up the gravel walkway, and barreled through the screen door, which closed behind me with a bang. I didn't even spare a thought for Grandma, who had expressly forbidden the slamming of doors and all manner of loud childish exuberance, or the pointed look she would be giving me behind the rims of her glasses that were shaped like cat eyes. I sought, with singular intent, the warmth of my grandfather's arms.

I found him where I knew he would be, with the *New York Times* open on his lap, settled into the vinyl La-Z-Boy in the corner of the living room. The year 1980 was an election year, I had been informed, which resulted in the inordinate fixation, from my view, that adults took in the tight rows of letters that, squid-like, released black ink onto the fingers when touched. "Grandpa!" I climbed up on his lap, displacing the newspaper, and buried my face in the soft fabric of his button-down shirt. I soaked the thin polyester material with my tears.

"Ketzele!" my grandfather said, alarmed, using his pet name for me (Yiddish for "little cat," a name I had earned by purring over my bottle as an infant). "What's wrong?"

"I saw . . . a squirrel, and he . . . he . . . was dead," I sobbed.

"Oh, Ketzele." His fingers soothed my sweaty hair. "Shhh, now, shhh . . . it will be all right." But it was hard to stop crying for this poor squirrel whose life had ended so abruptly. Did he have a family? Would they wonder why he never came back to their tree-house again with a nut or a berry in his mouth? *We would never know what had become of you.*

When he had rocked my tears dry, my grandfather fished my favorite library book, a children's version of a Justice League comic, from the pile that we kept on the coffee table.

My tension began to ebb as I listened to the familiar words. Soon, the sounds of all my summers lulled me into sleepy security. The *tch-tch-tch* of the revolving sprinkler and the purr of the occasional passing car gave way, as evening fell, to the clink of ice against glass in Grandma's gin and tonic and the chirping of crickets.

That night my mother's sleep was broken by the sound of my piercing screams. In the soft glow of the night-light, she inspected me for signs of illness or injury. Finding none, she inquired as to what on earth had happened to me. It was a dream, I told her when I finally surfaced from its grip, but like none I had experienced before.

"I was in a deep hole in the ground!" I sobbed. "There was fire all around me in a circle, and I couldn't get out." My brother had quietly joined us. The whites of his deep-set brown eyes seemed to float on his darkly tanned face. He did not tease me or make an ill-timed joke but stood there silently.

"It's just a dream, Miriam." My mother stroked my cheek gently with her bony hand, the knuckles too large, arthritic at the age of forty-five. She smoothed my hair back from my sticky forehead. "It won't happen in real life."

"But how do you know that?" I cried. "What if it becomes true for me?"

"Ah," she answered, smiling, "a dream always *follows* its interpretation. The sages of the Torah tell us that. What you see in your dream cannot happen if we give your dream a happy ending." I was skeptical. Those sages might understand about Hashem (a Hebrew word that refers to God), but what did they know of nightmares? I was, however, willing to try.

It was Uriyah who surprised us by supplying just the right resolution to my dream. "Superman," he said, and his hands flipped and rolled on imaginary cloud banks, "flies into the burning pit and pulls you out — just in time! He puts you down outside the ring of fire, and with one huge, super breath . . ." As my mother tucked my blanket around my shoulders, I could feel myself drifting off. I loved my new dream now, and as sleep swallowed me, I continued the story in my head:

I am flying high above the clouds on Superman's shoulders: "Hold on tight!" he says as the land below zips by faster and faster. Suddenly, I see the Kotel HaMa'aravi, the Western Wall, and my Jerusalem home far below in a neighborhood of stone houses carved out of the foothills of Mount Scopus.

"I live here!" I tell Superman and he obliges me by diving in for a closer look. Soon we can even see the lemon trees that grow in our yard, and, as we hover outside the window, I point to my father, who is seated behind his desk, his head bent over his Persian Judaica books, wire-framed glasses perched low on his long nose, preparing notes for upcoming university lectures.

"This is my *abba*," I say with pride.

• • •

My father never came with us to America. New York was my mother's land.

At the start of every summer, the cabbie would pile several large suitcases into the trunk of the *monit* (Hebrew for "taxi") and begin the long drive from Neve Sha'anan, our Jerusalem neighborhood, to the Tel Aviv airport, where we would board a colossal plane, leaving my father and my home with the lemon trees behind, the former smelling of cardamom seeds and pungent aftershave, the latter of salt and huge cool slabs of Jerusalem stone. In late August, when the evenings grew dark and chilly, we would board a plane once more, heading back to our home with sand in our sandals and the promise of the holidays of Rosh Hashanah and Yom Kippur ahead.

When the summer of my dramatic "near demise" drew to a close and we returned to Israel, I brought back with me the nightmares that had begun at the canal. They filled my sleeping head with outlandish and harrowing scenes. In these dreams, I would lose my mother or my brother to some horrific accident.

"For goodness' sake, where are you getting these awful images?" my mother would fret, upset at my distress. After all, none of my favorite TV shows — *Sesame Street* and *Mister Rogers* — or even my brother's superhero cartoons featured decapitations.

We developed a ritual. Each time I suffered from night terrors, waking up in frantic tears, I would crawl out of the lower bunk of the bed I shared with my brother and into my mother's arms, where she would give my dream its absolutely essential "happy ending." As she blanketed me with the enchantment of her words, I knew for certain in my heart that no evil, no force in nature or beyond, could harm our family.

It seemed that the rabbis had been right after all. It was how we interpreted things that shaped our reality. To my view, my mother seemed to possess a rare and potent magic — the power to rewrite the gloomiest of endings and ameliorate the darkest of dreams.

I was completely unprepared, therefore, when less than two years later, her powers would fail her, and my family would fall apart.

2

The Negotiation

How the days went
While you were blooming within me
I remember each upon each —
The swelling changed planes of my body —
And how you first fluttered, then jumped
And I thought it was my heart.

— AUDRE LORDE, "Now That I Am Forever with Child"

I T'S A STICKY JULY EVENING IN 2009, WHEN THE SETTING
sun turns the trendy chartreuse paint I'm slapping on our sun-room walls a radioactive, swamp-hued green. It suddenly occurs to me, halfway up the ladder, juggling a dripping brush in one hand and a coffee mug of Malbec in the other, that I may be pregnant again.

I've been irritable (insufferably cranky, according to Joe) for over a week now and while it's never regular, my period is notably late. I set my brush down on the tray and wipe swollen, green fingers on the wet rag that hangs over the top rung. After stretching my stiff back for a moment, I head upstairs.

The set of clear plastic drawers tucked under the bathroom

sink is stuck, as usual. I have to lift the entire thing out to pry the middle drawer loose. That's where I'm keeping my conception-related paraphernalia: the ovulation kit and the pregnancy-test pee-sticks.

None of these have been touched for nearly two months. A "hiatus," that's what we've been calling it, a break from the stress of meticulously timed, results-driven lovemaking and the negotiations that, while ostensibly resolved, had stirred a simmering soup of contention between Joe and me.

"If we're going to have a second child — and you knew that I wanted a big family; I told you so before we married, and you agreed — then we shouldn't wait much longer," I'd said. I was thirty-two, heading toward the promised precipitous drop in fertility.

Joe was bearish at the prospect of adding another child to our family so soon, when Ella, at seven months, had yet to sleep through the night. Our move from a condo in Cambridge to a small house in Melrose, Massachusetts, had also saddled us with a mortgage on top of the graduate-school loans we were still paying off.

"We're not making enough money," he said, letting the accusation dangle in the air for a moment. *What about vacations? World travel? Ella's choice of whatever college she could get into?*

"She'd have a brother or sister," I retorted. "Isn't that worth more?"

"I don't know." Joe's voice wavered. He was an only child, had always been jealous, according to earlier admissions, of kids with siblings. I could see him attempt to regain his balance. "Yeah, but having a kid's expensive and it's hard work and you're not working now, so we just can't afford it."

"It's either *hard* work or *no* work at all. You can't have it both ways."

"You know what I mean! We have one income right now and you'll have to go back to work if we have two kids."

"Fine. That's fine by me. I will," I said, knowing full well that when we sat down with a spreadsheet, childcare for two would eat up most of my salary as a second-year charter-school teacher.

I wondered if our different priorities were fundamental. After all, we came from such disparate worlds, Joe and I.

Joe's mom, Kathy, had long been the primary breadwinner, as her husband, Paul, had retired early. When I met her, she was an administrator at a top-rated long-term-care facility (she later became its CEO). Delighted to finally have a daughter with whom to share hard-won wisdom, she often advised me that women could, *if* they planned and prioritized carefully, have most of it all. "There are plenty of men waiting and willing to take you down a peg or two," she would caution me in her thick Boston brogue. "Never show weakness." Kathy's belief in the power of advanced planning extended beyond the workplace to her personal life. Shortly after Christmas dinner, she would be busy setting the table for Easter, a fact that provoked some good-humored ribbing from us.

While I admired her strength and foresight, I was far fuzzier on the strategic career planning, and when it came to the thought of children, it had never occurred to me that they, like holiday dinners, needed to be planned carefully in advance and with the help of a spreadsheet. Perhaps because of my own upbringing, in ultra-Orthodox Judaism where eight or nine children were the norm, and the birth of the tenth and the first were equal causes for celebration, this perspective seemed cold-hearted to me.

The negotiations began to tip in my favor when Joe considered the kind of adventures he could have with not one "little buddy," as he called Ella, but two. The truth was, I didn't need to make a hard sell, only a persistent lobby of the idea that a lively home, even one of less means, was a happy one.

Joe's pride and the enjoyment he took in being a father were unmistakable. He had decided when Ella was born that as dad, his role was to teach his children to take risks and push them outside their comfort zone so that they could achieve their dreams. To that end, he had taken to occasionally swinging Ella upside down in a "death spiral" (in high school, Joe had been a nationally competitive pairs figure skater, so I had to believe he knew what he was doing), and he encouraged her to climb up the sides of our couch before she could crawl.

Conception, however, proved more elusive this time around. Now in high-tech sales, Joe traveled frequently. Furthermore, as new parents, we were perpetually tired and stressed out, making the schematics of baby-making less romantic than they seemed.

After several months of trying, we had sheepishly confessed to each other that we were ready for a break. Officially "off the hook," we had taken our first trip sans baby to Buffalo, New York, for a friend's wedding, returning, I now suspected, with more than a bottle of premium hot sauce on board.

Staring intently at the pregnancy test that I've set on the counter near the toilet, I now watch as a pink cross materializes in the second of two windows. I wait, breathless, for something to change, but two minutes go by and nothing does.

I grab the stick and burst in on Joe in his office, where he's standing by his desk. Thankfully he's off the phone when I jam the stick up close to his face. He steps back, hands rearing up in surprise, but then, taking in my excited grin, he looks closer at the object in my hand. His eyes widen, then go soft. "Wow . . . that's just . . . *great!*" he says, to my relief, pulling me into a tight embrace.

We are quiet for a long moment, holding each other. Then he breaks the silence: "Hoo-boy . . . I'm going to be a father of two." His eyes widen again, and he looks kind of dazed and, suddenly, so adorable that I pull him down to me for a kiss.

A blood test the following week confirms the pregnancy. A few weeks later, an ultrasound shows a pulsating object roughly the shape and size of a cashew. One hurdle of many is passed. The creature inside me possesses a strong heartbeat.

I begin to allow myself to dream. Who is this person-to-be? What will he or she look like? Recycling my old pregnancy journal but using a different color ink, I write: *I think it's a boy. I feel so* different — *nausea so bad this time.*

Unable to wait until my eighteen-week ultrasound, I splurge for one of those IntelliGender tests that claim to tell you with 80 percent accuracy if you're having a boy or a girl. *Boy* say the results. "I knew it!" I crow to Joe, but he is immediately skeptical. "These odds aren't something to hang your hat on," he says.

"Oh, pooh to you, Mr. MIT," I tease.

When it's time for the determining ultrasound, however, Joe is proven right. The test was a waste of thirty dollars. Our technician looks at the screen and tells us we are having another little girl. I am visited by a twinge of disappointment. A brother would have been nice for Ella, one of each of a set — parallel but unique experiences. "Are you sure?" I ask and the technician nods, showing us the double lines on the screen that indicate the baby's genitalia. Perhaps she senses my disappointment, because her tone is reproachful when she says: "You'll be glad to know that everything is right where it *should* be and developing perfectly. Congratulations!"

"Two sisters are the best!" my mother-in-law exclaims when we call her up on the ride home. She hasn't renewed her concerns about the home economics of our having another child since hearing that I'm expecting, and I'm relieved that she seems genuinely excited now. "What a blessing for Ella to have a sister!"

Maybe it's the hormones, but I find myself choking up when Kathy describes how her own little sister, Ellen, is one of the greatest treasures of her life. By the time we pull into the driveway, my disappointment has been replaced by a heady anticipation. Sisters! Nothing could be more perfect, I agree.

When I put Ella down to sleep for the night, the baby-name

books are right where I remember leaving them, on the tall dresser in front of my bed. After bookmarking pages and searching online, I have my shortlist. Though Ava is a top contender, I soon cross it out because this year it's too popular. Joe uses his veto privileges to nix Emmanuella and Nuala. He declares himself the savvier in regard to playground etiquette: *"Really?* You want her to be called Manny or Noola-Droola? Seriously? We might as well call her Chuck!"

Finally, we both agree on a name and it feels perfect, clean and melodious, modern yet feminine. In short order we add a middle name, Irene, a nod to Joe's beloved French-Canadian grandmother, Mémé Irene. I sing the full name to myself, Em Irene Lemay, wondering what it sounds like from inside the walls of my womb.

When I tell my mother that we've chosen the baby's name, she asks what her Hebrew name will be. I don't plan on using the Hebrew often, as it's only there as a cultural touchstone, but I promise my mother I'll come up with one shortly.

Within a day or two, I've decided on Michal, short for Michaela, which is the exultation "Who is like God?" It's one of the names I'd envied growing up because, to me, it sounded strong and hip, the opposite of my given name, Miriam, which had clacked like false teeth and smelled like a dusty attic. I had harbored such a dislike for the name Miriam that in the fifth grade I had come to school one day with the request that, moving forward, people should call me by the nickname Mimi (rhymes with Jimmy).

To my joy, my teachers and classmates took immediately to my nickname, in common use for girls named Miriam. My mother, however, had flatly refused to call me Mimi, leading to years of awkward moments when new acquaintances would ask my mother why she referred to me as Miriam. "I *named* her Miriam." She would deliver the punch line, clicking her tongue and tapping her clogs in delight, while I stewed.

It's my mother who now suggests a Hebrew middle name for

the baby, Esther, and I must admit, it's a good choice. The baby is due on March 2, which corresponds to the Hebrew day for the festival of Purim this year. Purim, along with Hanukkah, had been one of my favorite holidays as a child. Neither required interminable days in synagogue or refraining from all work, including using electricity and driving cars. Purim was the fun holiday, a day of masquerading, where children in costumes paraded through the streets delivering baskets of goodies, called *mishloach manos,* to neighbors and friends.

Learning about the holiday's origin and meaning in school, I had admired Purim's gutsy heroine, Queen Esther of Persia, delighting in the overarching theme of the day: *Nahapochu,* whose closest translation might be an O. Henry–esque denouement where everything is turned on its head. Nothing is as it appears; in fact, everything is just the reverse.

In Esther's very nature, the sages of the Talmud tell us, was embedded the quality of hiddenness, like the masks we donned for Purim, those that shielded our true identities. In this central body of Judaic law and lore, the name Esther itself derives from the word *hester,* meaning "hidden." Unlike other open miracles we celebrate in the Jewish calendar, Purim's covert redemption is cobbled together from coincidence and spectacularly good timing. As such, Purim is the antithesis of the over-the-top Charlton Heston–type miracles of Passover, with its raining plagues, burning bushes, and parting seas.

In the Purim story, the young Jewess Esther, ward of her uncle Mordecai, is chosen through a bizarre beauty contest to be the new queen of Persia after the old queen, Vashti, is executed. Is it good fortune or merely prudence that accounts for Esther's decision to keep her Jewish provenance a secret from her royal husband? Hard to tell. What about the fact that Mordecai's long-standing archenemy, the anti-Semite Haman, happens to be viceroy to the king? It's a leap, but it's possible. Surely, it isn't likely that Mordecai would be the sole witness to a plot to kill the king that puts him — and Esther — in the position to deliver a coup de grâce to the evil Haman, saving the Jewish people from decimation? Perhaps, but not out of the realm of possibility . . . and so on.

Purim delivered on the message of deus ex machina, God's hidden hand, hence the meaning behind Esther's name. As a woman, she would further symbolize, the sages maintained, the feminine aspect of God, the Shechina, which follows the nation of Israel into periods of exile and darkness. She is the shadowy moon to the brilliant sun of Yahweh.

My mother is ecstatic with the Hebrew name Michal Esther and promises to start working on a speech for the baby's ritual naming ceremony, to take place within a few months of her birth.

I had initially objected to the large gathering she had planned for Ella's ceremony not two years back. "Please do this for me?" my mother had asked. "Kathy has Christmas and Easter and even all the Jewish holidays with you. This is the one thing I have." I bit my tongue at the time, wanting to remind her that her absence from our holiday table was by her choice alone, that she would be welcome to join us for a Passover Seder or a Rosh Hashanah dinner such as we celebrated them. Saying so would have been meaningless, I knew. Our holidays, like our home, were not kosher enough, stripped of the thousands of laws that dictated her daily life. If a baby-naming party was something we could share from our faith, then so be it.

It's been a fairly uneventful pregnancy, and finally, we are a month away from the birth. A second crib has been purchased and assembled; the fancy Bugaboo single stroller that I just *had* to have for Ella was sold on Craigslist for pennies on the dollar, and we've chosen a functional, pared-down double stroller as its replacement. And, surreptitiously, I have purchased matching dresses, outfits, and frilly hats for "the girls," as I now refer to them.

My hospital bag lies open on the floor near my bed, gathering toiletries and other supplies. Almost all conversation revolves around Em's arrival, with Ella asking several times a day: "Baby hee-ya?" "Soon!" I respond.

When my bellybutton finally protrudes, going from an innie to an outie, Ella, at sixteen months, has yet to walk independently. She's been receiving services from our local Early Intervention program for speech and gross motor delay and is making measurable progress in both but still hasn't mastered the coordinated dance of arms, legs, and trunk that walking entails. "I suppose that will come soon enough," I say. "Nonsense!" says Kathy. "You can't be carrying two babies and recovering from childbirth!" and so then and there, she gently props up Ella by the scruff of her shirt and commands in a voice that will brook no resistance: "*March!*"

I hold my breath as a look of fierce determination crosses Ella's face. She narrows her bright green eyes, her thick auburn brows knitting themselves into a single line. After a harrowing moment of buckling and swaying, she takes her first wobbly steps around the kitchen island. Joe and I lean forward, afraid to make a sound, not wanting to risk breaking her concentration. Within a lap, Grammy is able to let go of Ella's shirt and shadow her from behind. Despite a few near tumbles, I can see the fire lit in Ella's eyes, and just like that, she's walking.

"That's my girl," says Joe, beaming. Kathy too is flushed with pride, and with good cause. She has engineered this moment of triumph. She has taught her granddaughter to walk.

"You're *ready!*" I say. "Ella is ready to be a big sister!" Elated but exhausted, Ella drops to her knees and crawls over to me. Propping herself up, she places a small hand on my distended stomach. "Baby," she says. "Em," I respond. "Baby Em."

At that moment, I realize that we are all as ready as we will ever be and that this — all of this — is very good.

• 3 •

The Sabbatical

In that part of the book of my memory before which is little that can be read, there is a rubric, saying, "Here beginneth the New Life."

— DANTE ALIGHIERI, *La Vita Nuova*

A T THE START OF THE SUMMER THAT I TURNED SIX, MY mother, brother, and I once more crossed the Atlantic to the ranch house in East Quogue, Long Island. I thought nothing of the fact that we had loaded several extra suitcases into the *monit,* but when the evenings turned crisp with the promise of autumn, instead of making our way back to my father and the tiny grove of lemon trees, we headed northward with our belongings. Our destination was Boston, Massachusetts, and, more specifically, the town of Brookline, home to a small but vibrant community of devout religious Jews just outside the city.

"A sabbatical year" was what my mother called it. The time would be spent completing her requirements for a PhD in philosophy at Boston University so that she could work as a well-paid professor like my father when we returned to Israel.

We moved into a subterranean apartment on Beacon Street,

part of a string of brownstones owned by the Bostoner Rebbe and his sons. Rabbi Levi Yitzchak Horowitz was the leader of a small Hasidic dynasty and the shepherd of a modest flock living in Brookline; they had a school, a synagogue, two kosher food stores, and a purveyor of books and assorted Judaica. The rebbe let some of his apartments at a discount to impecunious Jewish families who came to Boston for its world-class medical facilities. Though our purpose here was not health-related, my mother, on her own with two children, merited similar consideration, and partly in exchange for the reasonable rent, she worked several afternoons a week as secretary to the rebbe.

After dropping our bags in the threshold, my brother and I excitedly checked out our new digs. "Ima!" I called to my mother, discovering that our apartment had one glaring deficiency. "There's only one bedroom! What about Abba? Where will he sleep when he comes?"

"He will stay in Israel for this year," my mother explained. "When he visits us, he can rent one of the short-term apartments in this building." "But . . . but he has to stay with us!" I stammered, the tears welling up. We were a family, and families lived together. That was the way it had to be. This plan for which I had been so excited was rendered terrible! Unthinkable! I imagined that if I cried hard enough, both my *ima* and my *abba* would change their minds. My mother laid this idea to rest, gently picking me up off the floor.

"Abba has an important job at the university," she said stiffly, referring to the Hebrew University in Jerusalem where he had created and chaired the Department of Judeo-Iranian Studies and where he was revered by students and colleagues, as well as presidents and prime ministers, for his knowledge of Iran. "He will come when he *wants* to come."

I dismissed the suggestion that he didn't want to be with us every day as ridiculous. I knew that my *abba,* who called me his

Maryam'eh j'an in a musical language and waltzed me on the tops of his feet while he laughed from deep within his belly, would wish to visit me frequently.

As the days coalesced into weeks, then months, I pined for my *abba*. As I fell asleep at night on the metal-framed cot beside my brother in the tiny apartment's sole bedroom, while my mother kept the watches of the night seated at her typewriter, sleeping on the daybed that would miraculously transform into our couch with the help of a kiwi-green bedspread and some artfully placed cushions, I would imagine what Abba was doing back in Jerusalem.

Was he dressed in army fatigues like the shadowy memory I had of him improbably filling our doorway on his way to the Negev or Golan for a fortnight of training exercises? Was he playing the violin whose mournful strains had soothed me during my frequent childhood bouts of respiratory illness? Perhaps he was serving up fragrant dishes overflowing with saffron rice, with various *khoresht,* stews of lamb or beans, to guests who came to sit on the floor and feast on ambrosia and my father's quick wit. While I knew little Hebrew (despite being a *sabra* — native-born Israeli likened to a prickly pear — it was my American mother who raised me) and no Farsi, I recognized my father's jokes by the sidesplitting howls of laughter that punctuated his stories. No, not this. I couldn't imagine Abba laughing without his *zhaleh,* the name my Persian *savta* (Hebrew for "grandmother") had conjured for me. "*Zhaleh* is the first frozen dewdrop of dawn," my mother had once explained.

As the weather in Boston turned cold, then colder, I experienced the enchantment of my first snowfall. My mother would take us for long walks over the frosty earth on Sabbath afternoons and we went sledding in Dean Park on Sundays, when we were allowed to carry our sleds without violating the Sabbath restriction of transporting objects over the threshold from public to private domains.

Despite these winter delights, I pined for Jerusalem and my father and continued to badger my mother: "When is he coming?" "When can we go home?"

One day I pushed her too far, crying: "Things were better when Abba was here!"

"You don't remember his anger," my mother burst forth, pausing with her lips pursed before saying, "or the way he teased and teased Uriyah until he writhed in pain, or the way he demanded quiet and obedience always so that he could do his work, which was all-important to him." She was right, I did not remember these things, though I held one memory gingerly by its sharp edges: the night my brother and I were giggling in our bunks past bedtime, and in punishment, my father brought a long wooden stick sharply against my backside.

Still, I would not let the matter go. It was my brother who finally broke the news to me. Perhaps he tired of hearing me beg or perhaps he wanted to make me cry, as he frequently did when the mood came over him. We were *never* going back, he said. We had left Abba and Israel forever. Abba and Mommy, as we had now taken to calling her in the way of American kids, were getting a divorce.

I cried heavy, despondent tears that day, at first refusing to believe my brother. "Mommy," I begged, "tell Uriyah he is lying!" My mother's silence indicated that he was not, so I beat my fists against her. I told her she had ruined my life. I told her she had ruined our family. But I soon tired of my rage and curled into her lap for comfort because I loved her deeply and needed her now more than ever.

I accepted that my *abba* was different than us in significant ways. He did not keep Shabbat, and when he eventually came and stayed for a week in the apartment down the hall, the lights would go on and off on a Saturday by the flick of his fingers as opposed to the elaborate system of timers that my mother had rigged up to our lamps and the hotplate that kept our Sabbath food warm.

My mother asked that he wear a yarmulke when he was with us, but what he would pull out of his pocket was a cheap white satin cap, very different from the large black velvet ones that the men of our congregation wore. His yarmulke frequently sat askew on his thick, slightly too long mane of salt-and-pepper hair, and he would laugh and joke about it as if this charade were just *too* ridiculous. My mother would press her lips into a thin line. "He doesn't respect our beliefs," she'd say, glowering.

When Abba was in the room she was noticeably less talkative, and when she did talk (mostly to us; she rarely addressed him directly), her voice seemed unnaturally loud and shiny. I felt torn during these times. It angered me when my father laughed at her or made her seem silly, but I also adored him, and I acknowledged that my mother was too strict, too unyielding. "Yehudit is a saint," my father would tell us, but like a martyr's, he believed, her life was extreme and joyless. He did not want to see us raised like that. "There is another way," he said.

Boston brought several subtle but significant changes to our family. While we were in Israel, all accessible food was kosher, or at least kosher *enough,* but now we had to check carefully for the kashrut symbols on the foods we bought at Star Market. I had discovered the distinction between kosher and *treif* — meaning "impure" — food at the day camp I attended in Boston while my mother settled us into our apartment. It must not have been a Jewish camp, for on a field trip to the Children's Museum, a kind counselor bought me a hot dog when I forgot my packed lunch on the school bus. That evening, talking a mile a minute about the day, I mentioned the delicious hot dog I had eaten, at which my mother, to my surprise, became upset. *Treif* was unhealthy, she explained, though not for my body, like sugar or food dye (my mother was an early believer in organic and health food) but for my soul. The following summer I attended a strictly Orthodox camp.

When we first arrived in Boston, my daily uniform was composed of shorts and short-sleeved T-shirts, suitable for both scorching, arid Israeli summers and hot and muggy New England ones. Within a month of my starting to attend the only ultra-Orthodox Jewish school in Boston at the time, known locally as Lubavitch, after the Hasidic sect that ran it, the T-shirts in my drawer were replaced with long-sleeved shirts and the shorts and pants with skirts that covered my knees, to be worn regardless of the season.

From now on, I would be expected to follow the rigorous laws of *tzniut,* modesty, in both dress and comportment. A woman's skin from her collarbones to her wrists and to the bottom of her kneecaps was considered *ervah,* of a sexually enticing nature. Of course, as a child of six I knew nothing and cared less about these things, and I chafed at having to ride my bike and swing from monkey bars in clothes that were clearly unsuitable for either pursuit. Adding insult to injury was the fact that my brother did not have to change a thing about his outer aspect save for the yarmulke bobby-pinned to his smooth black hair. It was there to remind him of God's watchful presence above, something, I would have said, that did not seem to be working at all.

Clothing wasn't the only way that my life began to diverge from my brother's. During morning prayers while I thanked God for creating me "according to His will," my brother would intone: "Blessed art Thou, O Lord, Master of the Universe, who has not made me a woman."

What was so bad about being a woman, I fumed, that it required a prayer of gratitude for having avoided such a fate? The women raised the children and kept the home, my teacher explained, and were therefore exempt from time-bound mitzvoth, commandments, such as prayers over the new moon each month. "The men are thanking God for giving them more mitzvoth to perform," she said confidently, but I wrinkled my nose in suspicion and she did not meet my gaze.

Perhaps the blessing referred to the *mechitzah,* I speculated, the tall curtain dividing the men's and women's sections at our synagogue. On interminably long Sabbath mornings, my brother sat with the men, beholding the beautiful wooden ark that housed the Torah scroll, and the *bimah,* lectern where the cantor would chant the long prayers and receive responsa from male congregants. Women were not permitted to join in the songful prayers out loud, as a woman's singing voice was considered, like her skin, *ervah.* Perhaps this then was the cause for blessing. Men were thanking God for the gift of raising their voices in song. I too enjoyed singing, but I knew that when I turned twelve, and bat mitzvah, my voice would no longer be welcome in public.

The synagogue became my least favorite place during the Sabbath and holidays. After I sat for several hours on the hard benches, my hindquarters would turn numb and my mind would wander. I itched to play with the other children who had long since fled their parents and were running up and down the hallways. Every so often an adult would poke his head out of the door of the prayer room and sharply rebuke whichever child was unlucky enough to have been caught passing by.

At these times my mother would bend her head and whisper, "I am proud of you," as she patted my hand. "You are civilized and well-behaved, not like those wild children."

Oh, but how I longed to be wild! The consequences, I imagined, couldn't be so bad if these children and their parents returned every week. Seeing my glumness, my mother would add, "Miriam, don't forget, you're *better* than that. Besides," she cautioned me, "our situation is less . . . stable than other families. We are here out of the kindness of the rebbe. We are living in his apartment for about half of what it's worth and we pay no synagogue dues."

I could not deny this argument. And being the daughter of the rebbe's secretary did indeed have some perks. On days when my mother typed up his correspondence and sorted through his mail, the rebbe's wife would sneak me helpings of hot, salty chicken or savory kugel that had been baked for the Sabbath or for an upcoming *simcha* (celebration). My mother was also able to save me piles of colorful junk mail to cut out and paste into scrapbooks, a pursuit that kept me happy for hours. If my boredom during Sabbath services was required, it was a price I would have to pay.

Despite my mother's expectations for her children's civility, a wildness seemed to afflict my brother. Barely a week went by that my mother did not need to beg forgiveness for his exploits either at synagogue or at school.

To make matters worse, the Lubavitch school, whose singular aim appeared to be the conversion to this sect of as many Jews as possible while providing the bare minimum of educational value necessary to stay open, had no idea how to handle my brother.

It wasn't just that my brother, who was bright and curious, couldn't focus on his studies, or that he refused to follow directions, or even that he would pull dangerous stunts, like climbing to the school roof or getting into fisticuffs with the gangs of Russian boys who proliferated at our school during the height of the Jewish diaspora from the Soviet Union. It was *all* these things combined and then an unquantifiable something more — what my mother would identify as my brother's faulty genetics. He was *like his father.*

The reason that my brother twisted the arm of my doll Becky and laughed while I cried was that he was *like his father.* The reason he was impervious to all the rules of civilization and thought that pulling the school fire alarm was a lark was that he was *like his father.* As my brother was condemned to follow in the path of a man whom at this point he barely knew, his fits of anger became increasingly violent and insupportable.

If I was lucky, I could forecast the coming storm and was able to hide, hunkering down behind a book. If I did not or if I dared stand up to my brother, I suffered the consequences of bruises and broken toys. My mother, while nursing my wounds and drying my tears, would beg me to stop provoking my brother. I learned to hate that word, *provoke,* with a passion. It meant that, somehow, I was responsible for bringing my brother's violence down on my-self. To my six-year-old mind, it became synonymous with injus-tice.

Although I often bore the brunt of his anger, my brother was also my closest, and often sole, playmate. No one could outdo him at fantastical Lego creations or at the elaborate space battles we enacted with our Star Wars action figures. We created kingdoms out of milk crates, taking trips to exotic lands in the airplanes we manufactured out of cardboard. Despite having little money to spare, my mother ensured that we had the tools with which to take these flights of fancy, subscribing to *National Geographic* and buying us books and maps.

Though I was keenly aware that my brother's behavior was, as my mother put it, "outside the norms of civilization," I still defended him vigorously, fists raised against schoolmates who called him "crazy" or "weirdo." With his dark skin, he was often taunted for being a *shvartze,* the Yiddish word for "black." He re-sponded with increased wildness and more dangerous stunts. Two years into our sojourn in Boston, Lubavitch closed its doors to my brother. Left with no other choice, my mother sent him to public school.

There were days when my mother worried aloud about the fu-ture, about whether we could "make it" as a family. As a single mother with two children, she had sacrificed a lot, she explained solemnly. A friend had even suggested that she "might have been better off having left the kids behind in Israel." Though I loved my *abba,* I was horrified at the thought that a mother could abandon her children and dumbfounded that this friend, a caring mother of eight, could consider a child expendable. If my mother herself hadn't told me, I wouldn't have believed it. My mother was quick to reassure us that she loved us too dearly for that; however, she expected cooperation. And by and large, that is what she received from me. While I was too frightened to prod her for details of what happened when a family couldn't "make it," my vivid imagination could conjure up plenty of undesirable scenarios.

Despite our tenuous situation, I was a cheerful, optimistic child, designated "Little Miss Sunshine" by a family friend. To be sure, I was far from perfect. Though generally eager to please, I was also given to pride and a sense of my own cleverness, and there was no dare that I could refuse, as accusations of cowardice were unbearable to me.

That's how I ended up rapping my classmate Vitali's knuckles with a ruler in the fourth grade and punching my friend Toby in the face (impressed with my follow-through, she forgave me immediately; our principal, Mrs. Hellman, did not). It was how I ended up sitting through my last few months of fourth-grade Hebrew classes banished to the third grade with the babies after the Israeli gym teacher the school had hired to teach us Chumash (the Five Books of Moses) took umbrage at a joke I made at his expense and threw me against a desk. The teacher remained, while I was confined to staring at the wall of the third-grade classroom for several long months, where I could not see, nor benefit from, any instruction. My failings notwithstanding, in comparison to my brother, I was the golden child; my mother frequently expressed her satisfaction with me.

By the time my brother neared the close of sixth grade and I the fourth, it was clear he was on the brink of expulsion from public school as well. He was seeing a therapist, someone my mother had found who, she claimed, respected our life as Orthodox Jews, and they had discussed sending Uriyah to a therapeutic school. I was hazy on the details of what therapy it was that could be applied to control my brother, but the prospect that I could lose yet another family member was stark and terrifying.

As many children do when faced with an unraveling family, I became the peacemaker. I begged my mother not to send my brother away, and I begged my brother to behave — to do his homework without a fuss, to chew quietly with his mouth closed, to say more yes and less no, to stop the troublemaking. I cowered before their rage, trying to soothe one and then the other. At night, in my dreams, both of them died over and over, and the terror of this experience was nothing a prayer could fully ameliorate.

On a particularly horrible, frustrating day, I heard my mother say something to my brother that seemed unimaginably cruel: "I wish you had never been born."

"How can you *say* that?" I asked, outraged. I felt cut, even though the wound was not intended for me. "It would be better for him not to have been born than to behave outside the norms of society like this," she explained. "He is destroying his own future."

My brother's behavior worsened, my mother continued to rue the day of his birth, and the question of whether or not my brother had a future became an anxiety-provoking speculation for me. And so I waited. I waited for him to fall into the path of an oncoming train when he danced, laughing, just out of reach of my panicked mother on the trolley platform. I waited for him to catch rabies from the raccoons and alley cats that he would corner and try to befriend. And I waited for him to be carted off by menacing men in white coats, perhaps in the middle of the night when we would least expect it, to some institution far away, there to be made into a new boy, a better version of himself. One that everyone would wish had been born.

• 4 •

Hello, Princess

One must still have chaos within oneself to be able to give birth to a dancing star.

— FRIEDRICH NIETZSCHE, *Thus Spake Zarathustra*

I am thrashing violently on the floor of the cold, dark ocean. No matter how hard I twist and turn, I cannot free myself, as I seem to be caught around the waist in a vise. Pain blooms in my abdomen, tentacles of blood unfurling in the water from a gaping hole in my stomach. I am wet and cold. I must be dying.

Sleep displaces reality which displaces sleep, for what feels like a long time until I drag myself into full wakefulness. My dream has fled but I'm still uncomfortably cold. And yes, I am indeed wet. How badly did I sweat in my sleep? I reach my hand down under the covers and discover that the sheets are soaked, as are my pajama pants. Too wet.

The pain blooms again from my midsection, a devastating wave that starts off as a massive cramp and ends in agony so severe that the pain radiates to the tips of my fingers. Finally, I understand.

"Joe!" I shake him excitedly, and it feels like an effort to reach across the narrow valley formed by our twin beds (the reality of pairing a light sleeper, me, with a shuffler, him). "Joe!"

He groans and snorts, rolls over, but does not wake.

"Joe! My water broke!" I wait.

"Whaa? Oh my God! Oh *my God*." His voice climbs as he leaps out of bed, his sudden verticality comical.

The February morning has yet to break. It is pitch-dark outside as, giddy and giggling, we bump into each other in the dim glow of the bathroom night-light. Sitting on the bathmat, on a pile of towels, I dial our obstetrician's emergency line. When the voice on the other end asks in a bored tone for the strength and frequency of my contractions, I become confused. Are they a five or an eight? Are they getting closer together or not? We were supposed to time this, I remember.

The on-call doctor phones back in a few minutes and it seems we are heading to the hospital today. I've got one C-section under my belt, and the doctor is risk-averse, so he wants me to come in. "I am going to try for a VBAC," I say, anxious to let him know that my preference is a vaginal birth this time, despite the previous surgery. "Come in as soon as you can," he says.

Nevertheless, Joe and I decide to shower quickly. It will be a long day. I even apply some makeup, conscious of the photographs I will want to take and disseminate when the baby arrives. Joe shakes his head wryly at my vanity. "You look beautiful," he says. "Let's go already!" But I linger, and it's not just because I want to apply my mascara and blush. I am struck that these are my last few moments as a mother of one. There is no denying the huge changes ahead, and in the near dawn I don't feel quite ready. Finally, we tiptoe into Ella's nursery; my mother is here visiting, and she'll stay with her. Joe bends low over the wooden crib rails to kiss her cheek, a feat I can no longer accomplish: "Goodbye for now, big sister," Joe whispers. I kiss my palm and reach down to plant the kiss on her soft skin. "See you soon, big sister," I whisper, and we slip out of the room.

It's nearly six thirty a.m. when we venture downstairs to grab our coats and boots. My mother is fast asleep in the sunroom, and yet, when we call her name, she emerges from the darkness with startling alacrity. The snood, looking like an old-fashioned nightcap, that covers her hair is askew, so short, pure white tufts stick up at odd angles. Blinking in the light, she reminds me of one of the dwarves from *Snow White*. I experience a rare moment of unencumbered affection seeing her so uncomposed.

The plan has been rehashed a half a dozen times, but my mother still peppers us with questions. Joe attempts to artfully disengage; I am more direct. "Stop it, Mom!" I say. "We're off!"

With kisses blown and assurances given for timely updates, we start down the driveway, bracing ourselves against the freezing February air, blinking at the sun that had, during our preoccupied moments, chosen to rise.

"You know, you could have been nicer," Joe says. "She's trying," he adds.

"Mmm," I mumble.

We decide to pick up a little sustenance before hitting the highway to Boston. Joe runs into our local café for raspberry croissants and coffee while I wait in the slowly warming car, my breath emerging in plumes over my phone as I send out messages to family and friends: *Today's the day!* My words sing. *Em is coming!*

We manage to beat the commuter crush and pull into the garage in the bowels of the hospital at a few minutes past seven. The contractions are persistent but the doctor who finally examines me declares my cervix uncooperative. A test, however, reveals the presence of meconium (indelicately: the baby's first poop) in my amniotic fluid, so an abridged countdown begins. I must deliver soon due to a high risk of infection. A little Pitocin is administered through a drip, and labor kicks off in earnest.

When the epidural's offered, I eagerly accept it to ease my pain, remembering the birthing class we took to prepare for Ella. Joe and I were each asked to rate what we estimated my tolerance for pain to be and write the number down on a paper. We laughed when we discovered we both had written a zero on the page. I had no intention of being brave; not then, not now.

Chills are the first indication that I have a rising fever, a symptom of uterine infection. Then the heart monitor strapped to my abdomen begins to send off little alarms as the baby's heart rate spikes and dips, spikes and dips, then spikes and remains elevated. A dose of Tylenol is applied through my IV, but my temperature stays high.

In a moment, without warning, I throw up the remains of my raspberry croissant, and the spew covers the front of my hospital gown. The wet towel that Joe and the nurse use to wipe me down hurts because it racks my body with chills.

The obstetrician comes back into the room and, sitting on the edge of my bed, takes my hand in hers. Her eyes are sympathetic, but her tone is brisk. "I know you wanted to have a VBAC . . . but for the safety of the baby and yourself, we recommend a C-section at this point."

She looks like she's prepared for an argument, but I'm shaking with cold and covered with partially digested raspberry goo, so I nod, grateful. Moments later, several orderlies and a nurse come to wheel me into the operating room, and with time for just a swift kiss, Joe is whisked away to scrub up.

They had reminded me that it would feel like someone was "moving furniture" in my belly. Now I am sure that these movers have dropped a piano. Sharp, intermittent pain tastes metallic in my mouth. The brows of the perky young anesthesiologist are furrowed. She adjusts the medication through the tube in my back, but I insist that I still feel the scalpel, so she and an assistant use a nasty-looking needle to inject the painkillers directly into the layers of tissue surrounding my abdomen. It's called a block, she explains. While it doesn't in fact block all sensation, the pain becomes more manageable.

Work continues. I close my eyes to marshal my senses back into the space in my mind that I am creating for this moment. It takes every ounce of effort to pull myself back from the bright lights, from the sounds of movement and purpose and electronic devices, from the cold of the operating room.

I find my breath and follow it, in and out, in and out, alert as I can be, waiting to catch hold of the sound as it comes fleeting through the operating-room din; I cannot see beyond the blue curtain that separates my head and shoulders from the rest of me. Seventeen months ago, in perhaps the same room, I heard Ella's voice for the first time. That high-pitched, furious caterwauling had shot through me like a cleansing flame, and I'd sobbed helplessly, feeling more ecstatically real, more joyfully alive, than I had felt before or since.

I want that moment back. It is for this sound that I brace myself. To my annoyance, I feel someone dab at my eyes, where the tears of anticipation have begun to flow. "Don't ruin your mascara!" a nurse remonstrates. I pull away, turning my head to the side. She is quiet. I hope I have not offended her.

All at once I feel it. A tug, a release — perhaps only in my head? But no, there is an increase of noise and movement, a countdown, the command to lift, and I know, I just know with a certainty, that my daughter, my Em, is out in the world. But as soon as I begin to crest this wave of joy, my heart thuds to a stop.

There is no sound. No soul-cleansing wail.

Speak, I will her, *speak or my heart will never beat again.*

This moment feels like death.

Then I hear it. It is not a whimper or a cry; it is neither a high-pitched keening nor a squall. It is a bellow of surprising strength, an angry roar, a trumpet heralding an arrival: *Here I am!* My feelings, overwhelming relief, joy and gratitude, are huge. It's not the experience I had anticipated, but still, infinitely precious. I begin to laugh while I am still crying, and the tears and the laughter mingle in the grace of this moment and this is, I am certain, all the heaven I will ever want, or get.

The moment is fractured again when my anesthesiologist calls from the poor vantage of my side of the curtain: "It's a *boy!*"

"*No!* Not a boy!" My voice is sharper than I intended.

"Oh, ah! Yes, not a boy," she quickly affirms, and I forgive her instantly, and we all laugh again. This story we will savor, laugh about, enjoy as we tell and retell our adventures in the days to come.

Soon, wrapped in a white towel with thin pink and blue stripes, a tiny bundle is placed by my head. It is time for a quick first kiss before my daughter is whisked away to be weighed, cleansed, and inspected. I turn my head, the only part of my body that moves under my direction, and gaze at the small face, now at peace, beside me.

She is so beautiful. A thatch of thick dark hair peeks out from underneath a pink knit cap. Her forehead is round and broad, her skin rosy and unblemished. Little eyelashes delicate as strands of silk lie on soft cheeks. Any inspection would be superfluous; she is perfect.

I brush her forehead with my lips, inhaling her sweet, musky fragrance.

"Hello, princess," I whisper. "I am your mama."

• 5 •

Down the Rabbit Hole

In another moment down went Alice after it, never once
considering how in the world she was to get out again.

— LEWIS CARROLL, *Alice in Wonderland*

ACCORDING TO MRS. STERN, IT WAS *HASHGACHA PRA'TIS,*
"divine intervention," that led her and her husband to take
up temporary residence in the adjacent apartment, though her elderly mother's doctors might have argued that it was her cancer
that drew them to Boston. Whatever the reason, the Sterns were
there at the period of my brother's imminent crash and burn, in
time to regale my mother with stories about the Orthodox Jewish haven of Monsey, New York, and provide an alternative to the
threat of therapeutic school.

To my nearly ten-year-old ears, Monsey did indeed sound like
the Promised Land. While Boston had a handful of kosher retail-
ers, Monsey laid claim to dozens of kosher food emporiums and
restaurants. In Boston, there were two Jewish schools (and the
good one, Maimonides, had been prohibitively expensive and too
lax in matters of religion); in Monsey there were at least ten in-

stitutions. In Monsey you could find *frum* (religiously observant) doctors, dentists, plumbers, EMTs, and bus drivers. If one chose, and many did, one need not interact with gentiles or secular Jews (called *frei*, for "free") at all.

Most significant, while Boston's *frum* community stood embattled against the pressures of outside influences, Monsey's had, through sheer numbers and by calculation, fought its way to *becoming* the establishment, occupying seats on city councils, zoning, and even school boards for institutions their children would never attend — positions that they used ruthlessly to their advantage.

By the start of summer, and with an offer for us to stay with them while we got settled in, the Sterns had convinced my mother to move to this land of opportunity. There was no school left for Uriyah here, my mother explained. In Monsey, we would have a far bigger community and access to many resources.

I was excited for our move, eagerly helping my mother pack the contents of our small apartment into discarded liquor-store boxes. With the proceeds from selling the color TV that my mother's brother Rick had given us, we hired a moving van to make the four-hour drive south to New York, where we moved into a neighborhood populated entirely by Hasidic Jews.

I spent a happy month playing with the local girls, several of whom came from families with fifteen to twenty children. Their homes were always bustling and busy in a way mine had not been. Despite having many mouths to feed, these families unhesitatingly made room for more, and we joined them for lively Sabbath meals with plenty of singing and delicious food.

I had never seen so many visibly Jewish people in my life, and though some of their Hasidic customs were different than ours, the myriad ritual laws that dictated all of our lives were fundamentally the same. I soon learned that the men of the Polish sects wore the tall black fur caps while the Ukrainians wore the wide-brimmed ones; I could distinguish between the black silk coats over culottes and white lederhosen the men wore on the Sabbath and the matte black frock coats of the weekdays. Some sects allowed their married women to wear somewhat natural-looking wigs; others, only braided cloth caps or kerchiefs over shorn skulls.

In Monsey, I also experienced my first self-segregated Hasidic ghetto. Crossing into the enclave of New Square was like being transported into a foreign country in a past century, and not only because of the garb. English was rarely heard; the vernacular was Yiddish, a lively blend of German, Hebrew, and Slavic languages. Men and women had separate, designated sides of the street to walk on, as any intermingling of the sexes was completely verboten. There were no televisions, secular books, or newspapers allowed. Married women, some of whom seemed to be in their mid- to late teens, pushed baby strollers down the streets, wearing long pleated dark skirts over "bulletproof stockings" — thick, fully opaque beige tights with visible seams running up their length, worn in the sweltering summer and the dead of winter. Lives revolved around prayer, Torah study (for the men), and the care of large families (for the women). There was no blending into the outside *velt* ("world") by design.

One day in early August my mother returned from apartment hunting flushed with success. She had found us a new home, just off the main street, for a reasonable rent. It was an unusual space, a repurposed, stand-alone two-car garage that, with the addition of plywood walls, had been converted into a one-bedroom apartment with a tiny living room/kitchenette and a small stall with a toilet and shower. It wasn't much, she admitted, but it would do just fine for now. My mother and I would share the bedroom and we would hang a curtain in the living space to create some privacy for my brother, who had turned thirteen in January and was therefore a man by the standards of our faith.

My mother found work as a secular history teacher at a local Hasidic high school for girls, Bais Rochel, and could now afford, with some financial aid and an interest-free loan from the local charitable Jewish lender, to send us to the largest mainstream, ultra-Orthodox elementary school in Monsey: Yeshiva of Spring Valley. My brother would start seventh grade in the boys' school, and I would begin fifth in the girls' school across the street from it.

We spent the last weeks of summer setting up shop in what my brother and I called "the Garage." The Garage sat at the end of a driveway, a pygmy to the side of a large Victorian that looked abandoned but wasn't. It belonged to our new landlords, the Bialiks.

Mr. Bialik, a dark and wiry man of middle age with sad eyes, appeared to me to be as closed and shuttered as his home. A recluse, bearing the physical and psychic scars of the Holocaust, he left the rent collection and most other tasks involving communication to his wife, a truculent woman with a ratty dark wig and a large mole on her face from which sprouted tufts of black hair. I did not like Mrs. Bialik. She wore a seemingly permanent scowl of suspicion and made a show of resentment at my mother's timid yet doggedly cheerful requests for repairs to our apartment. When water leaked through the ceiling during a rainstorm or an outlet went dead, my mother would sigh, square her shoulders, and seek out Mrs. Bialik for a tense exchange, following which, if we were lucky, Mr. Bialik would eventually come trudging up the driveway with his handyman kit and his son Heschel in tow, a sullen, menacing-looking youth of twenty or thereabouts, and together they would silently patch the walls or tighten bolts and then, just as quietly, gather their tools and depart. "Why is Heschel so weird?" I asked my mother once,

creeped out when I discovered him watching me playing outside the Garage from behind a curtain from the second floor of
his dark house. "The son has inherited his father's traumas" was
her cryptic reply.

When the weather turned chilly, the Garage became dank and
dim by the light of the naked bulb that hung over the card table
where we ate our meals and did homework.

"Can we buy a TV now?" I begged my mother. "The rules are
quite clear," my mother responded, reading off the pamphlet we
had received from our school: "'No TVs in the homes of any students, or the student may be asked to leave the school.'"

It would be hard to understand such punitive measures without
mentioning that in our lexicon, *influence* was a weighty word with
outsized consequences, so if you were accused of being a Bad Influence on others by dint of your parents' permissiveness, very
little — except possibly unusually large charitable donations or
your family's outstanding rabbinical pedigree — could wash the
stain off.

"How would they even know?" my brother asked, curious.

"They don't!" I retorted, privy to intelligence that several of
my classmates had televisions discreetly tucked in wardrobes or
locked cabinets in their parents' bedrooms. "We don't need a
TV." My mother put her foot down.

Regardless of school guidelines, my mother maintained that a
TV would never befoul our home again. It was the gateway to
the "superficial" life that she disdained, battery acid for the soul.
If my classmates' parents chose to allow corrupting influences to
dull their children's spiritual faculties, so be it. Her children were
meant for *more*.

Being meant for more was a family directive steeped in contradiction for me.

Rejecting the "modern lifestyle" that would allow for a tele-

vision, my mother denounced, with equal ferocity, the culturally narrow life embraced by our more pious neighbors. The one
practiced a watered-down version of Judaism; the other practiced faith by "rote," making little effort to connect on a personal
spiritual level with God and the truth. Hankering after the shiny
perversions of the world or being myopically focused on the performance of ritual were both manifestations of spiritual short-
comings. Neither led to fulfillment of a human being's purpose in
life — a deeply attuned, personal relationship with the unknow-
able Lord (my mother thrilled at this incongruity — that the pursuit of God was both unattainable but incumbent upon us).

There were subtle ways my mother set herself apart. To our ultra-Orthodox neighbors, she quoted Plato and Aristotle, while to
her gentile colleagues at Rockland Community College, where
she soon found work as an associate professor and later as a department chair, she frequently referenced the Torah sage Maimonides. Volumes by Thomas Aquinas and Immanuel Kant
rested on our bookshelf alongside the works of Rabbi Joseph Soloveitchik of blessed memory, and together they wielded inordinate authority over our daily lives. Like her, we were tasked to
straddle both worlds but belong to neither.

My mother's philosophy in life was accompanied by its own origin tale, one that I clamored to hear despite how little she would
divulge of it. It made me feel connected to a woman so parsimo-
nious in accounting for her past that the four decades preceding
my arrival were little more than a mystery to me.

"I first experienced, *definitively,* the presence of God when I
was four years old," the story began, "and this changed everything for me."

It was 1940 at the New York home of my mother's *bubby* and
zeide (grandparents). Judith Feinstein was four years of age when
relatives gathered at the bedside of her dying grandfather, Tzvi
Aryeh. He and his wife, Lena, were the sole relatives that she

knew of who lived according to the "old ways," the religious life that my mother's parents openly disdained.

While family members paraded in and out of the room to pay their respects, four-year-old Judy sat nearby, quietly absorbing. As she noticed the sun begin to set through an open window above the old man's bed, her *zeide,* who had likewise been fading, became extremely agitated, pointing to the dying sun. Lena hurried to her husband's side, propped the old man up with her shoulder, and, refusing assistance, moved him to a seat by the window and placed a prayer book in his hands. The time for the afternoon prayer of *minchah* was almost over.

My mother was mesmerized by the enactment of this ritual, and seeing an otherworldly joy on the praying man's face lifted her soul, she maintains, out of her body momentarily. "I was looking down at myself, sitting beside the bed, wearing my favorite powder-blue coat," she would add for dramatic effect, "and I knew, don't ask me how, but I did, that I was *in the presence of God.*"

When she revived, my mother explained, she had found that she could not "go back to the way things were" before her eyes had been open to a new reality, which included an omnipresent, beneficent Higher Being. As she grew up, the lives of her parents, who had long shed the rituals of their faith to chase American ideals and dreams, began to seem hollowed of meaning.

For their part, her comfortably middle-class, culturally assimilated parents and younger brother Rick could not understand my mother's strangeness or her obsession with the divine. She, in turn, was incredulous that people could walk about the earth while a God existed and *do nothing about it.*

"God became, to me, the only *really real* thing," she explained. She began a spiritual quest to understand and comply with His will and design. As a consequence, she admitted to me, deeper human connections were harder to come by. It was this loneliness, born of a quest for truth, that she now believed she had passed on to me. It was also something of which she appeared inordinately proud.

"*You,*" she would declare, holding me at arm's length, examining my face with satisfaction, then commenting as if discovering an endearing, congenital family trait such as one blue eye, one green, "*will never be satisfied with an ordinary life!*" I, she believed, was meant for something *more.*

It was only as I grew older that I began to suspect that these blessings of more might in reality confer *less* — less camaraderie, less by way of choice.

Over the years, the circle of singularity that my mother consecrated around my brother and me grew into a fence, then a towering gate, and, finally, an impenetrable wall. With my budding flesh and bone formed a sense of unshakable "otherness." When I was ten and living in the Garage, I could not tell you why I felt so *strange,* only that I did.

I would study the way the girls in my class giggled and tossed their hair, shrieked and elbowed each other, at ease in their surroundings and in their unexamined expectations of being and belonging. At times I resented what I imagined were their carefree lives; at times I pitied them, for, as my mother would put it: "They have never questioned their existence!" Always, I secretly envied them.

I knew even at this age that there was a way of being that was ordinary and uncomplicated and safe, in which the sun rose because the moon set, and the moon set because the sun rose, and mothers and fathers came home to you at night because they left you in the morning, and like the tides, they would be pulled back in.

Our family "situation," as my mother referred to it, appeared to compound this inscrutable apartness. In a staunchly patriarchal world where divorce was still highly scandalous, I had the misfortune of being a *fatherless girl,* she frequently reminded me.

"But I am not fatherless," I would say, bristling. "Abba visits us, and besides, he is alive, he *exists!*" My mother would look at me sadly and say, "Oh, Miriam, for all intents and purposes, you are."

How I hated her fatherless-girl trope! How I writhed at her pity. I felt that it pointed to a nakedness in me, a vulnerability, a thing that, as I grew older, I would attempt to weave into a story of hardship and heroism.

Ultimately it was the splinter of truth in her words that stung the worst. My father's visits were infrequent, once or twice a year and only for several hours at most, as he was en route to give lectures or do important university work in New York or Los Angeles. I soon tired of embarrassing questions asked by those few classmates who ventured over to the Garage about where my father slept, since it was abundantly obvious that our living quarters couldn't house an unbroken family. I stopped inviting classmates over altogether, rejecting offers to go to others' homes, rare though they were, for fear of the need to reciprocate. Potential friendships stalled as acquaintanceships, dying on the vine.

I too, it appeared, had inherited my mother's treasured loneliness, though to me it often felt like a curse.

Our first winter in Monsey brought with it howling winds that would batter the thin walls of our home and a pervasive damp chill that our space heaters could not muster enough enthusiasm to dispel. I began to dread the onset of shadowy evenings in the Garage.

I do not know if living there affected my brother the same way, and, I am ashamed to admit, I did not care much at the time. My brother, before we had unpacked all our boxes, had crafted a reputation for insubordination, one that, this time, the full weight of the school administration was happy to help him fix. I don't know if it was his frequent detentions or the hours of Talmudic study required of bar mitzvah–age boys, but I saw less of Uriyah than I had in Boston, and for this, I was, frankly, relieved.

However, as soon as the school bus dropped me off and I started to trudge up the long driveway toward the Garage, a mounting feeling of dread would come upon me so that by the time I dropped my school bag on the floor inside our door, accepting my mother's embrace and routine request to pick up my belongings and "stow them properly," I had begun to scheme for ways I could entice my mother to relieve me of the Garage for a few more hours. I would suggest a trip to Nagel's, our grocery store, or to Rickel's, the hardware store — anywhere but the Garage. "I won't ask you to buy me a thing!" I promised. "Well, then, why do you want to go so badly?" she would ask, puzzled.

At first, I claimed boredom, but the word was anathema to my mother and did nothing but provoke the assignment of chores. Finally, I gave up and described to the best of my ability the "yuckiness" that sat in my stomach like indigestible food and the heavy pressure that lay on my chest, tugging at the corner of my eyes as evening fell.

"If these feelings of unhappiness are within you," she responded, "then you must work on yourself to overcome them. External solutions won't fix internal problems." Despite the undeniable logic of this statement, I continued to wheedle and cry until I would break my mother down, and we'd discover that we were almost out of batteries or apples or peanut butter and then head out for those things. This, I suspect, began in me a sense of the "comfort of things," the anchoring stability that the contents of shopping bags would add to our sparse shack. It's possible they indicated a foreseeable tomorrow where a family would consume them, baking apple pies, packing lunches or powering flashlights, doing things that were safe and boringly normal, things that indicated that this family would "make it."

I had another reason to fear nightfall: too frequently, sleep brought with it frightful dreams. To these, my mother would always apply the balm of positive reinterpretation. No matter how grim the dream, she would clap her hands and marvel at how attuned I was to my subconscious. It was another sign of our shared profundity.

When my mother came down with her second bout of pneumonia that winter, rendering her too weak to leave the house for over a month and racked with a deep cough, her skin clammy and hot, I crawled under my blanket to bargain tearfully with the Almighty. "Listen, Hashem . . ." I began in the easy faith of childhood, never questioning that He was listening.

If my mother lived, I promised, I would be a better girl, a devoted girl, a more *eidel* (sweet and modest) version of myself, and I would stop nagging my mother so much for *things*.

God kept His end of the bargain. It was I who soon fell short.

Teachers were easy and enticing targets for my sarcastic wit, particularly those with rules they seemed to enforce for some kids and not for others. Sometimes they told you things that didn't make sense and then got angry when you asked questions. Soon, I had built my own reputation, to my mother's chagrin, for having chutzpah, a boldness that questioned authority. *Reputation* was a word with even more enduring consequences than *influence*.

It was also quite hard not to be seduced by *gashmiyus,* materialism. The bright storefronts full of unattainable *things,* the exciting, clangy music that strangers driving through our neighborhood brought when their car windows were rolled down, these all called to me with a Siren's song. At ten years old, I longed for *more,* but it was not the kind of *more* that my mother approved of. It was the kind that could get me in trouble.

• 6 •

Birthday Girl

Childhood has its own sweet secrets and confirms mortality,
and that mortality defines all courage and love.

— STEPHEN KING, It

February 23, 2011

Dear Em,

Happy first birthday!

You are a "tour de force," as your daddy says . . . a real force
of nature.

You are so loved. Daddy and I are deeply in love with you.

You are energetic, willful, bubbling with joy, occasionally
temperamental and gosh-darn stubborn.

We are so proud of all these qualities and we know they will
keep you achieving your dreams in life. We might need to work
on the anger management. ;-)

When you were born, Daddy and I dubbed you our "ptero-
dactyl." You were insatiable — always craning your neck like a
little bird searching for a worm with your mouth open wide. We
knew then that you would grab life by the horns.

Now you are nearly one. You are a powerful little baby. You can go from kneeling to standing, lose your balance halfway, and get upright again. You haven't decided to walk yet, but that's just around the corner. Truth be told I'm a little nervous; you seem to be unaware of fear when you launch yourself at things — and that's probably because of your helmet (your head was a wee bit flat for a bit but now it's perfectly round, so don't dent it — no "head-firsts," baby girl, okay? Your mama couldn't take it!).

In the past two weeks you have decided to play with us. You hold out whatever it is you have in your hands and yell "Ga" triumphantly. You like to drop presents in my hand: food, toys, pieces of dirt you managed to find and grasp in your little fingers. Then you take them back or wait for me to give them to you. You have started to play with those big chunky puzzles and have managed to work several pieces in at a time. At first I thought it was coincidence, but now I think you really get it. You seem to understand what to do with a pen or brush as well. You also love to take toys in and out of buckets. You tried to put Thomas the Train in the potty that Ella was trying to go to the bathroom in and you were so mad when I got in your way!

You clap all the time. For yourself, for us, for Ella, and when I put music on, which you love. Today, both Daddy and I swear we heard you say, "I did it," and "Yay!" clearly several times when you stacked those big cardboard blocks on top of each other. You are so proud of your achievements, almost as proud as we are! You are such a joy to behold. Such a love, such a dear.

So how much do we love you? Eternally, the length and width of the universe, and then some.

Love,
Mama and Daddy

7

The Condiment Thief

You shall not turn from the word they tell you, neither right nor left.   — DEUTERONOMY 17:11

IT WAS THE ORTS WHO RESCUED US FROM THE GARAGE, in the spring of 1987. Neighbors had mentioned that an elderly couple, Shloime and Rose Ort, who lived on a perpendicular street barely a stone's throw from the Garage, had an apartment soon to be vacant. Perhaps they wanted to find new tenants? They did. The apartment was on the second floor, bright and airy with a bedroom, a separate living room, and a back porch. Things were looking up.

From the moment my mother and Mrs. Ort sized each other up, a fast but unlikely friendship bloomed. The short Hasidic grandmother in her late sixties with the thick Coke-bottle glasses was at least fifteen years my mother's senior; she had gotten married in her mid-teens, had an army of children and grandchildren to show for it, and had lived the better part of her life in the hermetically sealed world of her sect.

Mrs. Ort, however, was anything but typical of the housewives in our neighborhood. She was an autodidact, sneaking newspapers (and romance novels!) into her home under her husband's watchful but myopic gaze. She knew things that were surprising, like who had won an Oscar that year, and she had opinions about almost everything, including celebrities and *goyishe* fashions. ("I don't understand the appeal of that Tom Cruise!" she would cluck. "He's so short and has an oversize head!" Or "Those huge shoulder pads are so ugly! They make a woman look manly!") She was also the author of scores of florid poems written in neat flowery script on the backs of envelopes and shopping lists and in flour-dusted spiral notebooks. Mrs. Ort had a sweet but wobbly soprano and would serve up a rendition of "Danny Boy" with heaping plates of homemade pastries.

Many an evening, after I finished my homework and retired to my room to read, my mother would disappear into the Orts' side of the house, where, seated at the kitchen table, Mrs. Ort and my mother would debate politics and bemoan the inevitable decline of societal values. Happy and humming, my mother would return late in the evening to kiss me good night. She had found a treasure of a friend in Rose Ort. In return, my mother, an avid gardener, set the Orts' yard ablaze with bright carnations, morning glories, and zinnias, flowers of every shade that drew applause from total strangers.

Rabbi Ort was a gruff grizzly bear of a man with a voluminous white beard and long curly sideburns. He was also plagued by narcolepsy that would cause him to fall asleep midsentence, bowing gently over his plate. When this happened, his wife would rap sharply on the table and call, "Shloime," whereupon he would awaken with a snort, look suspiciously around at us kids, frequent guests for the Sabbath meal, and resume singing hymns or speaking where he left off. My mother would glare at my brother and me when fits of giggles escaped, but Mrs. Ort would secretly egg us on, making faces or rolling her eyes. How we loved Mrs. Ort!

I made my first real Monsey friends that year, when I was in sixth grade. Alisa, Sarah, and Debra all came from more "modern" families and for that reason, they had quickly earned my mother's strident disapproval. I thought they were the coolest kids in the grade, with their narrow denim skirts worn once we shed our school uniforms and their (discreet) access to television and rock-and-roll music.

"These are the kids that *I* actually like spending time with and they like *me,*" I would argue, angry tears rolling down my cheeks. "You would make more suitable friends if you only *tried!*" my mother would snap back, shaking her hands in frustration. "Soon," she fretted, "when you get a reputation for hanging out with the *modern* crowd, none of the quality families will allow you near their children! They won't touch you with a ten-foot pole!"

I was in a quandary. I could not deny the severe consequences of having a Bad Reputation, which could be earned by talking to a boy who was not your brother, wearing a skirt that hit just at the knee and not the requisite three inches beneath it, or violating some other rule of the religious code.

However, I also knew that I would be at a social disadvantage hanging out with the more *frum* girls. As I was the child of a *ba'alas teshuva,* someone who had become orthodox later in life, my cachet was pretty insignificant with these "good" families to begin with. We were also missing that magical ingredient called *yichus,* which means "stock" or "lineage." Families with famous *rabbonim* (the plural of *rabbi*) in their ancestry would have scrolls mounted on their walls with commissioned, artfully rendered family trees proclaiming their pedigrees. The most significant privilege of *yichus* was that your children were virtually guaranteed to be sought after for marriage, and their little peccadilloes might be overlooked. In the ultra-Orthodox community, dating someone you met randomly was not allowed. All dates, called *shidduchim,* were arranged through parents and matchmakers, and an individual's *yichus* factored heavily in these negotiations.

Debra, Alisa, and Sarah became my constant school companions, as, armed with the angst that I recorded in my diaries, I inched my way into a tepid teenage rebellion. At recess our gang of four would slouch together in the hallway under the stairs, wearing different shades of denim jackets but identical scowls, chewing on straws and whispering about secret crushes that we had on boys. Since I wasn't permitted to speak to any flesh-and-blood boys, the objects of my affection were invariably cutouts from the teen magazines I would sneak into the house.

The arrival of high school broke up our small gang. Debra and Sarah were the lucky ones. Their parents sent them to Modern Orthodox high schools, one of which was even *coed*. The Modern Orthodox, or "Orthodox Lite," as they were sometimes disparaged, believed in young people earning college degrees and pursuing secular professions while learning Torah in the evenings and on weekends. Boys and girls were allowed to mingle in carefully controlled settings, and most homes had televisions and access to secular newspapers.

Alisa and I were stuck in Bais Yaakov of Monsey, a strict ultra-Orthodox institution run by the notorious Rebbetzin (you couldn't throw a stone in Monsey without hitting a *rebbetzin,* or rabbi's wife, but everyone knew *exactly* who you meant when you spoke of "*the* Rebbetzin." Like Cher, she didn't need a last name; unlike Cher, she inspired more terror than awe). Rumored to lift girls' skirts during surprise inspections in the hallways to ensure compliance with the over-the-knee sock edict, the Rebbetzin ran her high school with an iron fist. She was reputed to have networks of spies and collaborators who would report any infringements of the rules, both within and outside of school walls. Even the teachers were frightened of her, something that my mother, who had left Bais Rochel and now divided her time between teaching at Bais Yaakov and at Rockland Community College, thought was absurd.

• • •

My brother, earlier, had suffered his own rocky start to high school. My mother had finally made good on her promise to send him to a therapeutic school, but in his case the therapy was strict orthodoxy as administered by one *rosh* yeshiva (head of yeshiva) after another.

His latest school, Reb Chaim Epstein's yeshiva in Brooklyn, New York, had been suggested as a place where difficult boys could be sent to have their wrinkles smoothed out and the fear of God instilled. Reb Chaim, however, saw something in my brother that previous *roshei* yeshiva had not. He saw a brilliant boy with an unconventional learning style whose capacity to question what he learned could, if carefully directed, be his greatest strength. He took my brother under his wing. The change in my brother was almost immediate.

For the first time, Uriyah seemed to be taking his spiritual life seriously. Once the fire of devotion had been lit, my brother threw himself heart and soul into his faith. He began to pray for hours a day, and when his lips were not forming words of prayer, he was bent over a holy book, swaying back and forth and muttering questions and answers from the Talmud to himself, as was the style of learning in yeshivas.

At first, my mother seemed pleased to see my brother showing signs of burgeoning maturation, but as he began to reject even basic materialism — which, to my disgust, included showering and changing his clothes — and undertake repentant fasting, she became frustrated. Already thin and wiry, my brother became gaunt; twitches and tics emerged like bad prescription-drug side effects.

"You have become an uncivilized boor!" my mother would rage when my brother's eyes would glaze over in thought at the table and he would forget the plate of food in front of him, crumbs dropping from his open mouth as he chewed, or when he stepped off the bus on Fridays with dark, smelly pit stains on the shirt he had been wearing for days. Because the world remained so seductive to a boy of sixteen, my brother began to remove his glasses on the street so that he would not gaze upon women. This, above everything, rendered my mother apoplectic.

Still, she could not argue that my brother was impious or behaving *superficially,* as she could and did in my case. I had slowly toppled off my pedestal, and he had appeared to take my place.

I resented the fact that my brother had managed to switch roles with me to become the less problematic child. He took to lecturing me on immodesty, improper language, and the secular books I enjoyed, which were, he insisted, defiling my pure Jewish soul. On the weekends when he was home he would hand-deliver to me meticulously written letters of a dozen or more pages, feverish and mystical manifestos laced with sharp rebuke. I never replied to those letters. Sometimes I would skim them, rolling my eyes; other times I tossed them into the trash, unread. They were eerily manic, like the characters in the Dostoyevsky novels I would grow to love.

I did not need another parent, I concluded. I was making well above average grades, at least in the secular classes that I loved, and at fourteen years old, I had never even *touched* a damn boy. And *fuck* my reputation. This *had* to be enough.

But it never was enough.

Things came to a head in our home on a Saturday evening in January 1990. It was a Motzei Shabbos, the evening after the Sabbath concluded, and my mother had prepared us a dinner of hot dogs in buns. My brother asked me to pass the bottle of mustard. Perhaps I didn't hear him the first time, or maybe he hadn't asked nicely; regardless, I set the mustard bottle down well out of his reach. Staring at me angrily, he *demanded* that I pass the mustard to him.

Now, there was simply no way that I was going to pass that mustard, so I deliberately ignored him. He next appealed to my mother, who closed the book she was reading. She too demanded that I relinquish the condiment forthwith. I picked up my hot dog, studied it, took my first bite. I could feel them bristling across the table, and, I must confess, it amused me. That's when things went sideways.

My mother, turning to Uriyah, sighed elaborately: "I feel sorry for her."

"Me too," he said, shaking his head. Even with a quick glance, I couldn't quite tell if he was joking.

"Pretty soon," my mother added, "she'll have no friends left at all."

I calmly took another bite, trying to hide my smile.

"Yes, *nebuch,* it's a pity," my brother agreed.

"But the worst thing," my mother went on, her voice becoming more edgy and angry the longer I ignored her, "is that if she continues this way, *no one* will want to marry her. Or if she does marry, she won't be able to keep her husband. Who could tolerate someone who behaves like this? They won't touch her with a ten-foot pole!"

It was the "ten-foot pole" that broke me. I began to laugh, spitting out chunks of meat and bun. Incensed, my mother banished me from the table.

Left to stew in my bedroom, I began to record my family's bizarre behavior in my diary. As my pen tore into the pages, releasing my grievances, I grew angrier and angrier. I had to teach them a lesson. It was high time that they realized where in the hierarchy of things a mustard bottle lay.

I decided then and there, on the spur of the moment, to run away.

8

Honey Badger

His mother called him "WILD THING!" and Max said "I'LL
EAT YOU UP!"

— MAURICE SENDAK, *Where the Wild Things Are*

February 24, 2012

Dear Em, aka "Honey Badger,"

Oh, what a year it has been!

Daddy and I are so proud of you. You learned to walk well
this year — and gallop and run!

You are fierce, truly a force of nature.

We found a funny video in which we discovered that the
honey badger is the toughest creature alive . . . that's you, all
right, so that's what we call you! And *boy,* are you stubborn!

When you want something, you go full-out Attila the Hun to
get it. As Daddy says, "It's zero to sixty with that one — nothing
in between" (and yes, he truly loves it).

Sometimes you do this thing when you're mad where you
jump up and bring your legs up in front of you and land with a

crash on your bum — good thing you are still padded. You're well into your terrible twos, so that's a milestone you hit early. ;-)

We are all very proud of your strong spirit.

You are a loyal and loving little sister. You love it when Ella sings to you and you follow her around with stars in your eyes. If she gets hurt you come over right away and try to make it better with "kwisses" or a Band-Aid. It is so beautiful to see.

You have many words now. You know all your "major" animals and insects and you've started saying all these cute phrases, such as "I know!" and "Wayd'a minute!" You have the sweetest lisp. The other day you called me a "siw-bi-wy" (silly billy).

I think you're going to be a great big sister too. It might be hard for a while, because there are lots of changes coming up, but I think the Three Sisters Lemay are going to be wonderful friends. People keep reminding us that now we are going to be outnumbered, and I reply that we were "out of our league" already.

You are very excited for the baby. You and your sister made me pictures for "Pop-Out Day," when we celebrated that Mama's bellybutton is now an outie. You painted my belly with finger paint and we all laughed.

You *love* Thomas the Tank Engine and your train sets. You take them with you everywhere. You point to the wind towers on the way to Boston and yell, "Mama, ders'Ah *Thomas!*"

I think you're almost ready for potty training. You're very curious about the whole process.

You *love* your Buddy bunny and your Benin blanket. You take them everywhere, and even though it's awkward, you never let go — on the swing or climbing up a slide. You've gotten very good at navigating with something in hand. When Daddy climbed Mount Kilimanjaro you were ready to give him Buddy to take with him but couldn't quite let go, so he took

Backup Buddy instead. You were so amazed to see him waving a flag from Uhuru peak. Daddy says one day he will climb that mountain again with you, and I believe it.

We love you with everything, sweet, darling Em.

Happy second birthday, little love.

Love,
Mama

The truth is, Em's tantrums are *epic* these days. Nothing like Ella's, and she had quite a healthy dose of terrible twos. I've asked for advice from everyone I know, including all my mom friends and our pediatrician. It's probably her overall gumption, says Joe. Strength of character, says Kathy, adding, "And she'll need it as a girl!"

My mother says that it's my pregnancy, that as I get bigger, I am slowing down and I'm less available for play and this bothers my child. "She's sensing your weakness," she says. That's possible, of course, but coming from my mother, this advice is unwelcome because it implies that the dynamic between me and my challenging two-year-old is a function of my own inadequacy.

Her opinion is also, as usual, stated as unassailable fact. I had thought I was doing my mother a favor years ago when I suggested that she use the words *I think* and *maybe* more often in conversation, but that is not who she is, and I cannot change her, just as she can no longer mold me.

The kids, however, are a different case. They were supposed to be the clean slate between my mother and me, the Alka-Seltzer to our roiling discontent. Instead, I find increasingly that they are the subjects of a subtle tug of war between us during my mother's extended visits. Especially Em.

My mother's visits mark the changing of the seasons.

She comes after the Jewish New Year and Days of Atonement

but before the Festival of Lights, after the secular New Year but before Passover, between the Festival of Weeks and the dirges of the summer month of Av. She brings with her delicious recipes, an orderly house — and the painful memories that send me into a tailspin.

I marvel at how small I become when she is here, how I retreat in increments as she expands. "Settling in," she calls it, as each time the contents of half a dozen large suitcases, amassed over the years, find their way up from my basement in order to kosher the kitchen, establish a library of Judaica, and lay down her utensils — her godly things that supplant my ungodly things.

"I come here for you only," she says. "Don't mind me," she says. "I hate that I have to take over your space! If there was any other way . . ." And perhaps most meretriciously: "Just pretend I'm not here."

I am certain that the girls have started to notice the sharp edge in their mother's voice, the way their grandmother rolls her eyes and throws up her hands and emits those barely audible noises of derision. How can they not sense the flammability of the atmosphere, the acrimony a sharp scent in the air that leaves the room somewhat smaller, the parts per cubic inch of oxygen diminished?

And now, a most troublesome betrayal: Em's no longer the pliable, chubby, and cuddly baby, and my mother's pointed and reproachful remarks head, by and large, toward my younger child, whose constant shifting movements and imprecise aim scatter cascades of food about her like gastronomic crop circles.

To Em's increasing tantrums my mother assigns motives of deliberate insubordination. My discipline in these moments is deemed inadequate. And somehow, in the way of all self-fulfilling prophecies, the outbursts are longer, stronger, and closer together with Bubby as witness. When I come to Em's defense (*She's barely two, for God's sake*), my mother's response is a chilly withdrawal, a wholly dissembling "I bow to you." My mother's love and her anger, her generosity and censure; these make up the enervating concoction to which, before each visit, I promise myself full immunity, and fail.

Why can't I love you? I ask the empty air, closing my laptop on the birthday letter to Em, then pressing the spot between my eyebrows where I can feel the tension building. Worse than the anger I feel toward my mother, worse than the frustration, is the regret. *Why do we still do this to each other?*

9

Devotion

You try to be faithful
And sometimes you're cruel.
You are mine. Then, you leave.
Without you, I can't cope.

And when you take the lead,
I become your footstep.
Your absence leaves a void.
Without you, I can't cope.

You have disturbed my sleep,
You have wrecked my image.
You have set me apart.
Without you, I can't cope.

— JALAL AD-DIN MUHAMMAD AR-RUMI

I DIDN'T EXACTLY HATCH A PLAN FOR RUNNING AWAY, ONLY had some vague notion that I would make my way to a friend's house for the night and come back in the morning after my mother had had time to think about what *really* mattered.

I waited until she was occupied washing dishes, then I hoisted my school bag stuffed with a change of clothes onto my back and dashed out the door and down the porch steps, heart pounding. As I entered the woods behind our house, I heard her calling my name loudly, sharply, from the door to the porch. After a quick glance back to see that she made no move to follow me, I pushed on.

Snow had hardened to a shell on the ground in the patch of woods behind our house, causing me to wince in pain with each step as my heel broke through the ice. I was still wearing an air cast on one of my ankles, having sprained it a few weeks prior after jumping off a chair while playing air guitar to Billy Joel's chart-topping protest anthem "We Didn't Start the Fire."

I slogged painfully through the snow for over a mile until I reached a pay phone at our local strip mall. I figured that my mother had alerted the police already, so as I dug coins out of my backpack, I ducked my head, heart thumping wildly, with each set of passing headlights. But there were no blue flashing lights and no cars pulled into the lot at this hour, already past nine p.m.

I found myself regretting the fact that I had no real money on me, a result of the rule that proceeds from babysitting jobs had to be handed directly over to my mother. "I will pay for anything you need," she had said. Her view was that if I wanted to keep *my* money, then I was on *my own* for the things I wanted. I had felt that it was a bargain, of sorts. Now I felt like an idiot. Oh, why hadn't I skimmed off the top?

The friend I called was Debra. Her parents were known to be the most "chill." I hailed a passing cab and gave the driver her address. The man never glanced back at me during the entire ride, a blessing, because if he had, I might have jumped out then and there in the middle of the road. *Never take a cab on your own,* my mother had warned me several times. *Everyone knows half the cabdrivers work for the Russian mob. I don't even want to say what they will end up doing with you.* But she had told me, in frightening, lurid detail, followed by the inevitable, *And I will never see*

you again. "Good riddance," I now muttered, deep in the intoxi-
cation of my rebellion.

My cabbie, apparently of the 50 percent of cabdrivers lawfully
employed, let me off in front of my friend's house unscathed.
Debra was on the sidewalk, cash in hand to pay the virtuous
man's fare.

We planned to keep my arrival on the down low, but our plans
immediately went awry when the family dog enthusiastically heralded my entrance as I came through the basement door. Debra's
dad soon showed up to inspect his daughter's bedroom, perhaps
suspecting the presence of a male paramour. Instead, he found me
cowering in the closet. After some reparative cocoa and a brief
discussion, Debra's parents decided that I could stay the night so
long as I called my mother first thing the next morning.

She answered the phone after the first ring. Once she had inquired after my general welfare, my mother expressed little interest in hearing of the grievances that had provoked my abrupt de-
parture. "Come home, *then* we'll talk," she said firmly.

I thought earnestly about going home. I was scared. What had
seemed a fabulous idea last night felt like sheer insanity by the
light of day. There were so many reasons to head back home now,
prime among which was that tomorrow was Monday, a school day.

Something stirring inside of me, however, could not bear the
thought of slinking back to my mother with my tail tucked between my legs. If I returned home without any concessions from
her, then she could, and undoubtedly would, claim victory and
thus be encouraged to restrict my life even further. I could forget
about seeing my friends occasionally or going to the movies. If I
went back now, I was sure I would never leave the house again. I
hung up the phone.

The next ten days unfolded like a parody of a hostage crisis.
What I had found myself negotiating, rather ineffectively, was my
own return home. I would call each morning at eight o'clock sharp

and ask my mother if she had considered my list of requests. The list, which I had compiled after I hung up the phone that first day, was, in my view, pretty basic. It covered, in somewhat florid language, the "fundamental rights" that I felt were owed any fourteen-year-old girl: I wanted to wear clothes that adhered closer to the minimum, not the maximum, of the laws of modesty. On occasion, I would like to be allowed to see a PG-13 movie, and, most important, I wanted to keep my friends — with the understanding that they weren't corrupt or immoral people.

By day eleven, negotiations had clearly stalled. I came to the unhappy conclusion that, as long as my mother expected a morning phone call each day, she was disincentivized to come to the table. So this time, I hatched a plan. From a pay phone on the side of Route 59, I dialed my mother at her office, an hour later than our usual time. With the beeping of cars and the rumble of trucks on the highway as my backdrop, I told her that I was at a bus station, ticket in hand, and headed for New York City. "I won't be calling for a while," I said sadly. After what felt like an interminably long silence, my mother caved. "Come home," she said with a sigh. "Most of the things you ask for are . . . doable."

At this point I was exhausted and ready to fold. Quickly accepting the olive branch, I agreed to come home that day and hung up. My sense of relief was short-lived, however, as I realized that now I would have to face my mother in person, not just over the phone wires.

I swallowed my tears. She swallowed her pride. We hugged stiffly.

For days following my return home, my mother and I tiptoed gingerly around the house. Having each bloodied the other, we nursed our wounds in private, discussing little of what had taken place over my nearly two-week absence. My mother agreed to every item on my list, with some caveats. The one that irked her the most was my request to keep my friends Sarah, Alisa, and Debra.

"Just don't expect me to chauffeur you to their house when I don't approve of your friendship," she muttered.

Though our reconciliation had gone more smoothly than expected, something thorny *had* transpired that required immediate attention. The Rebbetzin had demanded of my mother an explanation for my absence. This battle-ax, as my mother had once referred to her (an act of rebellion that I had cherished in its rarity), was decidedly less inclined to let bygones be bygones. On a frozen day in February, my mother drove me to school and waited for me on the bench outside the Rebbetzin's office where we had both been summoned.

I had to fight off a rising panic as the door closed leaving me alone in the room with Rebbetzin Soloveitchik. The feeling grew more acute as she ostentatiously ignored me for three long minutes, arranging papers on her desk and making phone calls. While it was unlikely that she was a student of police procedurals, she was clearly allowing me to sweat it out before she finally addressed me, folding her arms on the desk and skewering me with a long, thoughtful stare.

"What are we going to do with you?" she asked, her thick accent New York by way of Lithuania.

I was rooted to the spot. I had no answer for her; none, anyway, that I felt she would appreciate.

"Miriam," she said (and I wondered briefly whether she was deliberately using the name I detested), her voice angry. "What you did was *sinful.* In no way the correct behavior for a daughter of Israel! Not only did you violate *kivud av va'em*" — the commandment to honor one's parents — "but you are on a destructive path. You may have forced your mother to allow *tumah*" — impurity — "into your life, but *I* will not agree to it."

She proceeded to tell me that if I wished to stay a Bais Yaakov girl here among her *eidel* students (at which I raised an eyebrow, feeling somewhat better informed regarding their virtues), under no circumstances would I be allowed to wear skirts that didn't cover, within a wide margin, my knees. Furthermore, were she to be notified that I was wearing makeup out of school, speaking to those inappropriate friends of mine, or seeing movies, I would be "out on the sidewalk" in an instant.

She finished her words, sat back, and smiled at me. There was something triumphant in that smirk that unnerved me, but beneath the smug satisfaction, I caught a glimpse of genuine anger, an anger that betrayed, what was it . . . worry? Yes. I could see now, clearly, that there was something she feared in me. She *needed* me to come to heel as much or more than she *wanted* me to. I was a threat to her reign of terror. I smiled back and took a deep breath so that when I spoke, my voice barely shook: "Well, I guess this is goodbye, then." I turned and walked out of the room, feeling the heat of her glare on my back.

In the outer office, my mother was still sitting on the hard reprobates' bench, waiting. She looked up and, after searching my face, gave a resigned sigh, picked up her pocketbook, and walked into the office. While the sounds that emanated from within were muffled, I could tell that neither participant in the conversation was happy. My mother emerged a few long minutes later and bade goodbye to the secretary, who stared after us open-mouthed. When the door to the school swung shut behind us, I reached out my hand tentatively for hers. She didn't grasp my hand enthusiastically, but neither did she push me away. She held on to the tips of my fingers with her own, as if she were carrying a delicate object that she did not want to drop.

In the car, my mother related some of what had transpired between her and the Rebbetzin. "I *warned you* not to push her to the wall," my mother had said to the principal. "I *told you* that the one thing that would cause you grief with my daughter is that she cannot tell a lie."

I was immeasurably happy to hear my mother say these words. To me they indicated that she valued a truth that led to discomfort over lies that led to conformity. I could not recall a moment that I had felt prouder of her.

Perhaps she saw the pride in my face because she let out a restrained smile. "I think she thought I came to beg her to let you back." She made a sound that could have been a laugh or maybe just a cough. When the euphoria of our stand faded, however, I was still out of a school. Public school was not on the table, nor would it ever be. My mother would rather have quit her jobs and homeschooled me than send her lamb in with the wolves. "I'll have to look at a Modern Orthodox school," she said, adding reproachfully, "if they'll even take you." She wasn't happy. Despite her spirited defense of me to the Rebbetzin, she continued to gripe about the way she said I had "burned my bridges," as indeed I had.

A week later, however, as I was in the process of rereading every book I owned and pounding my pillow in boredom, she called me from her office at the college, sounding practically excited.

We had an interview the following day with Mrs. Bak, the principal of Bat Torah Academy, a small girls' high school in Suffern, New York, about a fifteen-minute drive from our house. "Yes, it's more modern," my mother admitted, "but after talking to Mrs. Bak, it appears to me that at least they have a semblance of standards for their students."

The woman who greeted us at the door of the large Dutch colonial that was home to Bat Torah Academy was a vision in a pastel-colored suit, whose skirt, I noted immediately, hit just a fraction below her kneecap. She was plump and pleasant, wearing a platinum-blond wig, heavy, though artfully applied, eyeliner, and bright magenta lipstick.

The school, like its principal, was fashionably decorated in beautiful, glowing, feminine colors. The bell rang for the end of a period while my mother conversed with Mrs. Bak in her inner sanctum. I stared wide-eyed as girls erupted from doorways and rushed up and down the narrow, carpeted stairwell. Quite a few had long, flowing hair, *en vogue* tight denim skirts with back slits, and — oh, glory — bobby socks exposing tanned, athletic calves! Many even wore nail polish, and not just the clear kind! I smiled at them shyly. Several smiled back.

Mrs. Bak finally ushered me into her office. She told me that she was willing to give me a chance at Bat Torah despite my expulsion from Bais Yaakov, although it had given her pause. We could consider the next few weeks a probation period, during which she would expect me to comply with the school's regulations and try my hardest in all ways. "I will!" I promised breathlessly. I simply could not believe my good fortune. "Welcome to Bat Torah." She smiled.

In the coming months, I made good on my promise to Mrs. Bak. By the time my freshman year came to a close, I was pulling top grades in all my subjects, Judaic and secular, and was comporting myself as a model student in every way. I even joined the school newspaper in my sophomore year as assistant editor and was promoted to editor in chief in my junior year. After taking the PSAT, I became a National Merit Scholar. I found it easy to apply myself and follow the rules at Bat Torah, as there were a great deal fewer of them there than I had at home.

Miraculously, even my home life became somewhat more relaxed. When my mother saw that I was flourishing at Bat Torah without losing my sanctity, she loosened her grip in a few significant ways. On occasion, despite loud but halfhearted protests, she allowed me to purchase the *Vogue* magazines that I loved or the latest album from my favorite band, U2, and she accepted my Bat Torah friends into our home with only periodic warnings that I must not confuse their casually Jewish lifestyle with genuine Torah observance.

Once I found myself with a greater space to breathe and *be,* something odd transpired. I began to actually enjoy my Torah learning, deriving great satisfaction from those religious studies I had disdained while at draconian Bais Yaakov.

I was particularly drawn to the works of the biblical scholars and sages, referred to generally as *meforshim*. I loved their wrangling over picayune details of syntax and grammar in scriptural verse as much as I enjoyed their meaty fables and poignant allegories. I was breathlessly happy discovering new *gematria* (assigned numerical values for Hebrew letters used to decode biblical texts) or an apparent textual contradiction that could be resolved only by a deep dive into centuries of scholarship.

Packed into each skeletal Bible verse was a treasure-trove of historical perspective, psychological insight, and moral guidance if one followed the exegetical rules to dissect the sparse text. Studying the Torah in this manner, I felt, was to engage in a three-thousand-year-long debate, and at fifteen years old, I found this legalistic and philosophical exchange absolutely riveting. Though, like the rest of my classmates, I intended to go to college, perhaps even get a secular law degree, I began to hope that I might find some way to further my Torah studies after high school.

Although there were no ultra-Orthodox yeshivas for women that would lead to ordination, there were quite a few seminaries that would provide a yearlong course in Judaica for high-school graduates. Most were in Israel, a place my mother would not send me, as she feared my father's hegemony. Seminary in general would be too expensive, she said, and possibly unnecessary: "There's nothing you cannot achieve by studying on your own."

I finished my sophomore year triumphantly and headed up to the Catskill Mountains for the summer to nanny for a family with four young children at an ultra-Orthodox bungalow colony. From the top bunk in a room I shared with my charges, I wrote frequent letters home addressed to "my dearest," and so my mother had become: my confidante, my best friend, and my source of inspiration.

It was at the bungalow colony that I first heard tell of the legendary Gateshead Seminary.

In the evenings, after the young children had been put to bed, the women and older girls would gather in lawn chairs in front of their bungalows to gossip. A popular topic, other than *shidduchim* (arranged dates), marriages, and births, seemed to be whose teenage daughter had been accepted into what seminary.

One evening, a woman shared that her sixteen-year-old niece had just been accepted into Gateshead Sem, leading to a moment of collective admiration from all present. "Gateshead?" I asked, unfamiliar with the name since no one at my school had ever gone there. "What's that?"

"Gateshead Seminary? It's only one of the best in the world!" said the incredulous aunt. The women began to chatter knowledgeably about this place that I had never heard of.

"The level of learning is quite *phenomenal,* genuine Old World European style."

"Gateshead is *mamish*" — meaning "for real" — "the crème de la crème of seminaries!"

"No *rebbetzins* there, only very, very *choshove*" — highly regarded — "*rabbonim*."

"I heard that the girls come home with *almost* the same level of knowledge as the young men. Too bad it's in England. I don't know if I could send my Gittel so far."

"That sounds incredible!" I exclaimed. "How do I find out more about it?"

"Oh!" said the aunt, clearly taken aback. She gave me the once-over, taking in, no doubt, my slim-fitting denim skirt, the shirt-sleeves that barely covered my elbows, and my long, loose brown hair. "It's almost impossible to get in," she said coolly. "They are *very* choosy."

I understood her meaning, but it only served to whet my appetite. If Gateshead was the best place for a young woman to learn Torah, then I must go there — it was as simple as that. Surely my commitment to studying the holy texts would make up for my background? That the school was in England didn't daunt me either; in fact, it seemed a distinct perk for the Jane Eyre–Sherlock Holmes–Miss Marple–loving girl that I was.

As it turned out, neither eagerness nor good grades were sufficient to gain me entry into Gateshead's hallowed halls. I lacked, as a local gatekeeper for the school delicately put it upon my inquiry, the *yichus* and the *right* academic pedigree to make me a desirable candidate. It wouldn't be fair, he explained, for him to squander his capital in recommending a girl who *could never* get in.

"There's always a way!" I exclaimed, leaving him shaking his head. Unable to apply the usual way, via someone's recommendation, I appealed by handwritten letter directly to the school, whose principal or other administrators I did not know. In fact, I didn't know the school's full name either (Gateshead Jewish Teachers Training College), so I addressed the letter to the city where the institution was founded: *Dear Gateshead,* I began.

In the letter, I laid out the case for my acceptance in the following way: Unlike girls from families that had been solidly Orthodox for generations, I had had to fortify myself against the temptations of an irreligious world to which I had been exposed *by my own father.* For the first time, for strangers' consumption, I put into words the uneasy relationship he and I had.

He has offered me the world and a pair of skates, I wrote, a literary reference to Hans Christian Andersen's "Snow Queen," my favorite childhood fairy tale. I had resisted my father's worldly temptations, I elaborated, to build of myself a wall of virtue against the corruption of outside influences. My older brother had even been moved to quote a verse in reference to me from King Solomon's Song of Songs: "What shall we do for our sister on the day she is spoken for? If she be a wall, we will build upon her a silver turret, and if she be a door, we will enclose her with cedar boards." I was no door by which the world could gain entry, I claimed, but a fortress.

At the time, I felt little guilt speaking ill of my father in so public a fashion. Our relationship had become strained since the move to Monsey. For several years, long after my parents' civil divorce, he had refused my mother a *get,* the religious document that freed a Jewish woman to remarry. My mother's repeated warnings that he might kidnap me and take me back to Israel added to my growing unease toward him.

At first, I had openly scoffed at this absurdity. Kidnap me? How ridiculous! "Even if he wanted to, how could he make me get on a plane?" She had thought of that too. A drug in my drink or food, she explained, and I would be putty in his hands. He had powerful friends in Israel, she warned, who could make such a thing possible. Did I really want to risk never seeing her again? If not, then I must agree to see my father only under her watchful gaze. It was not until I was in my mid-teens that I was allowed outside the house, in the backyard, alone with him. I remember the moment well and the anxiety that accompanied it.

While I retained some skepticism about her kidnapping claims, I viewed my father with suspicion when he would visit me, one afternoon a year, on his way to California, where he taught summer semesters in Judeo-Persian studies at UCLA. I rejected offers to visit him there, in Israel, or even in New York City for the day. As my mother recommended, I claimed I was content in Monsey and had no desire to see other parts of the country or the world. I would sigh in relief when he finally left, deflated, to take a train or bus back to his Persian hosts in the city.

Within two weeks of posting my letter to Gateshead, the seminary gatekeeper called me back, his tone newly ingratiating. "Rabbi Miller," he said in awe, "the principal *himself,* called me and asked, '*Who is this Mimi Netzer?*'" I was in.

• • •

When my acceptance to Gateshead became official with a letter and a hefty invoice, my mother was overjoyed. "We'll find a way to pay for it!" she exulted. A daughter who was accepted into Gateshead Seminary was nothing to sneeze at. Only one hitch remained. The seminary was a mandatory three-year program, and girls would not be accepted past the age of seventeen. I would need to skip my senior year of high school, no small thing. When I first applied, the likelihood of my acceptance had been so slim that I hadn't concerned myself too much about it.

"Can I defer?" I asked. "It's nonnegotiable" came the reply. "If girls start at eighteen, they're likely to drop out in a year or two to get married." That seemed odd to me, as I had no intention of marrying before I finished seminary *and* college, but clearly I had no choice in the matter; it was either forgo my senior year or forfeit the opportunity to attend Gateshead Seminary.

My mother was less concerned than I thought she would be about this. She assured me that any college "would surely consider your years in seminary as equal to or above the last year of high school!" Since she was a college professor herself, the matter appeared settled to me.

Mrs. Bak was less sanguine about my leaving high school after my junior year to attend Gateshead Seminary. She begged my mother and me to reconsider. "She doesn't want to lose her best student," my mother griped. "She is willing to hold you back for her sake, and I find that disappointing." I had to agree. What were three years in the span of a lifetime?

Our minds were made up, full of fantasies of an existence in the inner circle of Judaic royalty where I'd be delving into the mysteries of the universe and living a life far from ordinary.

10

An Ordinary Life

"And I will not weep from despair, but simply because I will be happy in my shed tears. I will be drunk with my own tenderness. Sticky spring leaves, the blue sky — I love them, that's all! Such things you love not with your mind, not with logic, but with your insides, your guts."

— FYODOR DOSTOYEVSKY, *The Brothers Karamazov*

AS WE PULL INTO THE DRIVEWAY, NEWBORN LUCIA IN her car seat, I am already adjusting the dial on my camera, checking to make sure all the settings are correct. I plan to have the same photograph of all three girls coming home from the hospital for the first time; well, *nearly* the same.

In Ella's picture, it's early autumn and the sun burnishes everything a deep gold. The first falling leaves have yet to dust the steep, curving driveway that leads to the brick patio in front of our two-story home with the white vinyl sides. The tall crumbling stone wall that runs alongside our driveway is still festooned with summer ivy. Joe grasps the handle of a pristine gray car seat in his hand. The picture, taken from behind, is full of movement; we see the bounce in his step, his straight back and lithe, youthful form.

For Em's homecoming, the trees are barren, and above, the

sky is a blank canvas reflecting the clumps of snow that dot the driveway. The grass is bowed and matted under the frost. As Em rounds the bend for the very first time, her car seat, a little worse for wear, is also firmly clasped in her father's hand. His stride is narrower, more cautious. Perhaps there is ice on the ground. On closer inspection, one may note that, like his hair, the sky is shot with minute flecks of gray.

Now it is our youngest daughter's, Lucia's, turn to be welcomed home. I depress the shutter halfway and the picture comes into focus on the small screen. *Click.*

It is several days into May and the rhododendron bush is starting to bud, its magenta flowers just hinting. An uneven row of bright yellow daffodils lines the driveway (courtesy of one of my mother's visits), nodding their greeting in the mild breeze. The grass is full of weeds and overgrown. Who has time to do landscaping these days?

Now, two little girls burst out of the screen door to greet their baby sister. They are shrieking with excitement and pounding the pavement with tiny sneaker-clad feet. Joe gingerly places the car seat down and runs interference — his arms outstretched to catch the marauders before they can trample the little form under the tented plaid blanket. They wriggle out of his grasp and the car seat rocks as they paw at the blanket.

Joe shoos them inside with a promise that they can greet their baby sister momentarily if they go wash their hands. He hails my mother as she appears in the doorway: "Hello, Bubby!" She raises her hands in the air in response, shaking her fists at the sky. "*Bruchim habaim,*" she shouts, then translates automatically for my gentile husband: "Welcome!" Once Lucia is safe inside with her grandmother and sisters, Joe comes back down the driveway for me.

He hooks my elbow and we shuffle up the hill together. I wince with every step. I have been sent home from the hospital on the fifth day with a C-section incision that has barely begun to heal.

Staples and stitches have been ineffective. The cut, some six inches in length, is held together by bandages and tape like a toddler's art project and will require daily cleansing and redressing by a home nurse as it heals from the inside out by "secondary intention."

As we inch up the slope, there is a moment where I imagine us, stooped and gray, hobbling up this very hill because we have made it together through these crazy parenting years. There is a catch in my throat. *I can only hope.*

For now, the humbling reward that awaits us is the presence of all our children, together at last, in the cozy home that I have taken to calling our Castle on the Hill. Once inside, with a little effort and some strategically placed pillows, I am seated as comfortably as I can be on the couch in the living room, snapping pictures on my phone of this wondrous moment.

"Ooooooh! She's so *cuuuute!*" Em's low rumble reaches upper octaves as she squeals over her baby sister. I am relieved that right out of the gate, she seems to be bonding well with her little sister. So well, in fact, that a shoving match breaks out between Em and Ella over who gets to "cud-doo" the baby next. I'm afraid she will soon be smothered. "It's Ella's turn," I announce.

"Can we still call her Butterfly Girl?" she asks eagerly, taking Em's place.

"Why not?" Joe replies. He's fetched the last of our bags from the car and now he plops down on the couch next to Ella and the baby.

Lucia has been Butterfly Girl since the eighteen-week ultrasound revealed her sex. We had asked the girls what they thought we should name their sister. Ella came up with Butterfly Girl, which received a second nod from Em. After a moment of intense brow furrowing, Ella, then barely four years old, had perceptively asked: "Mama, Dada, how do you *know* the baby is a sister?"

"Well . . ." Joe and I glanced at each other. With a house of predominantly girls, this question had never come up before. "Girls have a . . . vagina and boys have a penis," Joe explained, which prompted the inevitable follow-up: "What's a *peanits*?"

"A penis," Joe corrected Ella, "is what a boy goes tinkle with." "Can I see your peanits?" Ella asked, wide-eyed. "Uh, no!" Joe quickly responded and I buried my face in the couch cushion, trying unsuccessfully to stifle my laughter. Rolling our eyes at each other, Joe and I cobbled an explanation together that seemed to satisfy her curiosity, at least temporarily.

Ella thought this new intelligence was hilarious. She began to prance around the house, sending up the rousing cry: "Peanits! Vachiiiiiina!" Eventually, even Em, who clearly hadn't fully digested the information, her face adorably perplexed, eventually joined in the fun and soon they were both doubled over laughing on the rug.

"They're *your* children." I turned to Joe, and he, playing along, took mock offense: "How *dare* you?"

And now, here we are, on a beautiful spring day, at long last a complete family. Joe has managed to hoist all three of his daughters into his arms for a snapshot. My mother, watching in the background, wrings her hands.

"Joe, be careful!" she fusses good-naturedly, adding a measure of comedy to the sweetness of the moment. The baby's head rests on Joe's shoulder. Above the blanket emerge fine auburn hairs in matted whorls on a head so small that it would fit into an adult palm. The girls are perched precariously in the crook of Joe's other arm like koalas clinging to a tree branch. "Hurry," he says to me, "before I drop them!"

The picture comes out blurry; everyone's in motion. There will be other photos, many. I unabashedly love taking pictures. I am hardly ever without camera at hand these days, as the self-appointed chronicler of every holiday, trip, or preschool performance. My obsession for cataloging our lives baffles Joe. "How can you be enjoying the moment when you're behind the camera?" he had asked. "Maybe that's *my* way of enjoying it," I had responded, though well understanding the futility of attempting to freeze time and memory.

"Anyone here hungry for Bubby Meatballs and Spaghetti?" calls my mother, back in the kitchen. "Yes!" we all scream and after she's plated and served the steaming bowls, she asks if she can hold the baby for a while. "Of course," I say, and so my mother sits on the couch and smoothes her skirt down vigorously, tucks stray white hairs under her snood, and arranges the collar of her shirt. Composed, she reaches for Lucia. As she sits and stares into my baby's hazy newborn blue eyes with a look of simple pleasure and immense satisfaction, I feel a stirring in my heart, love muted by caution.

After finishing my lunch, I return to the couch and my mother places Lucia gently back into my arms. She is whimpering, so I put her to my breast, already cracked and sore from days of hospital feeding sessions. This time, I have promised myself, if the baby cannot latch on or I cannot produce more milk with all the unguents, machines, and lactation consultants at my disposal, I will not punish us both for months on end as I did with her older sister Ella. Formula feeding may not be ideal, but it is more than adequate, I now know.

Such are the charms of third-time parenting, I think. We recognize at each stage its imminent passage, that time will release us from one challenge as it heralds the next. "Preparedness," as my mother-in-law was fond of saying, "is half the battle."

The baby and I retire upstairs for a nap. I swaddle her carefully, then gently lower her, already sound asleep, into the yellow and white baby sling by my bed.

As I settle into the pillows, I can hear the murmured exchange of my mother and Joe in conversation downstairs. I can make out what I imagine is the clomping of Em and the more delicate patter of Ella. Sounds of play. Sounds of a childish argument escalating, an adult intercession, followed by a détente as the voices calm once more.

In these walls is everything I care about in the world. My family is whole.

I am reminded, in the way that refrains from my past intrude on my present, of the words of the Passover song about gratitude sung at every Seder in my youth, "Dayenu."

"It would have been enough had God freed us from slavery . . . *Dayenu!*"

"Had He taken us out of the land of Egypt, but not passed judgment on them, it would have been enough — *Dayenu!*"

"Had He split the sea for us, but not brought us through it to dry land, it would have been enough — *Dayenu!*"

Had Joe and I met and fell in love, it would have been enough!

Had we only married, it would have been enough!

Had we had even one precious child, it would have been enough!

Usually, counting my blessings is an anxiety-provoking task accompanied by the nagging worry that perhaps I have mistakenly received *too* much and that, inevitably, some belated heavenly accounting will be done, and, like the unlucky Job, I will lose it all.

For years, as my earthly bounties had accumulated — marriage, home, and children — this fear had made me shy away from any form of prayer except at my deepest moments of joy or sadness. I knew well that I had wrestled choice back from a God who, I had been told, required of me that I give it up. Who was I, then, to commune with Him, to ask favors, and, possibly, to remind Him that I was living in rebellion outside the margins of my faith?

All these thoughts, of course, presupposed an assumption that had hounded me from the day I left my mother's home: that God was real. As unwelcome as this was to me, I had to admit that I could not shake off a sense of His presence. Unlike my mother, the existence of a God did not spur me to discover and live by His will; rather the opposite. I had taken up camp as far away from Him as I could; we are in limbo, God and I, circling each other at arm's length.

This unease has meant that God is not a subject often discussed in our home, and when it arises, it's quickly dispatched. "Some people believe in a God," I tell my children. "You can believe in whatever you want." "Do *you* believe?" they ask me innocently. The question turns my stomach.

It was Kathy, my Catholic mother-in-law, who surprised me by imploring that I pass my Jewish faith on to my children. "I don't care what God they pray to, only that they have a God." For Kathy, faith was a wellspring of comfort in troubled times. I had nodded mutely, appreciating her request yet feeling unable to fulfill it. What is my faith, exactly? It was Joe who pushed against this idea more decisively. He saw no purpose in indoctrinating our children with stories that might or might not be entirely fabricated but, regardless, could not be proven.

"I don't think you quite *understand* faith," I had murmured. But I had no heart left, no stake in these arguments. My faith had come to me by way of marrow and bone. I could not rid myself of it, but neither could I bring myself to pass it on or explain it, and I certainly took no pride in it. To me, my God was a whispering, nagging presence, a murmuring over the deep that was my ineffable soul, here whether I wanted Him or not.

But today, on this beautiful spring day, perhaps on account of the sheer exhaustion or the onslaught of childbirth hormones, I find my lips forming prayer, tears flowing helplessly, tributaries from a hidden stream.

Dayenu.

I have more than my fair share and I know it.

I have every blessing this world has to offer.

I am blissed out with my lovely, ordinary life.

• 11 •

In the Land of Mist and Fog

Gather to Me My devout ones, sealers of My covenant
through sacrifice.   — PSALM 50:5

MY MOTHER AND URIYAH ACCOMPANIED ME TO THE AIR-
port on a muggy morning in August 1993 when I set off for
the shores of England. They had chosen to take the taxi ride with
me from Monsey to JFK airport, enduring over an hour and a
half of traffic through several of New York City's most congested
boroughs. Although I wanted to cling to them as long as possible,
their presence also served to prolong the anxiety I felt in leaving
my home.

Our cabdriver, a rotund Hasidic man with long reddish side
curls, was warm and talkative. He regaled us with stories about
his various passengers and their exploits as we jolted and bounced
over each pothole in his dented, dusty station wagon. He stayed
with us in the airport, leaving to grab a coffee and say afternoon
prayers, but not before he obliged us by taking our photograph in
front of the security line.

My mother and I are smiling in the photo, but the smiles fade
just short of our eyes. A family of three does not lightly let one
of its members go. When it was time for me to pass through the
checkpoint, my mother turned to me, her eyes wistful, proud, and

pained. Clasping my head in her hands, something which under ordinary circumstances would cause complaint, she examined me, then drew me to her. I wrapped my arms around her, burying my face in her shoulder, inhaling the leathery scent of her worn black purse strap, the powdery smell of old hairspray on her wig.

My brother, looking insubstantial in his ill-fitting yeshiva uniform, a black double-breasted suit and a fedora, had tears in his eyes when it was his turn to embrace me. From him, I received the awkward over-the-shoulder squeeze, his back rounded, drawing me in and pushing me away at the same time. "I'm proud of you, sis," he said, nodding as if to affirm the truth of his words, then looking away.

I swallowed hard. This was different than going up to the Catskill Mountains for the summer. Coming home would now entail purchasing an expensive transatlantic plane ticket in addition to taking a series of train, bus, and taxi rides. Home would no longer be where I spent the majority of my days; at least, not until the three years of seminary were over. And then? College, perhaps, in another part of the state? Followed by marriage and a new home? I realized with an ache that this was the end of childhood. Seventeen, which before had seemed so grand, now felt awfully young. One lingering look back, and then I fixed my gaze forward, surreptitiously swiping at escaping tears.

Once on the plane, I took my seat and settled in. It occurred to me that it had been nearly a decade since my last flight; my grandmother had abruptly ended our summertime visits to Long Island in my eighth year. "Grandma has grown too sensitive to the noise and excitement of children," my mother had explained our disinvitation. I had reacted to this betrayal with fury, sitting down to write my grandmother and ask her why she did not love us anymore. My mother, who read all my letters before they were mailed, wisely refused to send this one. I never fully forgave my grandmother, and I paid her back at the age of ten by shedding no tears when I learned of her death.

Now, as the plane climbed and plateaued, dipping and swaying in the strong air currents, I loosened my grip on my armrest and opened my book of Psalms. Praying calmed my nerves from the turbulence, and it was also a soothing distraction from the discomfort I felt being seated next to a man, whose very proximity would keep me in a quiet state of anxiety for the full six hours of the flight. What if he tried to talk to me? What would I say? He must have noticed my reticence, or at least the fact that I was bent over a book, because other than politely passing me the peanuts and Coke, we had no interactions the entire flight.

After my prayers I scoped out the seating arrangements, looking for other seminary girls and judging whether it was safe to pull out my copy of *Jane Eyre,* tucked into my carry-on bag. I had hidden the covers of the secular books I had taken with me — *The Count of Monte Cristo, The Collected Works of Edgar Allan Poe,* and, of course, my beloved *Jane* — under thin gift wrapping topped with clear contact paper. I had been discouraged by those "in the know" from bringing secular works to seminary but I couldn't imagine a month, much less three years, without these dear companions. Best to do, I decided, and ask forgiveness later.

A reconnaissance stroll assured me that the two seminary girls on my flight, seated beside each other, were occupied in chatter, so I opened the book. I was soon absorbed in Jane's awful treatment at Gateshead Hall, her abuse at the Lowood School, and her early days as a tutor to the ward of the mysterious, darkly cynical Mr. Rochester with whom a mutual distrust would shift to admiration, affection, then love. *How romantic.* To think that I was headed to the very place where Jane's journey had begun!

"What are you reading?" asked a voice above me. I started and looked up to find Ruchie, the blond first-year from Borough Park, standing in the aisle. I shut the book quickly and, feeling somewhat anxious, I told her. She shrugged. "I never heard of it. Is it good?" "It's great," I answered. She shrugged again. "This flight is sooooo long. You should come by us to talk." She moved on.

When the plane landed with a teeth-chattering thump, I craned my neck eagerly for my first sight of this new country, but we had arrived in the predawn hours and the world beyond the airport was still cloaked in darkness.

When the sun finally rose outside the steel-and-cement block of Manchester Airport, I was too busy racing with my luggage and a gaggle of sem girls that had arrived from different countries, trying to catch the train to the city of Newcastle, just over the Tyne River from Gateshead. Finally settled into my seat, I gazed out the train window. I couldn't help but be disappointed by my first glimpses of England. What I saw was a city with dull brick buildings. Where were the Brontës' windswept moors?

The train picked up speed and we soon left the urban sprawl behind us. *This is more like it.* Gone were the tenements and modern buildings. We zipped past endless acres of farmland, crumbling stone walls, clusters of sheep and goats that seemed to have free rein in these rolling hills of Northumbria. Towns appeared and disappeared with speed, some charming and quaint, others large and more industrial. Their names were delightfully British, and I repeated them under my breath after the conductor, rolling them about on my tongue with what I imagined was an excellent Queen's English: *Leeds, York, Huddersfield, Darlington, Durham.*

I sat with the other sem girls, but I was too tired to join in much conversation. I listened with half an ear as the second- and third-year students filled us first-years in about the rabbis, their lessons, room assignments, and other particulars of dormitory life. I learned then that I could be assigned to a room with up to seven other girls! This was a worrying proposal, as I had suffered from frequent bouts of insomnia since middle school.

"Eight-girl rooms are the best!" chirped a curly-haired upper-classwoman, bangs sprayed into a stiff wave that arched over a mildly acned forehead. I took stock of her long navy-blue pleated skirt and white starched blouse buttoned high on the neck and at the wrists, and for the first time I questioned the appropriateness of my own white blouse whose huge puffy poet sleeves now seemed immodestly ostentatious.

"Are there single rooms?" I queried tentatively. "Oh, no!" said Curly, raising a pert chin. There were doubles, she said, but those went only to T-1 girls. T-1 girls were the third-years, as the classes went in descending numerical order: term three, term two, term one. "But you don't want a double anyway," she added decisively. "Making friends is what it's all about!" *It is?* There seemed to be vigorous agreement from the rest of the group.

Suddenly, I missed my mother so keenly that I pressed my hand to my heart to contain the hurt. I turned to the window again to mask my tears. *It will be fine,* I chided myself. *You haven't even gotten there. Give it time.*

After the train pulled into the Newcastle station, we hurriedly unloaded our luggage and stood in line for one of the large shiny black cabs that would take us to Gateshead. When it was our turn, Ruchie and I clambered into the back seat and were greeted by the driver who, when he opened his mouth, seemed to be speaking in tongues.

The thick northern accent was unlike any I had heard before, something in the neighborhood of a Scottish brogue but with words sliced up in odd places, randomly punctuated by a series of "eee"s and "aii"s. I had been warned by my travel mates that Geordie, the local dialect, would take several months to learn. Somehow, Ruchie and I managed to communicate our destination. Staring out the cab window, I gazed, rapt, at the city of Newcastle, formerly a medieval fort that had since erupted into a riot of different architectural styles, adding imposing Greek and elaborate Renaissance to its spindly medieval buttresses and looming gargoyles. Old buildings hugged narrow winding streets alongside immense, modern structures with large storefronts and bright signs.

The view in Gateshead was far less appealing, the buildings plainer, boxier, and repetitive. Once in the residential area, we passed street after street of brick row homes girded at one end by a church and at the other by a convenience store or pub. The symbolism of such a setup was not lost on me: church, home, pub . . . Life in this economically depressed region seemed squeezed into a cycle of the aspirational, the ordinary, and the baser of human pursuits. Aside from a few floral displays in front of public spaces, the only greenery seemed to be rows of boxy hedges that lined the fronts of private homes. It wasn't Newcastle, which I vowed to myself to explore, but I didn't mind too much. I hadn't come for the physical city, I reminded myself.

When we pulled up in front of the three-story brick row house about midway down broad Bewick Road, our driver declared that we had reached our destination by applying the brakes. Ruchie and I split the fare, handing the driver what seemed like colorful play money after he pointed to the meter. Passing through the front door, we found ourselves in the hallway of a house whose interior had been transformed into, on the left, the administrative offices of Gateshead Seminary and, on the right and up the stairs, three large lecture halls. We were greeted by girls with notepads who checked our room assignments and pointed to a bulletin board with details about orientation activities. We were each to check in personally with Rabbi Simcha Kohn, the vice principal and founder's son, as soon as possible, preferably within the next twenty-four hours. Until then, we were on our own to find our way to and from our bedrooms, the dining hall, and various introductory assemblies.

• • •

Gateshead Seminary sprawled from 50 Bewick Road down to 24, which was the home of Rabbi Roberts and his wife, who would act as our "den mother." The first two houses, 48 and 50, had been hollowed out to create the lecture halls, each of which would be filled by between one hundred and twenty to one hundred and eighty girls, depending on the year (despite the fact that parents vouched that their daughters would stay all three years, marriage would deplete at least a third of our class before graduation). On the first floor of all the row houses, a narrow patch of wall had been knocked down, creating one long hallway that served as a tunnel between the dormitories and classrooms.

My first room assignment was a small attic dormer about halfway down the row houses. I was immensely relieved to find that I had not, after all, "scored" an eight-girl room but rather a four-girl room, which I shared with another American, an Israeli, and a French girl.

Most of the four hundred or so girls at Gateshead Sem hailed from the larger British communities of Manchester or London; about fifty were local to Gateshead itself. The rest were Israelis, Americans, Continental Europeans, and a smattering of Canadians, South Africans, and South Americans. With the exception of Gateshead natives, who went home to their families in the evenings, we shared the cramped quarters, ate in the same large dining room, and prayed together.

Since I was the first of my roommates to arrive, I chose the bed closest to the window, from which, as evening fell, I was witness to the most glorious sunset of my life. I lingered by the window, transfixed, until the broad streaks of gold, orange, and violet faded into the blue-black of night. The sky had seemed impossibly close to my attic window, which I wedged open, then spread my arms wide, feeling as though I could sweep the clouds with my fingertips.

• • •

Skies aside, my first days in Gateshead were fairly dreary. Jet-lagged and homesick, I was unable to sleep a wink the night of my arrival. By daybreak, I couldn't keep warm, shivering under every blanket I owned plus several cardigans and a wool coat. I was teary and weak but afraid to leave my room and seek food because I did not want to cry in front of others. By the afternoon, having missed an orientation activity and not shown up to visit Rabbi Kohn, I was paid a visit by Mrs. Roberts.

The brisk but kind-mannered dorm mother was a pretty woman in her late forties with one of the sharpest chins I had ever seen and a patrician nose to match. Her London accent (the Jews never spoke Geordie, I discovered) was clipped but her tone was soft as she said: "Oh dear, we must get you some food and a place to rest." I gratefully accepted the offer of a bowl of hot soup and a blessedly quiet bedroom in her home, though I didn't think I would be able to sleep. However, when I opened my eyes, the sun had gone down again, and I was feeling warm and somewhat more human, ready to begin orienting myself to life as a Gateshead Sem girl.

The following morning, after a quick breakfast and prayers, we raced to the T-3 classroom for our first lecture. At the door was a diagram of the classroom seating assignments, and I found my place in one of the many row desks with interior slots for our notebooks and supplies. The desks were crammed in lines both facing and perpendicular to a raised dais in the middle upon which the rabbis' lectern and microphone stood.

Prior to our first lesson, a third-year prefect arrived to address the class and lay out the ground rules: We were to stand when a *rav* entered the classroom (preferably *before,* with the help of a scout by the door) and sit only once he was seated and had given us express permission. We were to address the rabbis in the respectful third-person, never referring to any of them as *you* but only as the *rav* or Rabbi so-and-so. "It may take a little getting used to," admitted our guide, "but it's the way we show our holy teachers the *kovod,* respect, they deserve." Venerating the rabbis was akin to honoring the Torah knowledge they embodied, which itself was equivalent to paying due homage to the Almighty.

We were further warned against speaking out of turn during lectures or displaying any lax standard of behavior, despite what might have been the norm in our countries of origin (and for an example of this, we were treated to the story of the American who had, *during* a lecture, no less, *put her feet up* on the chair in front of her). After these admonitions, we watched, wide-eyed and silent, as the first of our *rabbonim* entered the room.

I cannot recall who provided our first lecture that day. It might have been Rabbi Sternbuch, tall and slender, in his seventies, with an impressively Teutonic bone structure and a shiny, bald pate upon which sat a large black skullcap.

Rabbi Sternbuch taught us Chumash, the Five Books of Moses, speaking so softly that we strained to catch the words that even the microphone could not adequately amplify until suddenly, having reached a critical point, he would thunder into the mike, causing us to jump in our seats. Rabbi Sternbuch carried about him an otherworldly air, rarely gazing directly at students, so our class representative, sitting at the foot of the lectern, had the unenviable task of interrupting him when a girl raised her hand with a question. When he was thus disturbed from his train of thought, he would look momentarily dazed and, frequently, annoyed. This lack of focus on the students at his feet was evidence, I was told, of the man's holiness and rare state of perfection. He was a true *tzaddik* and we were lucky to have him teach us girls.

It's also possible that our first lesson was delivered by Rabbi Katz. Tall, gangly, with a light brown beard and a wide grin from which protruded an ample set of teeth, Rabbi Katz was our jovial and somewhat mischievous teacher of Jewish history. Fond of puns and full of interesting facts, he had recently authored a book attempting to distill the more theologically palatable basics of earth science and biology as seen through the lens of the Torah. Rabbi Katz would frequently enthuse that the material world was concrete proof, even at the subatomic level, of God's glorious plan. I welcomed his warm and humble manner, as well as his sense of humor.

Rabbi Katz's easygoing attitude, I would discover, belied a warrior-like commitment to maintaining the purity of Jewish youth. Shortly after a billboard featuring an immodestly clad model went up on a nearby road, the picture was vandalized, painted over in the middle of the night. The billboard was replaced by an identical one, only to have the same thing happen. The vigilante or vigilantes were never caught, but rumors abounded that it was Rabbi Katz, with the help of several Gateshead Yeshiva boys and an extension ladder, who had done the deed in sanctification of God's name.

In all likelihood, however, our first lesson was delivered by one of the Millers, father or son, Rabbi Miller or Rav Miller, as we called them to distinguish between the two.

Rabbi M. Miller was the father, wizened and arthritic but sharp as a blade, with a wry sense of humor that could be, at times, quite cutting if a girl hadn't thought through a question or response with sufficient care. Rav T. Miller was the son, slight and dark with a sparse beard that reminded me of King Tut's. He possessed a nervous energy and was rarely given to laughter or even a smile. Both were inspiring lecturers, but I preferred the son's classes. They were suffused with hellfire and brimstone, laced with deadly sarcasm and high drama.

More than the manner of delivery, it was the material in Rav Miller's lessons that seemed less . . . condescending than that in our other courses. Several of our rabbis openly nodded to the dictum of the authoritative twelfth-century Jewish philosopher Maimonides, who claimed that to teach a girl the Torah (outside of what she needed to know to fulfill her daily duties) was as if one taught her idleness and empty matters. She did not, Maimonides believed, have sufficient discernment or intellect to make use of such study.

Rav Miller did not seem, at least to me, to subscribe to this infuriatingly demeaning approach.

The lessons he prepared for us had many sources we would be unlikely to access elsewhere, from both the Talmud and esoteric works of Jewish mysticism.

Furthermore, the style of exposition in Rav Miller's classes was that of *pilpul,* from the word *pepper,* named so because of the sharp, incisive manner in which a biblical passage would be dissected. At the start of our inquiry, various sources would be brought in to aid interpretation, which would only lead to more confusion and questions until, using one of the many rules of interpretation, we would find some commonality between one verse or another, enabling us to tie the entire matter up into a lovely, elegantly scaffolded piece of intellectual and moral discovery.

Rav Miller's expansive teaching materials and methods received a mixed reception from seminary parents. Many fathers did not approve of their daughters' returning home for the holidays full of "arrogance," believing that the smattering of Talmudic learning gleaned from the ditto sheets they were handed before each lesson gave them an understanding of the Torah on par with their brothers. This perspective, so casually repeated by my classmates, revolted me. Many a time I had to bite my tongue to prevent myself from saying pointed things to a girl about her own father.

Despite Rav Miller's controversial teaching style, his position was unassailable. He was the son of the revered Rabbi Miller, who was himself a star pupil of Rabbi Elijah Dessler, who had brought to England the European Mussar movement, which held the belief that it was bad *middos,* character traits, and the replacing of the Torah of old with the Golden Calf of the Enlightenment that had set in motion the destruction of the Holocaust. It was essential for us to subjugate our personal will to God's so that no such tragedy could befall us again. This ideology of subjugation was foundational to everything we learned at seminary.

My daily life in seminary fell into a routine: morning classes, a break for lunch, then free time, after which the late afternoons and evenings were spent with an assigned study partner, a *chavrusa,* to review texts for upcoming lessons. Our days were capped off with dinner, an occasional lecture, evening prayer, and then bed.

We didn't see much of the Jewish Gateshead community outside our walls other than when we went to synagogue on the Sabbath or to Stenhouse, the kosher grocer on Coatsworth Road, where we made small purchases and timed our visits to avoid "boy shopping hours." Most girls also went "helping" each Friday afternoon at one of the homes in the community, where they would assist an overworked matriarch with the cooking and cleaning necessary for the coming day of rest.

While we had little to do with our Jewish neighbors, we had even less to do with the goyim, as we called the gentile community around us. Gateshead Jews, who had begun to settle here in the years following World War II, had never assimilated with their gentile neighbors, and tensions had metastasized over the years between the native Gateshead citizenry and the town's Jewish "interlopers," as they continued to be seen. Decades of poverty and governmental neglect following the demise of the area's chief industry, coal, had led to struggling schools, a dearth of well-paying jobs, and gangs of disaffected youth, many of whom turned their ire on any "stranger," including the seminary girls and yeshiva boys who showed up each fall in droves. During my tenure in Gateshead, I was frequently subjected to the spit, epithets, and drunken serenading of the local populace, even, on occasion, being pelted with stones. Because the streets weren't safe, we were warned to take walks in groups and never after dark or outside the area that we referred to as the "Gateshead Ghetto."

This uneasy coexistence served to highlight, for many of my peers, the existential differences between Yidden, Jews, and goyim, gentiles. Perhaps my high-school teachers had been carefully selective or maybe I had already been infected by what was referred to as the "sickness of the outside world," but I was shocked at the way my rabbis referred to those of different faiths and ethnicities.

This perspective, claimed to be supported by various passages in the Talmud and the most reputable *meforshim,* struck me as impossibly unjust. That gentiles had qualitatively lower souls, purposes, and value and were created as a means to an end to serve the Chosen People or that, likewise, women had an auxiliary purpose to serve men rankled my heart.

It was an oft-repeated refrain: A man's *tachlis,* or purpose, was to learn Torah, by which he would reach *diveikus,* a melding, to God Himself, through his intellect. A woman's purpose was to enable her husband's greatness by fulfilling any and all of his material needs and ensuring that the faith and values of her children remained intact. Since one's purpose was one's destiny, deviation from it could only lead to unhappiness and loss.

Most painful was the fact that my classmates not only seemed to concur with their demotion; they frequently seemed to take a perverse pride in it. "It's all very nice to learn these deep things, but really, is it practical?" I would hear one after another question. "We don't need to know this" was another common complaint. "Better we spend our time memorizing the laws of *kashrus*" — keeping kosher — "and Sabbath so that we can fulfill our *tachlis* to create a Torah-observant home." I wanted to shake them, to scream, to ask them how they could be so complacent about this belittling assignment.

I soon learned to keep silent about these and other injustices. One day, hearing the wail of a siren passing my dorm room, I said a prayer under my breath for the vehicle's unfortunate occupant. "What are you saying?" asked my Israeli roommate. "I am saying *tefilos*" — prayers — "for the person in the ambulance," I innocently replied. She was immediately concerned. "How could you use God's name if you don't know if it is a goy or a Yid you are praying for?" When I reacted with distaste to her question, she threatened to ask a rabbi to set me straight. I told her this would be unnecessary. I continued to pray for anyone in trouble, the difference being that, in the future, I kept my prayers, and my thoughts, inside my head.

As I entered the last trimester of my first year, I seriously considered leaving Gateshead for good. I didn't fit in here. Few of these girls were the independent-thinking personalities that I had imagined they would be, given the school's reputation. Also disappointing was the way the rabbis dangled carrots of knowledge in front of us with one hand while pushing us away with the other. To me, as I described to my mother in a letter, they were akin to Marie Antoinette, except they would say with disdain, "Let them *bake* cake."

It was my mother who urged me to reconsider leaving. "You must not confuse *Jews* with *Judaism*," she reminded me. The rabbis, she explained, were limited in their understanding of women because most women *were* stereotypically frivolous. I must forgive and overlook these things if I was to achieve my own greatness, because for that, I *must* drink from their well of wisdom. She chided me for having a tendency toward hasty judgment. She warned me not to let the "few things that disturbed" me make me "cut off my nose to spite my face."

I agreed to stay, to stick it out, to question only when appropriate.

When I returned to the seminary after summer break to begin my second year, it was as if I were two distinct people. The one was an enthusiastic student, praised by classmates and rabbis alike for her keen and insightful participation in class. The other, emerging only after class hours, was something of a recluse. She retired to her bedroom to nap, read, or write in her diary, skipping most, and eventually all, study sessions, often wandering the streets of Newcastle alone until dusk approached and she needed to take a cab or bus back to the seminary.

I always had an excuse at the ready for why I needed to go into town. I had to pick up a new notebook, a fresh set of nibs for my fountain pen, another incidental. Sometimes I returned home from these excursions with something extra, a classic from Henry James or Tolstoy purchased at the bookstore. I found increasingly, though, that I lacked the necessary concentration to finish these works. I imagined it was due to my never having fully adapted to my sleeping arrangements so that most nights I slept poorly, frequently coming down with bronchitis, tonsillitis, or, if I was lucky, some garden-variety cold. Whatever the reason, my mental state began to resemble the fog for which this region was known. I felt as though I were floating through the world, making landfall only during my favorite lectures, the rest of the time feeling insubstantial, disconnected, plagued by a pressing sadness.

I shared these feelings with a single confidante, my mother.

During our weekly phone calls she offered me various practical solutions for this growing feeling of "frustration," as she put it, like praying daily for greater understanding and acceptance of my role in life and, above all, choosing to view those things that bothered me most about my rabbis and peers with a practiced patience, a trait she felt I sorely lacked. Time would change everything for me if I let it, my mother promised. God had a plan, of that I could be sure. I must learn to surrender — or I might never discover it.

• 12 •

Changes

But whether small or great, and no matter what the stage or grade of life, the call rings up the curtain, always, on a mystery of transfiguration – a rite, or moment, of spiritual passage, which, when complete, amounts to a dying and a birth. The familiar life horizon has been outgrown; the old concepts, ideals and emotional patterns no longer fit; the time for the passing of a threshold is at hand.

— JOSEPH CAMPBELL, *The Hero with a Thousand Faces*

"MAMA! MAAAMAAA!"
Urgent screams pierce the night. My eyes fly open. The baby monitor on my bedside table is blinking madly. I stumble out of bed and follow the sound to the girls' bedroom. It's Em, of course, and she's in full-on panic mode. It's two a.m., so that means I haven't been asleep for more than an hour since Lucia's last feeding. *Damn.* I quickly shut the door to the baby's room and head toward the source of the tortured sound.

"*Shhh . . . shhh . . . shhh.*" I kneel beside my toddler, passing my hand gently over her wet face: "What's wrong? Did you have a bad dream again?" The glow cast by the ceramic Cinderella night-light, Em's favorite princess, a gift for her second birthday, barely enables me to see her small, shaking form, which I press to my chest.

"Mama, I need to change." She sobs into my T-shirt, her breath becoming ragged as she tries, unsuccessfully, to simultaneously push sound out and draw breath in: "I . . . need . . . to . . . change!"

A quick feel tells me Em's pajamas are dry; in fact, even her night pull-up is still pretty stiff and flat. Ella stirs uncomfortably in the opposite bed, the waterproof sheet beneath her crackling as she rolls over. I start to plead softly, hoping Em will mimic my hushed tones: "Go back to sleep, honey, please, your clothes are fine. You picked them, remember?"

"Noooooooooo," she keens. "They not fine, they *bad!*" Her voice begins to rise again, and I just know that in a moment Ella will wake up and so will the baby and this brief night will be over. "I *need*" — she pauses to suck in shallow breaths; her hands drag down her cheeks, bat at her face — "to *chaaange!*"

I clasp her small hands in mine, pull them away from her face, come to a decision. "Okay. Sh-sh-sh-sh-sh . . . If you are quiet *right now,* I will get you some clothes, but *I* will get you the clothes, no lights, no more noise."

I appear to have brokered a deal because we are both left in the near dark with her labored breathing. Feeling my way, I grab an armful of clothes from the girls' bureau and walk Em out into the lighted hall.

Her round face is tear-streaked and blotchy. Bubbles of snot emerge from her nostrils. My annoyance evaporates at this pitiful sight and what's left is a familiar, gnawing anxiety. *What is this, my love?* I reach to fold her in my arms again, but she pushes me away sleepily and soon hands me her outfit of choice for the second half of this interrupted night, an austere black T-shirt and dark yoga pants. Mollified, she waits patiently as I dress her, even letting me kiss her as I tuck her back into bed, smoothing her matted hair back from her damp face. I sit and wait by her side for a moment to be sure that she is at peace.

Joe's shadow momentarily blocks the light as he appears in the doorway to the girls' room. He shrugs his arms and mouths, *What happened?*

I register a flicker of resentment that he has arrived only after the night's headlining event is over. Em is asleep, her breath easing into regular rhythm, and Ella, blessedly, has not stirred again. "She needed to change," I echo Em. He rubs his face. "Has she ever done this before?" "What do you mean?" I reply sharply. "Only about ten times today." "No," he says. "I meant in the middle of the night."

Buzzing with thoughts, I toss the rejected clothes into a laundry pile on the bathroom floor and ease back under the covers. This *was* new, and yes, it appeared to elevate this months-long clothes-changing obsession into something a little more . . . concerning.

This is not normal, anxious-me says. *You're paranoid,* disgusted-with-anxious-me parries.

Em is . . . just Em. I rope myself in firmly. She's a two-and-a-half-year-old juggernaut with the fortitude of a weathered army general and the executive function of an excitable puppy. Add the hair-trigger temper and the need to have things "just so," and there you had it, a somewhat more resistant case of the terrible twos. I remind myself: Just because she's draining more than her fair share of my parenting reserves doesn't mean there's something wrong with *her.* Maybe it's I who am inadequate to the task. Perhaps I must think more, read more, ask around more.

I could talk to Ruthann again.

Our Early Intervention specialist is the one who pointed to Em's sensory-processing disorder as a possible cause for her constant clothes-changing. "She may feel the need for the additional sensory input that the fabric on skin provides," she had theorized after several hours of testing during which she and the occupational therapist observed things like Em's deliberate (and often bruising) crash landings into stationary objects and the way she would not, could not, sit still at all. A sensory deficit, they had explained, meant that Em didn't experience the same level of physical groundedness that most people took for granted, the comfort of floor against foot, chair against bottom, the weight of clothing on her back. It was the explanation for her "knock-abouted-ness," as Joe and I called it. "Have you ever seen this particular clothes-changing obsession before in a kid?" I asked Ruthann. "Well . . . not exactly in this way," she had admitted.

Yes, Ruthann will have a plan, I decide. I will get in touch with her in the morning after I drop Ella off at preschool. With this issue resolved, I fall back into a heavy, dreamless sleep.

"Does it feel like a *ritual?*" Ruthann wants to know. I assume her thoughts are headed toward obsessive-compulsive disorders. The thought had crossed our minds too. "The changing does, a bit," I respond, "but it feels kind of random at times, and she's not a particularly neat or compulsive person otherwise."

"Hmmm . . . write down when it happens," Ruthann advises. "Make a log and see if there is something that triggers it. Is there a particular time of day or activity?" And though I don't actually write it down, I take mental note over the next few days of when Em starts to fret and whimper about changing her clothes, and for the most part it does appear random. The only time I can predict its onset with accuracy is following a tantrum. And those, unfortunately, are all too frequent these days, triggered by a wrong look, a passing touch, anything, really.

"She's had a lot of changes to contend with," my mother says on the phone that evening. "A new sibling, being the middle child, toilet training, starting school in just over a month," she lists. "Plus she's a sensitive child . . . and," she continues, "I hope you won't get angry at me for saying this, but you're too lenient with her. She needs *you* to be the parent. You must set the boundaries of acceptable behavior and norms."

Too late — I *am* angry. "Oh, for God's sake," I retort. "You're not here. You don't see the multiple time-outs or any of that stuff. It's pretty easy to come up with 'just rein her in' over the phone!"

My mother's choice of words — "acceptable behavior and norms" — makes me stiffen. I remember how it was applied to my brother, who had come back into my life only recently after almost a decade of minimal contact.

Our near estrangement was not a choice I made. My mother had cautioned me against fully disclosing the extent to which I had left the faith, so when my brother and I spoke on the phone every few months, I found our conversations trivial and stilted. In my last year of graduate school, tired of the secrecy, I admitted to him that I had left our religious upbringing far behind. Imagine my shock when my brother confessed he'd done the same. He too had been advised against full disclosure. I was happy to welcome my brother back into my life, but I was sad to learn that his path into the secular world had been harder than mine. He had left the yeshiva world years ago, but he had not yet settled on a profession or found a long-term relationship.

Peripatetic, impulsive, unsettled; it could not be denied that Uriyah lived either on or outside some boundary where most people managed to dig out spots and build stable lives. Did my mother see the same wildness in Em? Is that why she was so hard on her?

When we hang up, I am still sulking and feeling shamefully adolescent for it. The following day, my mother's rebuke still ringing in my ears, I am testy and short-tempered with Em, and when she informs me that she needs to change, right after breakfast, at that moment when I am a whirling dervish trying to stuff backpacks, wipe faces, jacket children, and get out the door by 8:23 sharp, I drop to one knee and fix her with a wide-eyed stare, much as I would a disobedient puppy: "*No.*"

She lifts her fists, glancing past me to the stairwell. I am quick, catching her as she attempts to ram me aside. I hold her fists down gently as she screams, looking directly in her eyes again: "N-o," I spell. "No means *no!*" I am certain that the power of this mommy glare would have frozen a rabid Rottweiler, but Em's will appears unbroken. At the end of another five or so loud, harrowing minutes in time-out, from which there emanate howls and crashes that leave Ella cowering in the corner with her hands clapped over her ears and the baby in hysterical tears, I have had enough.

I pick Em up by the waist with one hand and the baby's car seat with the other, yell to Ella to "Get a move on, for God's sake, and don't forget your bag," and we burst out the door. Because she is flailing so hard, Em tips over and is hanging upside down from my arm. I proceed down the driveway in this fashion, wondering if I have pulled a muscle in my shoulder and all the while praying that my neighbor Christine is not hanging laundry at this very minute on the fence that separates our properties.

And that is when Em chooses to let go, and the warm malodorous wet spreads into the side of my hoodie, and now, at this blasted moment, I am closer to letting loose the foulest language on my daughter than you could pay me to admit. And because we are already ten minutes late, and because there is no way I'm going to let her add a "pee grenade" to her arsenal, I plop my wet child into her car seat and buckle her in.

I toss the dirty hoodie out the car window and peel out of the driveway in reverse. Em shrieks for most of the ride to school and when she runs out of steam and there is a momentary pause, Ella's small, frightened voice cuts in: "Em, you can change as soon as you get home, right, Mama?" Em looks at her sister reproachfully and then, leaning toward her as close as the seat belt will allow, screams loudly and wordlessly into her face. Ella shrinks away, her green eyes filling immediately, and I can see, glancing in the rearview mirror, that Em feels bad about it but she's not going to back down, not now. Her tear-streaked face is mired in truculence.

I sigh. "Ella, patient big sister, let's leave Em alone. She's having a difficult day." We pull into the small parking area by the side of the Purpose School. The one advantage to being this late is that the lot is nearly empty. As we walk up to the double doors of the white schoolhouse, I think about how miserable we must all look. Mrs. Kilty, the secretary, appears a few moments after I ring the bell. I fix a smile on my face. "Hard morning?" she asks sympathetically, glancing down at Em.

"I would say so," I answer, rolling my eyes, trying to make light of it all.

When Ella is safely handed off, we are once again on our way, but I am feeling resentful for my oldest child. This isn't the way I wanted her day to start. This isn't fair for her. After a relatively subdued ride home, I send Em upstairs and text Joe, who after a morning sales call is back and moving about in his home office: *Talk when you get off the phone?*

"How many days do we have left before she starts school?" Joe asks a while later, sitting on Em's bed. "About three weeks," I answer. "And Kristie wants her to come in for picture day next week." Since Em had missed the cutoff for the first day of school that year, she wouldn't be starting at Purpose School until the day after Thanksgiving, when she turned 2.9 years old precisely. The school's director, Kristie Colwell, had thoughtfully suggested that Em might be well served by coming in to meet her classmates on picture day. Now I wasn't so sure that this was a good idea. What if she pulled a stunt like the one from this morning? Would Kristie hand me my deposit back?

I couldn't imagine Em staying home another year.

Despite her increasing tantrums and odd behaviors, Em was a bright kid and quite capable for her age. Also, for the most part, Hurricane Em reached peak gale-force winds only *inside* our home, when lashing out at myself, Joe, and occasionally Ella. She was actually pretty manageable outside the house — if you gave her a little space and time when she started to fuss. I was also fairly certain she wouldn't lose her cool on another classmate. She was downright loving and gentle with "her baby," as she called Lucia, and didn't seem to show any animosity toward other children, though she didn't seek their companionship either. We decide to give picture day a go, preparing ourselves as best we can.

When picture day arrives, we choose Em's clothes with extra care. After all, they must last all the way through ten thirty, when we will have dutifully smiled for the camera and be on our way home. Em is visibly excited for the visit, though I can tell she's nervous as well. Her fingers keep wandering from Buddy, her well-loved, long-eared white bunny doll, to the tulle details on the light blue shirt from the Gap that she has chosen, which features three little ballerinas. After we drop Ella off at eight thirty we head to Pignone's Café for a special treat — a stack of Mickey Mouse pancakes for Em and corned beef hash and eggs for me. We have time for a rapid grocery dash and we're back at Purpose for the photo shoot.

Em stands at the doorway of the Beginnings Room and stares at the kids inside, who have already started to line up for the class picture. Mrs. Hunt and Mrs. Lovetere, her teachers, have arranged a row of tiny wooden chairs at the back of the room and now they are attempting to arrange two rows of nearly as tiny, dressed-to-the-nines children. There is a space for Em at the end of the top row and Mrs. Hunt, a trim, short-haired blond woman in her sixties with glasses and a kind face, warmly beckons her forth.

As I move forward Em pulls back and there's a moment when I almost lose my balance and drop Lucia. She tugs hard on my sleeve again, and I bend down.

"Can I change now, Mama?" she whispers.

Oh, crap. "Five minutes," I say, holding up my fingers. "Five minutes and then the photo will be done, and we can go home and celebrate, and you can change!" She tugs me down again. "But Mama," she says, her stage whisper wincingly loud. I can hear the kids start to lose their places in the row, the sounds of incipient unraveling, "I change *first, then* I take a photo." "No," I respond, and my voice is low and steady without a hint of give. "First photo, *then* change." I point to the kids, who by now are staring at us, and I can feel the sweat start to trickle down my back. She glances at me one more time to gauge my level of commitment, then moves forward.

Mrs. Hunt cheerfully introduces Em to the class and points to the empty space beside her, but I can see that Em's face is still pinched and tight. She shakes her head vigorously and when I step forward to intervene, Mrs. Lovetere, an auburn-haired, grandmotherly woman with smiling brown eyes, waves a warning hand at me. I back off. "My friend," she says, addressing Em, "you can stand *next* to us if you don't want to stand here, okay?" Em thus stands on the periphery of the group. When the rapid-fire flashes go off, I exhale. Em immediately bolts for me. Hanging off my legs she begins to beg, "Take me home, Mama, please, Mama!" I bid everyone a hasty but sunny "See you very soon!" and we make our exit.

When the pictures finally come home in Ella's backpack a few days before Thanksgiving, there is an undeniable comedic quality to the Beginnings Room class photo. In it, there are two poised, smiling teachers and two rows of neatly arranged children, a few of whom, despite having been instructed to look at the camera and say "Cheese," are gaping in curiosity at a pintsize brown-haired girl in a long-sleeved blue shirt who stands to the side, leaning as far away from them as possible without actually tipping over. She has her left elbow raised and bent in front of her, much as if she were warding off a badly aimed Frisbee or a misfired tennis ball, and her expression, a chin-raised wounded dignity, is, in its own way, utterly priceless.

• 13 •

The Circumference of Thine Feet

From thus distempered breast,
Adam, estranged in look and altered style,
Speech intermitted thus to Eve renewed:
"Would thou hadst hearkened to my words, and stayed
With me, as I besought thee, when that strange
Desire of wandering, this unhappy morn,
I know not whence possessed thee."

— JOHN MILTON, *Paradise Lost*

T WAS A BLUSTERY AFTERNOON IN THE LATE FALL OF 1994 during my T-2 year at seminary, when I headed out to Newcastle for my regular afternoon jaunt. After picking up my usual trifles, I ended up meandering a good deal farther down Westgate Road than I had before, a steep, bustling street that wound toward the banks of the Tyne River.

Although dusk was approaching, and I was eager to catch the next bus back to Gateshead, I was arrested by the words on a sign, engraved in gold, beside the imposing Greek columns of a large stone fortress, which announced with some grandeur that

I was standing on the steps of no less an edifice than the LITER-
ARY AND PHILOSOPHICAL SOCIETY OF NEWCASTLE-UPON-TYNE,
ESTABLISHED 1793. My curiosity piqued, I tried the door.

After passing through the lobby and going up a grand staircase ornamented with portraits of austere individuals and bas-re-
liefs of decapitated horses and centurions in the heat of battle, I
came upon a second set of doors. Within, I discovered a cavern-
like room, several stories tall, lined with books up to the vaulted
domed ceiling, crowned by several immense skylights. The room
was carpeted, quiet except for the rustling of pages. The scents
of old paper, leather, and library glue were intoxicating. No one
stopped me, so I began to explore the enchanting place, reading
the bindings on the sides of the volumes, some new, some quite
old. Glass cases housed curios, stuffed birds, and old manuscripts.
It had the air of a museum.

"Are you a member?" asked a whispered voice behind me. I
turned quickly. "Oh, no," I said, blushing furiously at the neatly
dressed woman with short, feathered gray hair who had addressed
me. "I was just curious." I backed away, preparing to leave.

"We're offering discounted memberships to students," the
woman said eagerly. *Membership? To this palace of knowledge?*
An image of myself spending those lonely afternoons in the company of books nearly made me swoon. I examined the form the
woman now handed me. The student membership fee was manageable. "It's only twenty pounds?" I asked, skeptical that this
small fee was all it took to access the treasures in this room. "It is
if you get the signature of your school's academic dean," she replied, smiling.

My hopes fell. I could never ask Rabbi Kohn to sign this.
Even the name of the place, the Literary and Philosophical Society, stank of heresy; to Orthodox Jews, *philosophy* connoted the
canon of ideas belonging to the secular world. Disappointed, I
thanked the woman and tucked the paper into my purse so as not
to be rude. On my walk toward the bus stop, I found myself un-

able to let go of the idea. *What if?* Could I make this happen? I began to plot out my request. I would not ask Rabbi Kohn, I decided, but rather the elderly Rabbi Miller, who, according to local lore, had been dissuaded from a promising career as a barrister to engage in Torah studies. He was known to have a soft spot for secular classics, and I had even heard him quote Shakespeare in class. By the time I returned to seminary, I was determined to ask Rabbi Miller the very next day, before I lost my nerve.

Rabbi Miller's eyes were bright and smiling when he welcomed me into his office the following afternoon. I believed that he liked me, appreciating the bold way that I raised my hand and asked unusual questions in class. "What can I do for you today, Miss Netzer?"

I carefully began the speech I had rehearsed.

"If the *rav* approves, I would like to ask the *rav* to consider signing this paper" — said paper waved about — "which would allow me to have a membership in the Literary and Philosophical Society of Newcastle."

I was met with silence and a blank stare.

"Most of the books are classical." I tried to sound casual as I went on, but my heart was pounding, and my words became rushed, knocking into each other in my haste. "It's not a regular sort of library. Membership only. Not the regular type of goyim going there. It would not detract from my studies . . ." I paused again. He was still looking at me. I could feel myself start to sweat. I rubbed my palms on my skirt and dashed headlong into what I imagined was my most compelling point:

"Rabbi Miller, I would like to learn what *others think* so that I can teach the truth of the Torah persuasively. If I want to return wayward Jews to the faith, I need to understand what they believe . . ."

The typing stopped as Mrs. Blum, the secretary, paused with her fingers above the ancient machine that she refused to replace with a newfangled computer. ("It has always been done this way. We didn't need *computers* in the time of Mr. Kohn and we don't need them now.")

I took a deep breath. "It says, right here, signature of academic dean." I thrust the paper onto the desk, careful not to pass it directly into his hand, which would be a violation of the laws of modesty.

I finally came to rest. Looking about me, I met Mrs. Blum's gaze. She raised one eyebrow with expression and began her typing once more, her ancient beehive wig bobbing up and down with each stroke. *Tap-tap-tap.* The sound grated on my already frayed nerves.

As I waited for his response, I cursed myself a thousand times for venturing on this hallowed ground with my impertinent request. A Gateshead Sem girl in a library of *philosophy?* Perhaps I should have asked him for his favorite pork recipe. Perhaps he was wondering how quickest to ship me back to America before I wrought irreparable spiritual damage on his *eidel* girls . . .

The rabbi sighed, making a clicking sound with his palate that I knew to be habitual but that somehow managed to convey the disapproval that I felt I had earned. He finally spoke. "Miss Netzer! Would you be so kind as to speak up? I hardly heard a word you said."

I nearly broke. After taking a deep breath, I launched once again into my pitch. Rabbi Miller spoke again.

"Miss Netzer, is there a family in Gateshead that you go to for helping?"

"A family? For helping?"

"Yes. A family. Do. You. Go. To. A. *Family.* Each week to do helping?" He enunciated each word slowly, as if it were I who was hard of hearing.

My heart sank. I had been exposed. Who had told him? I had gone only once to helping. I had hated the experience as an interloper in a happy, bustling home bursting at the seams with children whose exhausted matriarch, fingers sinewy and bony from labor, pointed at pots to be washed, chickens to be basted, and children to be bathed and dressed. But what one thing had to do with the other, I could not imagine.

"Miss Netzer. If you cannot peel potatoes, what will you feed your poor husband? He cannot eat your philosophy books! He will starve!"

Mrs. Blum's staccato laugh harmonized with her secretarial jangle. The remark was intended to be humorous and gently admonishing at the same time. Instead, it flagellated me from within, mortification rising in my gut. And then, worse, my body too betrayed me, tears clouding my vision. In a moment they would fall, consummating my shame. *You won't see me cry,* I promised. Then I did the only thing that my panicked self would allow: I turned on my heel and fled. I heard him calling my name, but I did not stop.

It was a Friday afternoon. Formal lectures were finished for the week and soon nearly four hundred teenage girls would be dressing in their Sabbath best. Now they were bustling to and fro in front of the row houses, some no doubt heading to their helping homes. *What the hell was wrong with me?* I bent my head down and allowed my hair to cover my wet face like a shower curtain. Thankfully, my roommate, a Montreal native with the unlikely combination of copper-red curls and deep olive skin, was out when I reached the room.

I closed the door — there were no locks here — and collapsed against it, folding my knees up to meet my chest, sobs drawing the breath out of me in huge gasps. When I had exhausted my reserves of rage and self-loathing, I felt nothing but a chill and a painful tingling in my fingertips.

I was wicked, I knew it. It was a tautology that could not be denied.

If Rabbi Miller was a saint (and surely he was) and *if* I hated him and everything that he wished of me (and at this moment I did), *then* it was I who was an abomination, fundamentally corrupt.

I came to my senses after the long cry. I had to apologize to Rabbi Miller for my mistake, at least if I hoped to continue my studies at Gateshead. I sat down and quickly wrote a letter asking him to forgive my behavior as I was not feeling myself due to a head cold coming on.

When Saturday night arrived a T-1 girl came to my room with a summons to the office. Rabbi Miller wished to see me. Ushered into the inner sanctum ahead of the line, already half a dozen deep, I was certain that my tenure at the seminary was coming to an end. A small part of me was relieved; the rest was scared stiff.

Rabbi Miller, when he looked at me, did not seem as angry as I imagined he would be. In fact, there was even humor in his voice when he asked: "Are you feeling better now, Miss Netzer?" "Yes!" I answered sheepishly, then laughed. "Oh, goody, then!" He attempted to pick up a piece of paper on his desk, but his fingers, bent from arthritis, could not find purchase. "Would you be so kind?" he said, sighing, and I started forward. Picking up the paper, I saw my library membership application and there, at the bottom, his signature: *Rabbi Mordechai Miller.* "Oh, thank you!" I cried, overjoyed. "Thank you!"

Rabbi Miller, however, was not smiling. He looked at me gravely. "Miss Netzer, do you remember the words of the sages: *Pa'les ma'agal raglecha?*"

"Yes," I said, inspecting my feet. How could I forget the lesson that he had recently given? The class was asked: "Is there merit to a Jew studying secular disciplines such as science or mathematics as long as they are not heretical in and of themselves?" I had answered enthusiastically to the affirmative, to which he had thundered loudly, to my shame: *"No!"*

He had quoted from the Talmud: *"Pa'les ma'agal raglecha,* consider the circumference of your feet, so that all your deeds will be firm." We must, he had warned, carefully narrow the circle of activity in our lives, limiting our access to outside studies and influences. Anything at all that sapped precious time and energy away from our primary purpose would reduce us, diluting our spiritual strength.

What shall we do with our sister? If she be a door, we will close her in with cedar planks . . .

Rabbi Miller continued to study me, his eyes grim. "Be careful, Miss Netzer."

"I will," I promised, then beat a hasty retreat with the signed application before he could change his mind.

I think I've discovered something wonderful, I wrote home to my mother the following month. My membership at the Lit. and Phil. had awakened an old longing in me; I had decided that after I finished at the seminary, I would go to college after all, maybe even to study astronomy, a subject I had taken an interest in. There was no need, I opined, for Torah and science to live estranged from each other. The entire world was a wonderful mystery, a conundrum gifted by our Creator to be unearthed and lovingly examined. I would, I declared to my mother, "have my cake *and* eat it too."

My mother's response surprised me. I had expected her to understand, even sympathize, with my decision. After all, hadn't she herself earned a PhD studying Saint Thomas Aquinas, who was not only a gentile but an *apikores,* a Christian, whose faith and ideas were heretical to ours?

Nonetheless, in her reply, my mother urged restraint. She asked me to distinguish between what was essential and nonessential to my being, and with those things that were nonessential, she begged that I tone myself down, react with more modesty, use softer speech and lighter tread so that I would not, God forbid, frighten my beloved away.

By *beloved,* she referred to my soulmate. Jews believed that each soul was born as a pair, male and female, who were destined to meet up on earth to fulfill their purpose. Talk of wanting to go to college and interest in subjects beyond Torah study could well scare away any potential suitor. As to the attitudes of the "Great Ones of the Torah" toward women? My mother recommended that I should focus on what I actually *was* assigned to learn, because even in that, there was enough, she wrote, *to drown in, to become intoxicated with . . . to live on, as with mannah.*

She closed the letter with a request. *Let us forget the issue entirely. It cannot be what it seems to be. It is only words. It is keeping us on one dimension, in one plane, or in a single concept. Let us expand. Let us break through the packaging and begin to trust that Hashem made things right. Our task is to discover it.*

Though her words were gentle, I still came away deeply disheartened by her response. Did she really expect me to ignore the way our faith regarded women as intellectually inferior for fear that I would lose my mate? This didn't sound like the mother I knew, or at least, not the one I thought I knew.

In her concern for me, my mother revealed my intentions to my brother, still in the throes of religious fervor, who had harsher words for me. His letter arrived within days, castigating me for my *stupidity and foolishness* and those fantasies that he said were *empty of understanding, like a brick.*

It is sheker, sheker, sheker! he wrote, meaning "lies." *Utter stupidity. You have absolutely nothing in a university and it is believe me an utter waste of a life no matter what thought and "goals" you have.* If I didn't heed my *rabbonim,* he further warned, I might well be on a path that would, God forbid, send me straight to *gehennom,* hell. He asked me to forgive his bluntness, as his admonition came from a place of love, and no one else would be as truthful with me as he was.

It was clear to me that no one approved of my desire to expand my intellectual horizons past seminary. That the rabbis felt this way, I had come to expect, and even my brother could be dismissed — but my mother? Furthermore, why was she so concerned suddenly with my finding a husband when I was barely eighteen years old? No matter, I decided. In just over a year and a half I'd be back in the States, and I'd be able to take my life in whatever direction I willed it. One thing my mother said was certainly true, I comforted myself. Time, even patience, was on my side.

• 14 •

The Doggy Sweater

"Stranger,
You are no longer what you were just now!
Your cloak is new; even your skin!"

— HOMER, *The Odyssey*

EM'S FIRST DAY OF PRESCHOOL!
I have the planner entry penned in purple Sharpie with a smiley-face sticker. I've even allowed her to color on the page, November 26, 2012, to mark this momentous day when she will finally join her sister in school as a *big kid*.

Now the hour has arrived, and I watch as Ella leads her sister down a set of steps to the Beginnings Room, holding her hand proudly. I capture the moment in a photograph: Ella is one step ahead, bundled up in a navy-and-pink Boston Red Sox argyle knit cap and pink puffer coat, cherry-red pant legs sticking out the bottom. She is smiling broadly and looking toward the open door of the classroom to the teacher who stands there waiting to welcome her sister.

Em, a step above her sister, has shed her coat already ("I is hot!"

she always complains, regardless of season) and stands ramrod straight in gray yoga pants and a cornflower-blue short-sleeved sweater with a puppy dog embroidered on the front. She too is looking toward the open door but with a close-mouthed hint of a smile. Her chin is tucked, buried in the sweater's turtleneck collar, and her black Mary Janes are so close to each other that they overlap. She appears both apprehensive and excited.

Mixed feelings accompany first days of school for me as well. I am proud of my children, yet I miss them keenly, not only their physical presence during my morning routines but the fully mine aspects of babyhood, where all of it — the feeding, toileting, comforting, and redirecting — is performed by me. From eight thirty until noon three days a week, someone else will now do these things for Em. I feel the lump in my throat. I'm determined not to cry because she isn't, and I want it to stay that way.

"Please call me if she becomes too upset or if the changing thing comes up," I ask Mrs. Hunt. We had already rehearsed what to do if Em demanded to change clothes midday, but I'm keeping my fingers crossed. Our thrice-a-day-only changing plan seems to be working, and it's manageable. There's an extra set in her school bag, the same as for every other child "just in case," but that's it. One and done. She'll have to learn to deal with the clothes she has on, her sensory issues or anxiety notwithstanding. Mrs. Hunt must have seen the look on my face because she says, "We'll be okay, Mama." With the ease of practice, she stoops to shepherd Em in with one hand while gently closing the door on me with the other.

"It's just us now," I tell Lucia, six months old and strapped into her bucket seat. She gazes at me quizzically. I imagine she is asking herself in whatever prelinguistic thought-language she possesses: *Why is Mommy crying?*

"I'm a little sad," I admit to her. The latest parenting manual I'm reading tells me parents should acknowledge their feelings, admit to moments of discomposure. Nonetheless, I hastily wipe my face.

When noon arrives, I can hardly imagine where the time has gone. The girls come out of their classrooms bursting with words. I am embraced, showered with excited love. "I missed you, baby-cakes!" I swing Em up in my arms and cover her face with kisses. She endures this for a moment then wriggles until I have to let go. "How was your first day?"

"It was good, Mama."

"It *was* good, Mom," Mrs. Lovetere confirms. "We did fuss about going to the toilet and we had a moment where we missed you, but we sat in the writing corner and took some time to ourselves coloring until we were ready to join our friends again." She hands me a ditto sheet with the printed words *This Is Me!* and beneath it, Em's attempt at a self-portrait. It is a lopsided circle, two dots for eyes, a dash for a mouth, no nose. Fingers sprout from the side of the head, like hair out of an old man's ears. The body is a stick emerging from a giant head, the stem on a cherry. "It's *gorgeous*," I gush. And it is.

A great first day.

The next morning, Em refuses to get ready for school, because she is *not* going. "Honey" — I am as gentle as I can be — "you're such a big girl now. You need to learn new things and have fun with new friends." "You learn me!" she says with wide-eyed sincerity. "You is my friend!" And my heart hurts. School is not a choice, I clarify. I watch her cloudy face as this news sinks in. After a moment, she stands, heads purposefully right past the bureau to the pile of yesterday's laundry, and pulls out the inside-out, crumpled dog sweater. "I wear this," she declares, holding it to her chest. "I *on'y* go to school if I wear *this.*"

Her face is set in a stubborn scowl, the one that is increasingly present as she careens toward her terrible threes (at this point, the assumption that they'll be terrible seems like a safe bet), yet I can't believe how easily she has folded. If the sweater is what it takes to get this show on the road, then so be it. Ella opens her mouth to argue and I quickly put my finger to my lips. "That's fine," I say as I help Em ease her substantial head ("We bought you in a bowling alley," jokes Joe) into the narrow hole of her turtleneck. "It's still clean." We struggle comically for a few seconds and then, *pop,* she is through. Her fine brown hair rises in a cloud of static that we all find hilarious. I breathe a sigh of relief. Day two is a go.

When I pick her up at school, Em's wearing the doggy sweater, of course, but a different pair of pants. Mrs. Hunt hands me a plastic shopping bag with the damp clothes, smiling apologetically. "She insisted she didn't need to go." *Oh, yuck.* "It happens," Mrs. Hunt says. More and more, I have noticed. Lately, we seem to have reversed all the gains of the potty training we did this summer. I make a mental note to talk to Dr. Harper, our pediatrician.

When day three arrives, the Doggy Sweater, as it had now been designated by its owner, is *not* clean. Nevertheless, Em demands to wear it. I shake my head. "I'll wash it today while you are at school," I promise. This is not acceptable to her. She yells: "No! I wear it *today.*" Folding her arms, she plonks herself to sit on the carpet, legs crossed, reminding me, improbably, of a furious Buddha. "You can't wear it!" Ella wags her finger at her sister. "Mama said!"

The noise brings Joe out of his office. "I'm on a phone call," he says, exasperated. "What is going on here?" "I'm sorry!" I had forgotten his early-morning sales call. (After business school at MIT, Joe switched from programming to high-tech sales, with an eye to a future entrepreneurial venture.) "Em wants to wear the same top to school today that she's worn for the past two days."

Saying it aloud, it doesn't sound like that big a deal. "Let her!" Joe echoes my thoughts. Em perks up, looking hopeful. "*Last day, miss!*" I say. "None of your fussing tomorrow, you hear me?"

"But you wash it today." She looks up at me innocently. "You say so."

At drop-off, I find myself apologetically explaining to her teachers why Em is dressed the same today, embarrassed by a food stain on the front of the sweater that I had only managed to spread further with a wet sponge. "Well," offers Mrs. Lovetere kindly, "that's a pretty shirt. I love dogs. What kind is that?" Em ignores her and moves farther into the classroom. She is looking hesitantly at a group of kids with a tub of toys spread out on the rug. It's time for my quick exit.

"Mum," Mrs. Lovetere says to me softly as she accompanies me to the door. "Sometimes when things are new, kids will latch onto something familiar, as a comfort. Pick your battles," she says sagely.

By Em's second week of school it is abundantly clear the Doggy Sweater will play a recurring role in my daughter's wardrobe. In fact, it is all we can do to stop her from wearing it at night on top of pajamas. Thankfully, I have a second one, as I'd been buying matching clothes for Ella and Em since before Em was born. "Twins!" people assume when I take them out together, and it's something that I always love hearing. Although Ella has reddish-brown hair and green eyes and Em's hair and eyes are darker, they are practically the same height, and Em has several pounds on her daintier sister. But even the second sweater brings little laundry relief as the days go on. With food splatters, paint, the top barely makes it through one day. I decide to go on eBay and see what I can rustle up. I try several search combinations until I hit the right one. Bingo! I purchase two more sweaters and even find matching brown-and-blue polka-dot pants and socks.

Friends have started noticing the omnipresent Doggy Sweater

when I post pictures of the girls and it's become a source of spec-ulation and commentary. I decide to embrace it. I even joke that I will soon have to create a photo retrospective with Em in the Doggy Sweater in all manner of places and activities. It's just part of what makes her a little "kookster," says Joe. I have to agree. Our Em is one quirky gal. She's no princess like her sister, that's for sure. In fact, she's only picking boy parts for role-play these days. She's even taken to asking us to call her James or Jackson, even when no one else is involved in play-acting. And she says she *hates pink*. "*Hate* is a strong word," I tell her, laughing. "I never liked pink either," says my German friend Cornelia, up from DC for a visit. "I went through a goth phase when I was in high school." "Really?" I laugh, having a hard time picturing my long-haired, elegant friend in heavy Doc Martens and spiky black hair. I could, however, see a future where Em is dressed this way, as-suming that she gets over the Doggy Sweater, that is.

Amanda, the girls' dance instructor, is thankfully pretty chill about the sweater being worn over Em's leotard during ballet class. "Just not at the dance recital," she warns. That's so many months down the line that I am not too concerned. Surely this ob-session will fade, just as the clothes-changing did. Another dance mom, my friend Leigh, shakes her head, looking at Em and smil-ing. "I just love her. She's so unique." She adds: "And you're such a good mama for rolling with it." "I don't know about that!" I laugh. "What else can I do?"

I suppose I am rolling with it. I'm not even upset when Em de-clares that she will wear the sweater over her Christmas outfit to visit Santa at the mall. Of course, this will mar the look of those three darling Christmas dresses (black and gold this year), but I think I get it now.

Em *is* a unique spirit. She has her passions (which admit-tedly border on obsessions) but this, if managed, can also be her strength. She will never half-ass anything, says Joe. For quite a while now, we've taken to calling her "Honey Badger," after viewing a viral YouTube video, a spoof on an Animal Planet–type show, where the honey badger is declared to be the world's fiercest animal: "Honey badger don't give a fuck," intones the narrator. Joe and I whisper this to each other and laugh. This is our Em, a force to be reckoned with, barreling through life on those chubby, adorably clumsy legs.

"Pick your battles" has become a large part of Em Management, and there are certainly plenty to choose from.

Thresholds

Come and see! Woe is to the man who does not know how
to beware the evil spirit that lies between the doorposts,
and does not mark the gates of his house with a holy
supernal name, for they [evil spirits] will denounce him,
above and below ... They prosecute him by day and by
night distress him in his dreams.   — *Sefer ha Zohar*

MAZEL TOV!" MY FRIEND HADASSA SPOTTED ME AT MY
desk and ran over to give me a big hug. "You're one of us
Gateshead town girls now!"

"Almost!" I reminded her. The wedding wasn't until June, but
news of my mother's engagement to a local widower, Ephraim
Pinnick, had spread like wildfire in the small community. There
were women I didn't know who stopped to congratulate me at
Stenhouse when I went to pick up snacks.

"I guess you *really* didn't want to leave Gateshead after sem!"
Hadassa teased me, a twinkle in her hazel eyes. What I liked
about my friend was something she was constantly trying to sup-
press. Shy of five feet, she had unruly curls nearly bursting out of
their elastic and an irrepressible personality to match. Once she
confided to me that her parents thought she "needed taking down

a peg or two" for speaking her mind too frequently, I had always felt protective toward her. "I'm stuck now," I said, laughing.

I was still in a state of disbelief over my mother's engagement despite having had a hand in setting her up with her fiancé, a Gateshead resident. It seemed meant to be, *bashert.* Her fiancé, a widower, had five children, the youngest of whom was a twelve-year-old girl. Roselyn had been, for some months now, my sort-of ballet student, owing to a request that had come from Mrs. Roberts, whose daughter was at school with the girl. At first I had demurred, explaining that I had never set foot in a ballet studio. Perhaps Mrs. Roberts assumed I had because I'd helped choreograph a dance for a seminary celebration? "She needs a mentor more than a dance instructor," Mrs. Roberts had responded, then explained the girl's unfortunate circumstances. Now I was to be her stepsister. How mysterious and wonderful were God's ways!

During the winter break of my second year, my mother had arrived in Gateshead for her first visit to the town. Our hosts for the vacation were the Hirsches; their daughter Raizel was a classmate and friend. Toward the end of the week, Mrs. Hirsch, a shrewd woman with a flyaway blond wig that she kept comically knocking askew with her hands, pulled me aside: "What do you think," she began, eyes narrowing, "of your mother and Mr. Pinnick?"

I was excited by the idea. I had pretty much given up on seeing my mother married because more than five years had passed since my father had finally granted her a *get,* and worry about what would happen to her as she entered old age was never far from my mind. Still, at sixty years old, my mother was sprier than most women of forty (old age, my mother insisted, would arrive only if *she* let it).

Mrs. Hirsch and I went through our checklists. She asked me if my mother was a good cook (my honest and enthusiastic response was in the affirmative) and a hands-on parent. I asked her if Mr. Pinnick was both intelligent and intellectual and would be amenable to learning Torah on occasion with my mother. She said that she couldn't imagine that he wouldn't be open to the idea. The Pinnicks, though a Gateshead family for decades, were not of *rabbonishe* stock, she explained; that is, Mr. Pinnick was of the minority who had money-earning jobs outside of learning and teaching Torah. However, he was intelligent, she promised, and he loved learning, spending every evening immersed in Torah study with his learning partner. It was agreed that my mother and Mr. Pinnick would be suggested for each other. When my mother announced cryptically that she was going out on the last evening of her visit to ask a *shai'lah* (a request for a *halachic,* legal, ruling) of a local rabbi, I bit my lip and smiled.

For the next several months, Mrs. Hirsch and I kept in communication about my mother and Ephraim. I got a kick out of playing secret matchmaker, as my mother did not choose to discuss the progress of her *shidduch,* courtship, with me. Finally, shortly before Passover, my mother broached the subject. She hoped I would be happy, she began tentatively, to learn that she was considering becoming engaged. "I know!" I burst into peals of laughter, and I told her then that my heart was the happiest it had ever been for her and for us as a family — and it was.

I traveled home to Monsey for Passover that year full of a strange mix of emotions. Now that our life as a family of three was officially ending, I found myself nostalgic for those intimate moments, those years of reliance on one another through thick and thin, even for the loneliness we had endured.

I would miss our small apartment, I realized, and my grandmother's watercolor paintings on the wall of my bedroom, the small blue rug that I had rolled up many evenings to practice the ballet that I had taught myself from a book. All of these things were precious. What changes would accompany this move? I would be gaining a stepsister and four stepbrothers, most of whom were older than I. There would be a new bedroom in a new home in a foreign country. For my brother, an even bigger change pended, since he would be moving from his current home in New Jersey's Lakewood Yeshiva to Gateshead sometime this summer. "This is good for Mom," he reminded me and, I suspect, himself. "Yes," I agreed. It wasn't good for a woman to be alone, and the fact that my quirky, hopelessly abstract mother had found someone felt like a miracle.

The Passover sermon I chose to deliver at our Seder table that year addressed the ambivalence that we were all feeling. "In the Passover story," I began, "God commands the Israelites to sacrifice the Paschal lamb and smear its blood on the doorposts of their homes, so that when the Angel of Death came for the firstborn of the Egyptians, he passed over the homes of the Jews, sparing them." Up to this point I was repeating familiar material, something that every Jewish schoolchild knew. The blood on the doorpost became the commandment to affix a mezuzah, a scroll with the words of the holy prayer Shema Yisrael, "Hear, O Israel," in the doorway of every Jewish home.

What I delved into now were some of the more esoteric reasons that the *Zohar* (Judaism's primary work of mysticism) gave for the necessity of this amulet at the doorway to our homes. It was at thresholds, I explained, both physical and experiential doorways, where one was most vulnerable to the predations of evil spirits and negative influences.

A threshold was, in essence, a way station or point of transition from one domain to the next. The space between two realms was vulnerable to evil because *ra* (the Hebrew word for evil) was nothing more than the *absence* of God's presence, a return to the chaos of *ex nihilo*.

Mind the gap.

Throughout Judaic ritual practice, those places, times, and states of being that are in limbo required special protections. For example, the hour midway through dusk and dawn, the "threshold" of night, was fixed as a time for the most devout to rise and recite a midnight prayer called Tikkun Chatzot — literally, "repairing the breach of night" — in the hopes of averting God's judgment.

This principle also held true for life's great transitions. A bride before her wedding day, a corpse prior to interment, a baby boy waiting for his eighth day to be circumcised — these vulnerable liminal states required an appointed *shomer,* guardian, to keep vigil until the threshold was safely passed. The mezuzah, with its declaration of faith inscribed within, was a talismanic guardian to the physical threshold of our homes.

My mother too was passing into a new life, I said, smiling at her across the table, as a married woman, and she was taking us with her. It would be our faith in God that would act as a talisman for us, as it had for our people throughout time. When I concluded my piece, I received enthusiastic praise from my mother and brother.

My mother had been moved to tears. Her eyes glowed as she exclaimed, "Miriam, this is remarkable! This is precisely the meaning of 'The Dark Night of the Soul'!"

Saint John of the Cross's poem was one of several works from the foreign faith of Christianity beloved by my mother, and its message had frequently been used to comfort me in times of stressful uncertainty.

The fourteenth-century Spanish mystic wrote of his soul leaving all earthly matter and sensation in his pursuit of communion with God. Bereft of everything familiar — unable to see the road ahead but having left the well-trodden path behind — the mystic felt as if his soul had entered a "dark night," a metaphorical cliff over a vast emptiness. This, my mother had interpreted for me, was the stage that the faithful inevitably encounter after reaching the upper limits of the soul's capacity to comprehend God and over which they must launch themselves, unknowing of their fate.

It is God who catches the devout and transports them across the threshold to a higher level of being, the bliss of a new dawn.

As soon as the first days of Passover ended, my mother, brother, and I headed to Gateshead for the ritual celebration of my mother's engagement, called a *vort,* Yiddish for "word," as a betrothal was a giving of one's word to marry. I was proud to have been granted the role, along with Zissy, the wife of one of my future stepbrothers, of carrying the china plate that my mother and stepfather would step on, the ritual that reminded us to raise the memory of the destruction of the Temple in Jerusalem above our greatest joys. The *vort* was wonderful and both my brother and I found our new family welcoming, to our great relief, though Roselyn was unusually distant. *Poor thing,* I thought. This had to be hard for her. After the second days of Passover ended, my mother and brother returned to America and I to my dorm at the seminary.

My mother's wedding to Ephraim was scheduled for June, in Monsey. As the time drew close, I began to ask pointed questions, looking for information about what role I would play in the wedding. My mother hemmed and hawed for a while before quietly admitting that none of the children, hers or Ephraim's, would be invited to the ceremony. "*What?*" My voice rose sharply, despite the lack of privacy in the seminary hallway where the pay phones stood. "How could I not be there? Don't you want me there?" I was hurt. "It's not that I don't *want* you." My mother sighed painfully.

There was a *minhag,* custom, she explained, that children didn't attend the remarriage of a widowed or divorced parent out of respect for the deceased or separated parent. It was a minority opinion, she admitted, but they had decided it was for the best in this case to follow it.

That my mother had chosen to deny me the pleasure of being there seemed cruel, particularly since I had been instrumental in arranging the marriage. I demanded further explanation. Our future stepsiblings had been "difficult," my mother put forth reluctantly, during the *shidduch* process. It was best for Ephraim and my mother to get a fresh new start without any interference. "I can count on you to understand, can't I?" she asked. "I've always counted on you, always been able to. You are my remarkably mature and thoughtful daughter."

She could, sort of, but I challenged the assumption that this was a mere matter of tact or maturity required of me. I would be forfeiting my last chance to see my childhood home and would not be able to pack up my belongings. "We'll get your friends from Bat Torah, the twins, Arielle and Janina, to help," my mother decided. I could hear the pleading tone in her voice, so I told her that I loved her and would cooperate. She *could* count on me.

That was how it came about that on the day my mother married Ephraim in Monsey, I was sitting on the roof gable of my dorm house, over three thousand miles away from the wedding, passing about a bottle of sickly sweet Tia Maria liqueur with friends and with each "L'chaim" getting progressively more inebriated. I had never had more than a thimbleful of Kiddush wine in my life and didn't understand the effect it could have on me. I loved the feeling of freedom and giddy wildness that came with the alcohol, but the next morning when I awoke, the hangover was a brutal surprise. Since it happened to be an exam day, I flunked Rabbi Sternbuch's Pentateuch test. Although grades didn't matter at sem (in fact, girls were discouraged from asking for them), I did care about these things and retook the exam the following day.

A few short weeks after the wedding, I moved out of my dorm room into the corner row house on Saltwell View, on the fringe of the Jewish ghetto, opposite one of the most spectacular parks in northeast England: several kilometers of floral walkways, ponds, and gardens. My new bedroom, at the top of the stairs on the second floor, had a window that overlooked a tiny patio with several fruit trees surrounded by brick walls and topped by shards of broken glass stuck into cement to keep out enterprising burglars.

I liked my stepfather, Ephraim, right off the bat. He was kind and friendly, if a little shy. When he asked me if I would like to call him "Daddy" like the rest of his children did, I told him I would be happy to. My stepsister, Roselyn, however, a newly minted teenager, appeared to view my mother and me as unwelcome interlopers. From the day we moved in, she went to great lengths to remind my mother and me that we did not belong. At first, I exercised patience, reminding myself that her resentment was only natural. I hoped that with a friendly and accommodating attitude, I could win back the shy but well-mannered girl who had been my student. However, tensions continued to escalate in our home as Roselyn drew her brothers into battle with us, issuing edicts about where and how much of our belongings we could bring with us and refusing to allow my mother to insist that she do anything, even a thing so simple as coming to the dinner table. Ephraim's peaceful manner became a deficit in this regard, as he refused to stick up for my mother, something that wounded her deeply.

I, however, felt more than adequate to the task. "You need to lay down the law," I told my mother. "Just confront her, and if you don't want to, at least let me do so. I promise to be gentle."

But my mother was afraid to take action in any way, even to openly acknowledge my stepsister's mean-spirited barbs and complaints. I suspected that the need to take matters into her own hands would add insult to the injury of Ephraim not rising to protect her. "Don't you dare rock the boat!" she admonished me. If I opened my mouth, she would pack up her things and leave, she vowed. I watched in concern as she became increasingly angry and suspicious toward her new family yet struggled to present a cheerful face to them.

The current of my mother's anger, I suppose, had to seek a safe place to ground itself. When Ephraim was in his office or visiting the flats that he rented and my stepsister was at school, my mother would shut the door to the kitchen behind us and release her frustration in a torrent, forensically analyzing each slight while claiming to be well above being emotionally affected. The only safe response was to express subdued sympathy, and even then, there was little I could do to avoid her ire. Much of the advice I offered incensed her. I loved her so much that I would have done anything to help, but the one thing she asked of me, my silence, was, I knew, a recipe for prolonging the agony, and it was not in my nature to submit.

Several months into our new life, I could no longer restrain myself. The first time I snapped at Roselyn, my mother became apoplectic. "Now I will have to leave!" she raged at me. "I know . . . I *know.*" She shook with anger. "That's what you wanted all along, isn't it? You *want* this marriage to fail so you can have me back for yourself."

She couldn't have hurt me worse if she had punched me in the gut. In significant ways I felt that I *had* lost her, but I had given her freely to Ephraim, with an open heart. I had even worked to secure her happiness. When she calmed down, she gave me an apology of sorts. "I should have left when I crossed the threshold that first night," she said despondently. "I'm sorry that I uprooted you from a perfectly happy home. Look what I've done! I've destroyed your life."

"You didn't destroy me," I responded, hugging her, though I knew she would push me away. Public displays of affection, my mother had decided, were not allowed in our new home. "Look at me!" I smiled at her through my own anger. "Do I look destroyed? Also, Mom, don't kid yourself," I added more lightheartedly. "It wasn't perfectly happy."

The truth was that I had no real home left, just a place to lay my head down at night and park some of my belongings (many of which were still in packing boxes and would remain so). I escaped to the seminary during the day and tried to keep my Newcastle trips up in the afternoons, but that had become harder now that my mother had no independent bank account or even a debit card and had to ask Ephraim for cash each week for my bus fare.

I was delighted when my brother moved to Gateshead with us at summer's end, enrolling at the prestigious Gateshead Yeshiva. I would finally have someone else to share the emotional burden of our home life. Soon the sounds of strife emanating from the kitchen were between him and my mother. My brother, by far the more forgiving of the two of us, returned again and again for the daily torment.

My reprieve, however, was short-lived. The following year my brother secured himself a spot in the renowned Mir Yeshiva of Jerusalem. I let him go reluctantly, envying his ability to escape the home before marriage. We had become confidants now that my talk of going to university had ceased (my new home was Gateshead, and in my mind, and in that of others, no doubt, that made me a Gateshead Girl, with most of the attendant prestige and all the obligations and expectations). Alone once more, I would lament: Why hadn't God caught us when we crossed the threshold? Why had He inflicted such misery on an innocent like my mother? Had we been lacking faith?

My worries at home that had initially served as a distraction later served to exacerbate the growing concerns I had over my spiritual health.

As we neared the end of the second year of seminary, our lessons began to coalesce sharply around the topic of how best each of us could serve as an *ezer ke'negdo,* a helpmate, to our future husbands. Every reference to the lives we would lead and the husbands we would obey felt like a shard of glass piercing my heart. There was no other way; of this I was sure. This was as it had been ordained from the start of time. My purpose in life had been assigned by God Himself, and surely, He knew me better than I knew myself. God did not make mistakes, therefore it was I who must be fundamentally flawed.

It never occurred to me that my rabbis could be wrong. They had pointed to the works of our holy sages to support their assertions, sages that were comparative angels to the fleas that we knew our generation to be. *Why can't I accept God's will like the other girls?* I would ask of myself bitterly. No one else seemed bothered. I knew there was something wrong with me and that it must be rooted in my psyche. It was clear to me that I was somehow corrupted, but if I could not find the source of the flaw, how could I hope to fix myself?

• 16 •

The Talisman

"Can you see that sentry crouched at the entrance? What
a specter guards the threshold!" — VIRGIL, *The Aeneid*

February 24, 2013

Happy third birthday to the incomparable Em Lemay!
 We are so proud of you.
 You are an ardent individualist.
 You love things with a passion.
 Your favorite color is gray.
 Your fervor for Rudolph and all things Christmas keeps the
holiday going.
 You've worn the same Doggy Sweater for four months, day
and night.
 You love Scotch tape and sticky-note pads.
 You are kind and empathetic.
 You insist you are a boy.
 Your favorite headgear is a propeller beanie, not a tiara.
 You are a terrific little kid and wonderful sister.
 Daddy and I hope you always stay true to yourself.

Twenty-seven little celebrants line up at the door, shining with
sweat and anticipation. They've expended the last hour on a fa-

miliar drill: careening in, on, and off room-size inflatable slides and bouncy castles. When the whistle blew, they raced for the exit like hounds chasing the scent of fox.

The long-awaited moment has arrived. Candles are lit! The decadent prize is gingerly and ceremoniously presented to the birthday girl perched on the painted wooden throne at the head of the long table. The ritual entails that if they sing the song with sufficient gusto, each will receive a piece of the coveted cake.

Except this time, it's a little different.

Parents help me distribute the little cellophane packages that curious hands tear apart. Red foam balls are fixed on small noses and straps adjusted around sweaty hair. Murmured conversations commence as adults explain that this day, to earn the treat, they must sing a different song. Little faces look sweetly perplexed, then tentatively excited. They are game, I realize with relief.

Em is bouncing up and down and sideways on her birthday throne like a demented pogo stick, the Doggy Sweater soaked from earlier exertions. I make a mental note to inquire whether she needs the potty, but I can't stop the momentum, so I raise my hand for silence, then wave it in the air like a conductor.

Slowly, we wobble into our song:

Rudolph the Red-Nosed Reindeer

Had a very shiny nose . . .

Little voices collide with big ones as everyone scrambles to re-call the lyrics in the right order. A few confident carolers distin-guish themselves early. Ella is leading the pack, dramatic hand gestures evolving to the point where I'm afraid she'll club the ap-prehensive-looking boy to her left. She's been trilling this song since October. Reflexively, my gaze shifts to take stock of her less confident sister. Em seems . . . temporarily content. I look for signs that she will repulse this impromptu choir in her honor, but there is no gravitational pull on the corners of her mouth, her telltale left elbow is slack by her side, and while she is barely singing, she does have a soupçon of a smile on her face. My diaphragm releases.

• • •

Rudolph had become a fixture in our lives in the late autumn of
2012. As in years past, I could hold back only so long before I began to pine for the holiday tunes that lit up the darkening days
with some joy and the promise that we would get through the dol-
drums of a diabolical Northeast winter with an infusion of cheer
and, perhaps, a little faith.

Not my faith, of course, but despite my upbringing, I have always loved the tinsel and the tunes of the Christmas holiday that
I adopted along with my gentile husband. It remains a standing
joke in Joe's family that I have more enthusiasm for the trappings
of Christmas than any of the jaded Catholics in his clan. I am the
Jewish Christmas junkie, each year lugging several huge bins of
decorations down from the attic before our Thanksgiving turkey
is fully digested. Then, in Joe's wry words: "Our house looks like
a red-and-green glitter bomb hit it."

And so it came to pass that one of my birthday presents from
Joe during the summer was a collection of Christmas-movie classics, including the tale of an unfortunate reindeer with an aber-
rant red nose. One deliciously chilly late-October afternoon, the
five of us finding ourselves with hours to spare before bedtime
but all played out, I had slipped the DVD into the player. We
had settled down to watch, swaddled in fleece, popcorn effervesc-
ing from large buckets into the nooks and crannies of our beaten
leather couch.

Lucia had fallen asleep within minutes, her sweet breath warm
on my chest. Ella had thoroughly enjoyed the show, giggling at
Rudolph's clumsy antics and clutching my hand and shrieking
when the Abominable Snowman chased Rudolph and Hermey
across the frozen wastelands.

Em offered far less commentary, unusually intent on the unfolding story. I stole a glance as she sat, wide-eyed and tense,
when Rudolph first took flight in front of his compadres. I noticed as her eyes darkened and pooled when he sadly trudged

away from his home to the Island of Misfit Toys, cast out for his troublesome nose. The return of the prodigal reindeer and his triumphant Christmas save at story's end brought a huge grin that lit up her round face, narrowed her warm almond eyes to slits, and caused her nose — not mine and not her dad's; perhaps an atavistic throwback to my Persian grandmother — to scrunch up in a way that endearingly emphasized its girth and unusual slope. She would not let me turn the TV off until every last credit had rolled. And from that moment on for Em Lemay, it was all Rudolph, all the time. And so it became for us.

Our paperback copy of *Rudolph the Red-Nosed Reindeer* slowly decomposed from incessant readings. Em carried Rudolph (in the form of a bug-eyed Beanie Boo doll) to preschool in the side pocket of her school bag. We listened to his anthem on car rides and crooned it in lieu of a lullaby at the day's end. Rudolph further accompanied us to the park, to gymnastics, to family gatherings, and on the occasional playdate. He had with unnerving speed supplanted Buddy, to whom even I had formed an attachment by this time. I never thought I would see the day when the great white bunny would lie discarded in a heap of blankets on her floor, but, sadly, it came.

The day of the town's Halloween Trick-or-Treat Parade had demonstrated to us how essential Rudolph was to Em. We were all dressed up and ready to go; at least, all the human members of our family were. Rudolph, it seemed, had been temporarily misplaced, leading to several minutes of frantic searching. As the hour wound on, I had faced my sobbing daughter and suggested that she allow Rudolph this time to enjoy playing with his other friends in the house while she went solo to the event. Even the best of buddies, I reasoned, can benefit from time apart. She had other dolls.

It was then that she drew a stuttering breath and spoke tearfully, with unsettling gravity: "I want to, Mama, I really, really want to. I want to so badly, but I *can't* go without him. I just *can't*."

Looking into her eyes, I had seen neither stubbornness nor pique but desperation, perhaps even fear; it sent my heart fluttering, and I had not stood my ground. *This we save for another day.* Luckily, after a few more minutes of upending and scouring, someone spotted a red nose. We were on our way to the parade, Rudolph in hand.

So complete was Em's preoccupation with Rudolph that it wasn't long before every narrative in our evening ritual of storytelling was routinely interrupted by the entreaty: "Then did you see a glowing red nose?" At first Joe and I vied for who could come up with the most creative insertion of a flying reindeer into a bedtime tale (pulling a rocket ship orbiting Saturn's rings? Rock climbing Yosemite's cliffs?), but we soon tired of Rudolph's misappropriation of all our family moments. We anticipated that Rudolph's privileged status would soon abate, but when February and, thus, Em's third birthday rolled around, the love had not waned between this eccentric couple.

Therefore, when it came time to choose a theme for Em's third birthday, Rudolph was the obvious choice. Christmas decorations were selling for pennies on the dollar, and my idea for the extemporaneous choir bloomed when last-minute shopping at a party store yielded a bounty of bargain-bin red noses.

I'm sitting on the couch at the end of hours of birthday revelry, and I can't quite peel myself off to clean up the wreckage of wrapping and ribbon that litters our living-room rug. Despite being exhausted, I am basking in the rare satisfaction of having pleased my increasingly captious child.

The day had gone well. Em had even displayed a rare degree of magnanimity by deciding to part with a good number of her birthday toys (mostly the pink and purple ones), to Ella's and Lucia's delight. She'd lingered longest over a gray stuffed schnauzer with a pink-and-white-paisley carrying case and a matching collar. "I can cut the collar off and make you a blue one," I offered. She hesitated momentarily, then slowly placed the stuffed dog in her older sister's eager hands. "Thank you, Em . . . *thank you!*" Ella had gushed. I decide to view this unusual act of philanthropy as an indicator of her generosity, that Em's enjoyment of the day had provoked a desire to share its largess. *We're doing well,* I tell myself. *Look how giving she is.*

Don't kid yourself, my more cynical self cuts in. *She thinks pink is a girl color. And she hates being a girl. Nothing new here.*

I turn back to the book I am reading, one of my favorites dating back to when I was a rebellious teen before Gateshead, Stephen King and Peter Straub's *The Talisman,* and now I think with a sigh of the acronym King employs in several of his books: SSDD (for "same shit, different day").

I grin, conjuring up an image of the birthday girl that I had, moments before, tucked into bed, her diminutive hand clutching Rudolph. I marvel at her no-holds-barred attachment to the objects of her affection. My smile barely falters as I consider how increasingly difficult it is for us — her flesh-and-blood people — to capture anything close to the intensity of this devotion. Buddy, Rudolph, the Doggy Sweater that has been a constant for four months now — their significance to Em seems to run deeper than merely loveys or a favorite shirt. These objects are *essential,* and without them she becomes unmoored, on edge.

"If she brings an ounce of this passion to her life and career, there isn't anything that can stop her!" Kathy had speculated, grinning. "If it doesn't kill us first," Joe had quipped in return.

The next thought, when it arrives, isn't full-fledged or even minimally fleshed out. It's probably an association I've made because of the book in my lap, but it feels like an intuition I shouldn't dismiss, a tickle that raises the delicate hairs on the back of my neck.

A talisman.

That's what it is. Rudolph is her *talisman.* The Doggy Sweater is her *talisman,* an object imbued with protective powers. But . . . if Em needs a talisman, then Em is afraid.

What does Em fear?

I feel a sudden urge to check on my sleeping child. The girls' room is still and quiet when I enter on tiptoe. As I gaze, Em's chest rises and falls in a steady rhythm. I take the measure of the room quickly and am assured that there is no danger here, but the hair on the back of my neck will not stand down. *There is no danger here,* I repeat to myself, and to make it thus, I whisper it out loud: "There is no danger here."

As I continue to gaze at her peaceful form, my fear evaporates. No, there is no danger here, no need for a talisman, if one even existed. What can my daughter comprehend of thresholds, crevices devoid of self-love where, without vigilance, the *ra* sets in?

What, then, troubles her innocent heart? Perhaps she is merely afraid of growing up, of the implacable march of time. Perhaps she fears the double-edged sword of independence that I must gently thrust into her hands.

Taking care not to rouse her, I climb beside her on the bed and lay my head down next to hers, watching for several minutes as her chest continues to rise and fall with ease. Seeing her so, I am visited by a sharp pang of gratitude that squeezes my heart. However brief, at this blessed moment, she is at peace, sprawled in her little bed, one arm splayed out carelessly, the other bent, and in its crook nestles an object of great worth.

17

The Other

All they who serve are telling me of Thy unnumbered
    graces;
And all wound me more and more,
And something leaves me dying,
I know not what, of which they are darkly speaking.

   — SAINT JOHN OF THE CROSS, *The Spiritual Canticle of the Soul*

RAV MILLER SWEPT HIS FINGERS REVERENTLY DOWN THE pages of the large leather-bound book. There were several on the lectern, arranged in order by their hierarchy in our lives. The Five Books of Moses, the Pentateuch, would always remain on top, as its holy words had been given directly from God's mouth on Mount Sinai, followed by the books of the Prophets and Hagiographa, such as the scrolls of Ruth and Esther, then the Talmud, and finally, at the bottom, latter commentaries, luminaries like eleventh-century Shlomo Yitzchaki, known as Rashi, and the sixteenth-century Rabbi Judah Loew, the Maharal of Prague.

Together, these volumes were an unbroken chain of custody over God's law, known as the *mesorah,* that extend from Moses's tablets, walking a treacherous and blood-soaked tightrope through the ages to today's houses of learning, where the next

gadol hador, "great one of the generation," was wrestling meaning from the Torah's cryptic text. As women, we were not a part
of the chain, though our lives were to be devoted to the service of
its links.

"Arba'ah Nichnasu L'Pardes."

His voice boomed into the microphone, a mincing British accent that still managed to roll each *r* and savor each *s* for dramatic
effect: *Parrrrrdesss,* Paradise.

"Four entered Paradise. Ben Azzai, Ben Zoma, Acher, and
Rabbi Akiva." When Rav Miller came to the third name, Acher,
he paused momentarily, flicking an invisible speck of dust off his
cuffs and fixing us with a look of suspicion, as if to say, *Are you*
truly *worthy of this lesson? Can you* handle *these secrets?*

Yes! I am, and I can, and I will! I wanted to shout, heart beating
a tattoo in my chest, because nobody ever taught us girls about
Acher. Of course, I knew *of* him; who didn't? He was the boogey-
man of Talmudic lore, a heretic so evil that he was rarely referred
to by his birth name, Elisha Ben Avuyah; instead, he was called
by the pseudonym Acher, meaning "Other." All the spiritual gi-
ants of his Talmudic era lay on one side and this man on the *other.*

Rav Miller continued with the legend of the four sages in Paradise, a most tragic one, for three of the men, at least. Beholding
God on His heavenly throne, the sage Ben Azzai dropped dead;
his friend Ben Zoma went mad; and Acher, in a rampage, uprooted the saplings that grew in Eden. Only Akiva, most worthy
of souls, exited the Garden as he had entered, unscathed.

"We will concern ourselves only with Acher today," said Rav
Miller as I had hoped he would. Uprooting the saplings, he elu-
cidated, was argued as either a reference to Acher's rejection of
God or to the actual murder of young Torah scholars, compared
to saplings, whom he had delivered to the Romans to die. For his
sins, Acher hears a *bas kol,* a heavenly voice, that proclaims, "Return, all wayward sons . . . all except Acher." Acher alone is be-

yond forgiveness. He has removed himself from the community of the saintly and can never be redeemed.

Referring to the pile of books on his lectern, Rav Miller began to piece together a chronology of a life of enormous potential gone terribly awry. A variety of reasons were offered for Acher's heresy, but to these Rav Miller shook his head and clicked his tongue. "Too easy!" he cried. "Acher was no simpleton. He was one of the greatest sages of his day, the holy teacher of Rabbi Meir Ba'al Haness, the miracle worker!"

It behooved us to explore further.

Forty minutes later, we students found ourselves among the shambles of several attempts to unravel the mystery of what had caused Acher to turn on his God and his people and in what way he was deemed unforgivable. Finally, we uncovered a signpost — a commentary pointing us to a similar paradisiacal visit drawn from a passage in the Book of Kings. Because of shared language and content, the stories, according to the rules, were permitted to aid in each other's interpretation.

The Talmud tells the story of the Israelite king Jeroboam, an evil idolater and the archnemesis of the king of Judah, David, son of Jesse. In a vision, God comes to Jeroboam and "grasps him by the hem of his garment," asking of him to repent; if he does so, he will earn the opportunity to walk with God Himself in the Garden of Eden: "I and you and the son of Jesse will walk together in the Garden." This is clearly the sweetest of deals, a shot at not only forgiveness but also sublimation with the Almighty. "But who will walk first?" demands the arrogant King Jeroboam. "The son of Jesse," God answers. "Then I shall not repent," decides Jeroboam, sealing his fate.

Jeroboam is clearly capable of greatness, since he is invited to walk with God, but he cannot abide that his nemesis David would achieve greater heights than him. "Arrogance!" Rav Miller shouted, using the Hebrew word *ga'avah*. He struck the lectern with his closed fist. Acher, too, devoted himself to the study of Torah, but not for God's sake, *L'shmah* (literally, "for His Name"). He did it for the pleasure or power that it gave him, Acher. Because of his selfishness, the roots of his Torah study were corrupt, hence the reference to his uprooting the saplings in Eden. His journey to Eden had revealed to Acher that he would be sharing his relationship to God with his compatriots, one of whom, Akiva, was even worthier than Acher. This he could not tolerate, and so he turned his back on God altogether.

God and the human ego cannot coexist, warned Rav Miller, glaring at us. One must go. If ego cannot be subjugated to God, then essentially, one has already "othered" oneself beyond redemption, as did the sinners in these two stories.

My heart raced. Thoughts had begun to coalesce; ideas knit themselves together.

Rav Miller concluded the lesson with a surprising, rather haunting tale.

Acher, now an old man, dies and is buried. Flames rise up from his grave, indicating that his soul is lost in the torments of *gehennom*, hell. Rabbi Meir, loyal to the end to his former master, refuses to leave Acher's grave, lying down beside it and quoting from the Book of Ruth: "'Stay here the night, and in the morning, perhaps your redeemer will come for you.'"

Rabbi Meir's humility, his love, and his piety cancel out Acher's sin, releasing him from hell. As day breaks, the flames subside. Acher is finally at peace.

The hall, following this moving denouement, was momentarily silent. I turned my face downward, shielding it with my hands. Tears had begun to fall. I was shaken by this story, excited and profoundly sad at the same time, a feeling I could not account for.

The bell rang, startling me. Rav Miller stacked his books back up in their order and stood, leading to the cacophony of over a hundred chairs scraping as we followed suit.

This is one of only a handful of pictures of my parents together with my brother Uriyah and me. I must be about one and a half or two years old here, circa 1978. You can just see the stone walls and fruit trees of our Jerusalem neighborhood in the background.

My brother and I in East Quogue, New York, in 1979. The boat was part of a playground near my grandparents' home.

My mother and brother saw me off at JFK airport for my first flight to England and Gateshead Seminary. I had turned seventeen just days before.

Gateshead Seminary celebrated its 50th Anniversary in 1994. All of our *rabbonim* sat on a stage and gave speeches. Here, Rabbi Kohn is helping Rabbi Miller down from the podium.

With my mother, stepfather Ephraim, and brother Uri in 1998. This would have been shortly before I left for Boston and my new life.

During my last year at seminary in Gateshead, at my desk in the T1 classroom. You can see the papers passed out for the upcoming lecture — all of our sources were photocopied on the sheet, as girls were not meant to study Talmud from the original texts.

My mother and I outside our house on Saltwell View in Gateshead. My mother was an artist with her gardens. This picture was taken shortly after my broken engagement, in 1997, when I was twenty years old.

What a different woman we see here, just a few short years after Gateshead.
A young photography student took this portrait at the start of my senior year
at Boston University. Coincidentally, it was the very week I met Joe, in early
September 2001.   © 2001 CHRIS AKELIAN

Joe and I got engaged at the start of summer 2004, a few weeks
after I graduated with my master's degree. Behind us are the
seagrass and dunes of his family's beach house in Seabrook,
New Hampshire.

My father was so proud walking me down the aisle at my wedding. He lived only three more years and passed away when I was pregnant with Ella, in early 2008.

STACIE ANN SMITH

The rain held off. The day couldn't have been more magical. Newburyport, Massachusetts, August 20, 2005.

STACIE ANN SMITH

This picture was taken by our friend Thais the summer after Jacob turned five. I love the expression on Jacob's face: it is relaxed and confident and perhaps just a bit cheeky.   TDM PHOTOGRAPHY

Once he had marched out and the chamber resumed its bustle and noise, I remained rooted to the spot. I felt breathless, on the verge of a discovery of consequence, and I needed to continue my thoughts in privacy, away from my classmates. I picked up my notebook and tape recorder (we frequently taped lessons for later review), dropped them into my bookbag, and slipped out of the room.

Shrugging on my navy wool pea coat, I snuck out a door, hoping no one would notice me leaving. I couldn't bear to drop the gossamer threads of thought that had begun to wind themselves into a coherent theory. Once on the other side of the tall hedges, I set off briskly, no clear destination in mind.

I must have walked for several miles, deep in thought, ignoring the harsh wind that tore at my cheeks and my gloveless fingers. I began with a deep intuition that Acher had rejected second place not because, as Rav Miller's sources had posited, he craved stature or reward but, I felt certain, because he loved God with an intensity that refused limitation. If that was the case, he was to be pitied, not reviled. *God broke this man,* I thought, and a wave of bitterness swept over me. He created a being with enormous ability and unquenchable love but put a cap on what Acher could achieve — go this far, but no farther. A thought made my heart leap with sudden certainty: *Acher wanted to burn.* Yes, surely. He would not have wanted a heaven where he was denied intimacy to God. Had his unraveling not begun in Eden?

I stopped short as another piece of the puzzle fell into place.

Rabbi Meir!

Of course! It *must* be Rabbi Meir who redeems him, and not only because Rabbi Meir was Acher's favorite pupil. Rabbi Meir was the husband of Bruriah, a brilliant woman whose Torah scholarship was so sought after that Rabbi Meir's students would come to their home and beg for her teachings as she sat behind a curtain for modesty. Bruriah, who had the temerity to argue with her husband that women's intellects were not inherently weaker than men's as was believed. Bruriah, whose husband, in order to prove her wrong, disguised himself as a stranger and seduced her. Bruriah, who committed suicide in her shame after Rabbi Meir revealed himself to her.

Bruriah and Acher are alike, I thought triumphantly, *they are of a common essence and spiritual temperament, and Rabbi Meir is their connection.* While he was able to redeem his master, Rabbi Meir had been unable to save his wife. In fact, it could be argued it was he who pushed her to her death. Is that why he was so determined to save Acher's soul? Was this act not one of compassion or reverence for a former teacher but one of repentance on Rabbi Meir's part?

When I next became aware of my surroundings, it was late afternoon, and the last of a fiery sunset was sinking into deep purple dusk. A cold drizzle had begun to fall. I didn't recognize the street I was on, as it was well outside the Jewish area. My hands and feet were icy but my head felt strangely flushed and hot.

I don't know exactly how I made it back to our home opposite the park that day. Perhaps I wandered a bit farther and found a landmark I recognized, or maybe I asked a kind stranger for help. I know that by the time I climbed our front steps, it was early evening and my mother had just finished making dinner. I begged off dinner, claiming fatigue. After taking a closer look at me, she felt my forehead, then sent me to bed with paracetamol, where I slept heavily until morning.

I woke up the next day feverish with a sore throat and a nasty cough, and I was soon on antibiotics and ordered to rest. While I lay in my bed, I reflected bitterly on the fact that no medicine could cure what truly ailed me. It could no longer be denied.

I was a heretic in my own way, much like Acher.

We both believed in God. We knew too much to deny Him. But just like Acher, I did not want to be second place in the spiritual voyage that was my life. And as a woman, that's exactly what I would be, both here and in the afterlife. Yes, I had been told that a virtuous woman would assuredly collect an *equal portion* of her husband's rewards, but if the true joy of paradise was intimacy with God, the "walk in the Garden," how could this be conferred on me for a greatness I had not achieved? And if it were "granted me" regardless, would I want it? Not, I realized, if God had not wanted *me* enough in my life to desire that my intellect be the instrument of our intimacy. I was too proud for that.

Therefore, I was doomed.

I could see now that if I continued down this path, I would be irretrievably lost, like Acher. Unless, that is, I could find a way to save myself, to overcome the ego that refused to submit to my purpose.

As fate would have it, an opportunity soon presented itself. It came in the guise of Benjamin Bonn, and I held on to it as a drowning man would a floating log that suddenly appeared.

18

Boy Band

Has anyone seen my chameleon this morning?
He has to be hiding somewhere.
He asked me if we could play hide-and-go-seek,
and then disappeared into thin air.

I've looked high and low in the yard and the house
and it seems like he's nowhere around.
He's probably hiding right out in the open
but doesn't yet want to be found.

— KENN NESBITT, "Has Anyone Seen My Chameleon?"

THE MORNING THAT EM EMERGES FROM HER ROOM WITH-
out the Doggy Sweater begins like any other. It is one of those
chilly spring days that coats unsuspecting flowers with a deadly
frost. I take note of the sweater's absence, but I am silent as I
set out breakfast. Today we have Bubby Brown Bread, my mother's combination of cake mix, almond flour, and walnuts that she
bakes in batches and stores in the large tub freezer in our basement. For a few weeks after she leaves, while they last, these loaves
are a great boon to our morning routine. All the girls love them,

even Lucia, who at nearly one crumbles the cakey bread between her fingers and takes small bites.

I am cleaning up after breakfast, and the Doggy Sweater has still not made its appearance. I continue my charade of breezy indifference, afraid to comment on the missing element of Em's attire, until she finally addresses the topic herself: "I don't need the Doggy Sweater anymore," she says defensively. She goes over to our accessory drawer, fishes about, and finds a turquoise-blue satin elastic headband topped with a ludicrously large rosette in the same shade. Pulling it over the top of her head in the style of a tennis sweatband, she announces: "This is my *boy* headband."

I look at her, tilting my head, and as I digest this intelligence, two thoughts compete for the fore. The winner: Surely she *knows* that boys don't wear headbands, especially huge, frilly ones. The runner-up: The Doggy Sweater was her *boy* sweater, and now it has been replaced with another "masculinizing" item. Perhaps noticing my expression, she repeats, firmly, "This headband is my *boy* headband." I look away, at a loss. "Okay."

At least, I realize, her boy headband will have the unintended effect of making her look more feminine. Over the past months, with the exception of Christmas and Easter, Em has chosen to wear clothing (under the Doggy Sweater) that reflects her stubborn assertion that she is a boy. The clothes are plain, in somber hues of blue, black, and gray. I have long given up on the cute matching clothes. Now I am merely waiting out this tenacious obsession, this "boy thing."

She's aware that she's not *actually* a boy, I am sure of it.

Joe and I have a pact of honesty with our children (with a loophole for Santa Claus, the Easter Bunny, and the Tooth Fairy, white lies I had initially resisted telling). We had gently pointed out to Em on several occasions that her body shared some defining parts in common with her sisters. She had looked at us stone-faced. "I'm still a boy, and you're wrong." I could see, though, that the words had sunk in. She walked away looking sad and pensive. I wanted to gather her up in my arms, had in fact tried, but she had screamed and roughly pushed me away.

What were we supposed to do?

"Here, let me show you how to put that on properly." I stretch my hand out toward the headband. *"No!"* she yells, pulling away from me. Her hair is rising like a mushroom cloud above the blue elastic and she looks ridiculous. "Come here!" I insist, vexed. I follow her, snatch the headband off her head, lift my finger up in warning as she turns on me, her arms raised, and say: "Stop!"

It seems that I have won this battle of wills, because she stands sullenly and allows me to slip the headband over her head like a collar and then pull it back up over her face so that her brown hair falls neatly in soft waves over the band. "That looks pretty!" *Wrong choice of words,* I realize, too late. Stepping just out of reach, she rips off the headband with a growl and readjusts it. The mushroom cloud is back. "Fine," I say, gritting my teeth. Feeling mean and frustrated, I mutter, "That looks silly."

"She doesn't look silly, Mama!" Ella, who has stopped to watch the proceedings, is offended that I have broken the family rule forbidding disparaging language. "She looks like a very pretty girl."

Oh no.

I'm not quick enough and Em reaches Ella first; she shoves her back so that she tumbles onto the carpet, which doesn't fully muffle the *thonk* as her head hits the ground.

Ella's eyes go wide in shock and her face crumples up silently, the precursor to a scream. I run to lift her up, pointing at Em, who, holding her hands out, appears shocked at their strength. *"Time out!"* I scream, and the sound is so loud, so much louder than I intended, that it hits Em like a slap. She recoils but nevertheless stands her ground. Her face trembles and her eyes narrow as she looks up at me, arms crossed. Ella is still crying but I let her go for a moment as I swoop in on Em, lift her under the armpits, and march her toward the sunroom couch. I deposit her and exit swiftly, and it takes every bit of self-restraint for me not to slam the glass doors behind me. I assure Em that she will stay there until she calms down and can apologize to her sister.

I gather Ella up in my arms and lay my chin on her head. As I rock her back and forth she asks: "Why doesn't Em like me, Mama?" *Oh God.* "She loves you!" I assure her. "She's just angry." "Why is she so angry?" Ella persists, her breath still ragged. "I don't know," I answer truthfully. "Being three is hard," I manage. "Why is it hard?" she asks. A wordless shrieking has begun from the other side of the sunroom door. I hear a crashing noise and turn around to see that Em has upended a bucket of Legos on the ground. A small fist batters the door. *"I hate you!"* she says, sobbing. *"I hate you!"* But she is running out of breath, fast losing steam.

Ella starts to cry again, her eyes wide with fear at this terrible word, this end-of-the-world word, *hate.* "Does she mean it, Mommy?" She breaks free from me and runs to her sister. "Em, you don't hate Mama! You don't hate us! I love you, Em!" and she does. Passionately, helplessly, selflessly, she is bound to her sister in a way that is a marvel to all who witness it. "Ella," Em sobs back, falling against the door.

I buckle. I open the door and allow Ella in to comfort her sister, knowing that in this power play called parenting, I have ceded valuable ground.

As I fail to bend my child to my will, I see my mother in the corner of my mind's eye as if she stands there leaning against the cherry mantel, pale face hooded by a dark kerchief, her bent frame supporting the straight one, a Samson in the picture books of my childhood. On her face is a look of undisguised disgust as I fold to a three-year-old's tantrum.

I shake the specter away along with the surge of anger that accompanies it. *She does not understand Em.*

But do you? I must ask myself.

19

I Am Benjamin Bonn

I am not what happened to me, I am what I wish to become.

— CARL JUNG

I SAT ON MY BED HOLDING THE GREEN POLYESTER SASH and makeshift cardboard cap in my hands, as I had done each day for the past week. Closing my eyes, I whispered:

"I am Benjamin Bonn, son of Herr and Frau Bonn of Hamburg, Germany, father to an infant son. I was born on the fifteenth day of Adar and I died on the fifteenth day of Adar." After tucking the pieces of costume back in my drawer, I rose, brushed my teeth, and went downstairs seeking breakfast.

The decision to become Benjamin Bonn had been a spontaneous one.

Every year around the festival of Purim, in the Jewish month of Adar, Gateshead Seminary put on a theatrical production. It was a huge affair, held in a rented hall and attended by most of the women and girls in the town, as it was one of the few sources of public entertainment all year.

Every girl had a role to play, whether it was acting, singing, dancing, or scenery and costume creation. Spare moments from Hanukkah to Purim were donated in preparation for this grand event. I had held a major acting role in the play in my first year and dance and choir roles in my second. During my T-1 year, I had auditioned for the play and been assigned the part of Benjamin Bonn.

Bonn was a fairly complex character for the tiny genre of Orthodox Jewish teen fiction out of which he rose. He was born in seventeenth-century Germany at a time when heresies, like that of the false messiah Sabbatai Tzvi, were tearing the Jewish diaspora apart.

Bonn, young and foolish, had fallen prey to his evil inclinations and poor choices in friends, becoming entangled in the Sabbatian heresy and engaging in thievery — looting homes to buy nice things for his pregnant wife. One night, he and another Jewish robber friend are caught in the act and dragged before a local tribunal in chains. Being that this was seventeenth-century Europe, and according to the tried-and-true plot lines of these books, there was a wicked Catholic priest on hand who offered the young felons a choice: Renounce Judaism and kiss the cross or die by hanging at daybreak.

Bonn's friend renounces his faith in an instant and is spared. Bonn spends a long night of remorse in his cell, praying to God for forgiveness and clarity (accompanied by a soulful choir). By morning, his mind is made up. He will not renounce God. He will die *al Kiddush Hashem,* a martyr with God's name on his lips. In a moment that's straight out of *A Tale of Two Cities,* he announces that this act will be not only his last, but his best, the only worthy act in a life of degradation.

According to the stage direction, I, playing Bonn, was to stand frozen in the spotlight as the choir finished its song, then I'd duck behind a curtain, recite the Shema (the Jewish declaration of faith), and kick over a chair. The bang of the chair hitting the stage would represent the floor opening up under the hangman's noose. Taking some artistic license, I added a long, strangled gasp that brought my audience to its feet in a frenzy of clapping. The outer curtain dropped, and we broke for intermission.

Though the scene went just as we had practiced it at rehearsals, something odd happened to me up on the stage that evening. I felt a disembodied sensation, a no-longer-me moment as I stood in the glare of the bright lights facing the amorphous audience of dark shadows. I felt like someone with *clarity,* someone whose internal peace came from anticipation of his soul's release from the bondage of sin and this world. In effect, I felt like I supposed my character, Benjamin Bonn, would feel before ascending to a martyr's death. And with this sensation came a fleeting peace. When I packed up my bag, accepting the congratulations of friends, I found myself dreading a return to my own reality.

What if? I suddenly thought.

What if, unbeknown to others, I continued to play this role for, say, a day or two? What if I pretended, for a while, that I actually *was* Benjamin Bonn? No one but me would know. Could I hold on to this feeling a little longer perhaps, just long enough to subdue the strife within me, providing a critical respite from the noxious self that had led me down such a dark path? Maybe the sense of peace would provide a small window in which I could circumvent my faulty circuitry and repair myself? I *had* to try. There was no denying the danger I was in. Rav Miller had confirmed it.

After recovering from the illness that had left me bedbound for days following our lesson on Acher, I had made an appointment to visit Rav Miller during office hours, held at his home.

I had thought long and hard about how to frame my most burning questions. In the end, I had written down the following: *How could a good God assign people roles that made them spiritually lesser? For example, if God made the goyim of baser material, then why were they punished with a lesser piece of heaven? Had He not designed them this way? How could this be fair? And what about women? If they were merely helpmates, then they were essentially secondary and lesser.*

Rav Miller had listened to my questions quietly, squinting down at the table and occasionally pressing his steepled fingers to the glasses at the bridge of his nose. He shook his head several times, and when I finished, he launched, to my disappointment, into an all-too-familiar and facile explanation: "The body has different limbs, but all are needed for the functioning of the whole," he began. I was not having this today. "The brain and the hand are *not* equal," I said firmly. "One can *live* without a hand."

Rav Miller spent a long moment in thought, attempting yet again to find the elusive piece of dust on his sleeve cuffs. When he looked up at me, he sighed, and it was he who appeared disappointed.

"I'm afraid," he began slowly, "that what *you* are attracted to in the study of Torah is the mental *gymnastics.*" I was cautiously intrigued. "When we say that every Jewish *neshama*" — soul — "was present at Har Sinai to accept the Torah unconditionally, we are not speaking metaphorically, Miss Netzer, but quite literally. I was there, and you were there. It is the memory of that moment that allows us to accept what we learn completely, with full hearts, without needing so-called proof or intellectual answers for everything." He added hastily, "Not that using your intellect is *wrong,* but it should not be *necessary* to accept and to do God's will.

"It appears to me," he concluded, giving me his diagnosis, "that your problem is you do not accept the truth of every word of the Torah with your heart. You demand intellectual satisfaction from your learning. It has become a matter of, as I say, mental gymnastics."

I was stunned and angered.

How could he accuse me of learning merely for *intellectual* fulfillment? Did my heart not soar and dive with every treasured word? Furthermore, if my heart wasn't in it, would I be so desperate to fix myself?

Mulling over our conversation on the way home, I discovered that there was a strong element of truth to Rav Miller's rebuke. I wasn't happy with the lesser intellectual role I had been given. If I'd had a faithful heart, surely that would not have been the case.

Now, with Benjamin Bonn, I saw a possible, rather creative solution. I would circumvent my own corrupted consciousness to assume the identity, even briefly, of a true believer. It might, *just might,* be possible for me to affect an eventual change to my mind this way. Perhaps all I needed was a break from *her.*

I started the morning after the play. "I am Benjamin Bonn," I would begin my incantation. I would affirm my identity as Bonn in my diary, signing his name instead of my own.

Life, I found, was easier as Bonn.

He was impervious to my mother's ricocheting moods. He enabled me to nod at her silently and in genuine sympathy. When my stepsister behaved cruelly, he smiled at her with equanimity. Even Bonn's handwriting was small and neat, the sign of a tranquil and organized mind. I attended every evening study session at seminary, a practice I had previously abandoned. I said my daily prayers in the morning, afternoon, *and evening,* an act of worship that had fallen by the wayside. I even set my alarm clock for the time of Tikkun Chatzot, the prayer at night's threshold. Despite my middle-of-the-night activities, I awoke refreshed each morning, a new energy in my step and a secret to my smile.

The secret was simply this: I had gotten rid of *her.* I was enjoying a reprieve from she who in her stubbornness had afflicted my life with pain and doubt.

My diary reflected the difficulties I encountered subduing Mimi.

It is so difficult to eradicate M.

For the first time since the transformation, M.'s mother has really lowered my guard. She is very tense, distraught. When she is critical and biting at me, M. responds. It's hard for me to have a say at those charged moments. I am quietened, pushed away, and the monstrosity called M. emerges.

The girl who wrote these things never actually believed she had metamorphosed into a fictional character. She was too intelligent, ultimately too grounded. This, I suspect now, was her last-ditch effort, the miracle she was praying for: to sublimate herself into another being less rife with contradiction and forbidden yearning. I admire her. I am sad for her. She could not hold on very long to Benjamin Bonn. He wasn't real enough, and she was.

Indeed, I could not keep Benjamin Bonn with me. Try as I might, after a mere two months, he slipped away; only a patina of his magic remained.

June 1996 brought me to my last month of seminary and, with it, a frenzy of picture taking, gift giving, and lamentation that our days under the wing of our great rabbis were soon to be over.

The highlight of those last few weeks were the *shiurei prei'dah,* farewell lectures, which delivered to us each rabbi's heartfelt instructions and parting tokens of wisdom to take with us into the next anticipated stage of life: dating and marriage.

If we weren't busy with arranged dates already, we would be soon. We were expected to marry within a certain amount of time, approximately two years post-seminary, tops; after that, our eligibility would drop precipitously and finding a mate would become increasingly difficult. This was referred to as our "shelf life." Our parents, acutely aware of the ticking clock, would be calling matchmakers before we'd finished packing our bags to go home.

One of those last days, when spring had all but turned to summer, I entered the lecture hall for Rav Miller's class and set down on my desk my notebook, pen, and tape recorder, as usual. When Rav Miller took his seat, he bent toward the class representative and whispered, shaking his head. She began to turn off all the recorders that clustered around his podium, helped by nearby girls. *Click, click, click.*

Heart pounding with guilt, I slid my recorder into my desk and depressed the button as softly as I could. Whatever secret material was presented in this lesson would be wonderful, I was sure.

When I left the class that day, I was of two minds. One, furious, betrayed, wounded beyond measure, announced: *I will* never *get married. Never. I'd rather be alone forever.* The other shot back: *Who are you kidding? Do you want to stay in Gateshead for the rest of your damn life?* While they were thus engaged, a third, less strident voice spoke: *There is another way out.* But that third way was too horrific to contemplate, so I dug a trench in my mind and buried it.

20

Pitending

"How does one become a butterfly?" she asked pensively.
"You must want to fly so much that you are willing to
    give up being a caterpillar."
"You mean to die?" asked Yellow, remembering the
    three who fell out of the sky.
"Yes and no," he answered.
"What looks like you will die, but what's really you will
    still live."

— TRINA PAULUS, *Hope for the Flowers*

WE ARE SEVERAL WEEKS INTO THE NEW SCHOOL YEAR and I'm just starting to catch my breath when Em spills the beans to fellow occupants of the Star Room. She tells them that they have been mistaken about her bona fides, that she is, in fact, a boy.

"We were splitting the kids up into groups," Mrs. Shea confides to me sotto voce as we stand in the classroom doorway at pickup. Her brows are furrowed, but her tone is still lighthearted, almost amused. "She didn't want to leave the boys and line up with the girls, so she said, 'I'm a boy.'" Mrs. Shea's bright turquoise eyes are searching my face for a reaction, a hint as to how I feel about this, and I realize by the sensation of heat rising under my skin that what I'm feeling is embarrassment.

She continues: "I told her to line up with the girls anyway, that pretending was okay during free play, but that now she needed to stop and get in line. I hope that's okay?" Mrs. Shea's whisper of a smile is still there, an invitation to treat this matter lightly, to get it over with, to tell her that I, too, am not on board with Em's shenanigans.

I accept. Rolling my eyes, I let out a nervous laugh. "Yeah, that's been an ongoing thing lately at our house." I hasten to add, to make sure that she doesn't think I'm going along with this charade, "I explained to her what's real. I'm surprised she brought it up in school. I'm sorry!"

Damn.

"That's fine!" Mrs. Shea assures me. "I just didn't want to say something that you weren't okay with. Frankly, I wasn't sure what to do." She taps me lightly on the arm, a gesture of solidarity. "That's you and me both, then," I say, laughing again. I collect my children, one an effervescent pink powder puff of confident femininity and the other, just as precious, a mystery wrapped in blue denim overalls and an outlandishly large floral headband.

Looking at Em closely as I buckle her seat belt, I can see that her face is pinched, her eyes sad, as if a hidden weight tugs at their corners. Suddenly, sour guilt floods me, the feeling of having betrayed her. Seriously, though, can she expect everyone to fall in line with this? Home is one thing, but school?

On the car ride home, I think about ways to broach the discussion about what transpired, this new hiccup in the road. Things had been going so well this year. If anything, I was more concerned about Ella, who had cried at drop-off each day for the first two weeks. Em had seemed to part with me more easily, her difficulties at school having more to do with knowing when to use the bathroom, as she was still refusing to do, to everyone's frustration.

Ella has just finished a funny story about the class pet, a guinea pig, when I catch Em's eye in the rearview mirror. I decide to go for it. "Em, honey . . . did you tell Mrs. Shea that you were a boy today?" She looks down at her lap. "It's not that you did something wrong, sweetie," I add. "It's just, well . . ." I pause. "What did you think about what she said to you?" I ask frankly.

"She told me I pitended," Em admits, her face stormy. "I *not* pitending." She stares angrily at the back of my seat, then kicks it for good measure. We pull into the driveway and I let the engine idle after I put the car in park. "Em." I speak as gently as I can. "It's one thing for us to use your . . . boy names at home, but we can't expect Mrs. Shea and Mrs. Zipper to use them."

James, Jackson, Max . . . at first we were playing, or so I thought. But these days, forgetting what name Em requires of us could lead to tears and recriminations. I can only imagine how disruptive it would be if every child switched names on a daily basis. Though it hurt to do this to her, we had to keep this boy thing from spreading, at least until we figured it out. As parents, that's what we needed to do.

But not every child is Em.

She looks so angry, so betrayed, that my eyes fill. I unclip the car-seat restraints and Ella and Em head up the driveway as I hoist Lucia into my arms. Tomorrow isn't a school day. This will give me time to think, time to mull this over. Time to come up with a plan.

"So what if she says it in class?" That evening, when the kids are all in bed, Joe and I discuss the day's events.

"*So what?*" I say. Inexplicably, I feel annoyed at Joe's reaction, which sounds cavalier. He's not taking into account the fragile balance of the preschool ecosystem. "She's going to alienate herself from everyone! She has a hard enough time as it is." While Ella has regular playdate requests, Em has yet to talk much about friends or be invited to social events. I was disappointed when the one good friend she had made last year, Katherine, moved into the prekindergarten class with Ella.

Joe takes off his glasses and rubs his eyes. He suddenly looks older than thirty-five. I can clearly see the gray encroaching on his temples. "I don't know either, Mimi. I just don't know." And then he says that word again, the one that has slowly crept into our conversations, the one that drips acid into my stomach: "It's possible she will be transgender someday. Right now, there's nothing we can do about it but wait and see."

The T-word. I can't remember which one of us brought it up first. An internet search for *girl who insists she's a boy* yielded a mélange of first-person accounts, ads for sex toys, and Yahoo queries containing the word *transsexual* or *transgender*. And images, mostly of drag queens in pancake makeup. Surely not? This could have nothing to do with my baby girl. Whatever this world was, it wasn't hers.

The word *transsexual* also conjured up images for me of the first time I had heard it, watching the psychological thriller *The Silence of the Lambs.* In the movie, a serial killer nicknamed Buffalo Bill skins his victims to create a "woman suit" because he has been denied the surgery that will give him a vagina. *It puts the lotion on its skin or else it gets the hose again.* Those words had become a cultural meme for human depravity, and depictions like this had given me the impression that being transsexual was, at best, some kind of fetish. How could anything in the remote universe of *this* apply to my innocent baby? The links I found all seemed to refer to adults or, at the early end, those in their teens. Em has no inkling of or inclination toward sexuality yet. She doesn't even seem to have those innocent preschool crushes that moms talk about.

There just *had* to be other reasons why she was obsessed with this boy thing. Something more age-appropriate, I felt. It could even be a combination of things; the concatenation of a mild obsessive disorder with middle-child syndrome, perhaps? Who knew? We just needed to keep digging until we located the spot in her psyche where the tension had coalesced into a knot. Then we needed to massage it out carefully.

We needed to fix this.

"I not pitending!"

Halloween is now days away and my daughter refuses to shed her daily cosplay. Not the Iron Man costume we bought her for our family's superhero theme this year, but the one where she is a boy.

Not pitending. She is clear, crystal clear, clear as a freshly wiped pane of glass as she informs us, patiently, angrily, sadly, exhaustedly, again and again, in all caps: "I AM A BOY."

The set of her huge, defiant brown eyes, the jutting of her chin, the elbow held afore at a ninety-degree angle, all of these become the early-warning system, the DEFCON 1 that heralds the impending mushroom cloud of wrath.

Hurricane Em strikes again, reads a text I send to Joe, and much like a hurricane, Em's anger batters the occupants of the house and leaves a trail of broken toys, bruised limbs, and fear in its wake. Even her burgeoning art has begun to reflect her stormy demeanor; she draws almost exclusively in black and gray, and the humanoid shapes have frowns, gashes, or, often, no mouths at all. There are zigzagging lines, storm clouds that gather, I imagine, over their heads. She bears down heavily on her writing instrument, often tearing a hole in the paper.

"Tell Em she is just pretending!" Ella says.

Ella is frustrated, having just been yelled at for using the wrong *nom du jour.* "I have, Ella." I pull her onto my lap. Em is in the sunroom with the door closed, stewing in a time-out for pushing her sister. "Em knows deep down that she is a girl, but this is important to her," I explain, but then I hasten to add: "She still had no right to shove you." Ella melts into my shoulder and clings to me, still upset. I place my chin on her head, and I whisper, though

Em cannot hear beyond closed doors: "She'll get over it, love. We just need to be patient."

Ella lifts her head suddenly and searches my eyes. "Don't worry, Mama." She reaches out her small hand and strokes my hair, much as I did a moment ago for her. Her hand feels insubstantial, like a dove's wing, no more than the weight of a feather. "I'm not worried," I say, smiling at my intuitive child. In another minute the timer goes off and Em presses her face to the glass door, chastened and ready for play. Ella is wary but forgiving. Lucia, as she is most of the time, is unperturbed by the drama. She pulls herself up to the side of the couch and wobbles, her hips jutting forward, backward, side to side, like a contestant in a Hula-Hoop competition.

Later, I overhear Em give a pep talk to her baby sister, who sucks on her pacifier intently as she listens. "If you want to do something, Lucia, I say go for it. If I want to be a boy, I say, 'Go for it!'" I cover my face with my hands and the sadness flows over me. *Oh, baby.* If only it were that simple.

One morning something odd occurs. I sit down to write Joe, who is out on a call, an e-mail:

Joe the creepiest thing just happened.

Em, out of nowhere, holding an acorn and a little pinecone and a rock said:

These things I had a long time ago when I was different. When I had a different mommy.

I said: You had a different mommy?

Em: Yes, and I had a sister, her name was Rose.

Me: What was your mommy's name?

Em: Her name was Rose too. I was different. I had no hair.

Me: No hair at all?

Em: No hair, my head looked like this (pointing to her skin).

Me: When were you different?

Em: It was a long time ago. It was before God was here.

There were no yellow and white stripes on the road. God didn't come yet and paint stripes on the road. The road was only gray.

Me: What was your name . . . ?

Em: Ben . . . garbled . . .

Me: Back when you were different, were you a boy or a girl?

Em: A boy . . .

I seriously don't believe in past-lives shit but the roads having no stripes is *creepy*. Going to ask casually at school whether they discussed lives of pilgrims etc. What do you make of this?

What Joe makes of it is that "either she remembers a past life or she has a great imagination," but for about a day, desperate for answers, I seriously entertain the possibility that my child has been a boy in some earlier iteration. However, I soon let the idea go. I don't really believe in past lives, and even if I did, it wouldn't help me deal with this one.

As Em's moods increasingly dictate the course of our daily lives, I begin to fear for my more temperate child, for the toll this must be taking on her. There are times that, after bearing the brunt of Em's wrath, Ella still welcomes her sister back with open arms. Em, for the most part, accepts Ella's love while she continues to reject her parents'. One day I can eke out a hug or a kiss; the next, I am pushed away brusquely.

The baby, thank heaven, Em continues to adore, and she won't raise a hand to her in anger. "*My* baby," Em calls Lucia, and as she strokes her head I can visibly see a melting of the tension that she carries. She's got a series of silly names for her, Flashlight and Cheesestick, among others. I am so grateful that she still shows a sense of humor and that she is able to accept love and give it, even if toward me she is increasingly hostile.

Joe fares the worst these days. While I can usually garner a stiff hug and good-night peck, he has been booted off the short list of those whom Em will touch. "It's probably the sensory thing,"

I say, trying to comfort him. But we both know that that's not it, that in some way, he has been rejected. "She was my Buddha baby," he says to me one day, and the hurt in his eyes is almost too much to bear. "She'll come back," I respond, giving him a hug. "She'll come back."

But Thanksgiving is just around the corner and she hasn't come back. In fact, she has picked up a new, peculiar habit of barking at people. "Hello, Em," says an acquaintance at the coffee shop where I am buying the kids muffins. "Arf! Arf!" Em cries, loping around in a circle like a puppy chasing its tail.

Life has become an endless merry-go-round of names: Jackson, James, Max, over and over. Sometimes a name will last several days; other times, only an afternoon. There are a few moments, scattered here and there, when she goes back to being Em at home. During briefly lived names, I invariably screw up. Instead of Jackson I call her James or, worse yet, Em. Then she either corrects me forcefully or yells, swinging her fists, and is on her way to the inevitable time-out. I don't know who I am going to get each day, not the moniker or the temperament.

When she leaves the house, she is Em. Always Em. I will not play this game in public, and she hasn't asked me to since bringing it up at school that day.

"Have you asked her *why* she wants to be a boy?" inquires my friend Jill. "Of course," I answer glumly, "many times, but she always says different things. It's hard to tell which, if any, is the reason." One day, boys have better toys, the next day they have more toys, and another time, girls are stupid. Joe is overly generous when he responds, "But Mommy is smarter than me!" and I am quick to add that we have different strengths.

Regarding the toys, I point out that Em's sister, who is older by seventeen months, has more toys than she does (a dangerous statement, but I'm that desperate) and that there truly isn't such a thing as a boy-only toy or a girl-only toy. "You can play with whatever you want!" I tell her again and again, and just to settle the argument definitively, and in case she's hearing otherwise elsewhere: "Anyone who says something is *just* for boys or *just* for girls is st — is not being smart." The girls look at me suspiciously, and I know they are wondering if I almost used what they've taken to calling the S-word that's banned in our house: *stupid.*

Though it's aggravating that cultural gendering seems to be tampering with my daughter's psyche, at least, Joe and I decide, this gives us a way to combat it, and so we go about transforming our home and lives into a gender demilitarized zone. Our gender DMZ means that there are no hard-and-fast rules regarding toys or even clothes. No gender rules, that is.

I search on Amazon and in the bookstores for picture books that highlight women who "broke the mold," buying a cute graphic novel about Amelia Earhart and a picture-book biography depicting Jane Goodall's early life, among others. Women can do what they want, wear what they want, and be what they want. We are firm and consistent with this messaging, to the point that it becomes something of a family dogma. Ella is an enthusiastic proponent of this idea, as she can see clearly how it benefits her. She corrects us when we slip up (as we still do) and assume some object is for a boy or a girl.

Ella has become my loyal partner in crime as we conduct conversations within Em's earshot about why we just *love* being girls. Joe is a good sport when our conversation turns to why being a girl can be *"so much better,* even," than being a boy. Em observes our efforts with stonefaced scrutiny. I try to shake the disturbing feeling that to Em, it is not her but the rest of us who are putting on a performance.

One day, Em gets her first invitation to a classmate's birthday party. I click on the link to the invitation but my heart falls when I read the words: *Calling all princesses! Dress in your finest!*

A princess party, just great.

When Em sees the theme of the party, she shakes her head. "Honey," I say, "you can go as a prince. What about that? "No, Mama." Still, I am determined that we are *going to make this work,* come hell or high water.

I sidle up to Lindsay, the birthday girl's mom, after drop-off the next day. "So . . ." I start. "This is kind of silly, but Em is very much *not* into the princess thing. I wonder, would it be okay if you had a pirate or something at the party too?" "Oh my God!" Lindsay says, beaming. "Of course!" She admits that she was a tomboy too as a kid and wouldn't have put on a princess dress if you paid her, and now that her daughter Sage is into that stuff, she's kind of at a loss. "Don't worry," she says now, "I have some ideas! Tell Em we would *love* to have a pirate at our party."

"We will be there! Thank you!" I give her a spontaneous hug.

When we show up to the party it's Princesspalooza, fresh flowers and tulle everywhere (the benefits of working in a flower shop, explains Lindsay). My little pirate hesitates on the doorstep and I give her a tug over the threshold. Before we've crossed the hallway, we are nearly barreled over by two identically dressed princesses in yellow dresses and little slipper heels. Their hair looks professionally done and they are iridescent with glitter. They stop and stare with open curiosity at Em. For a minute I think of cutting and running, but Lindsay appears, takes our jackets, and welcomes us in with a huge smile. "Em, you look great!" she says, and I know she means it.

Em seems content, but as usual, she's not mingling with the other kids. She holds my hand for a few minutes, then settles down with a cup of popcorn. I'm surprised by how many moms give me the thumbs-up for "letting" my daughter be a pirate. Some of them also have stories about not being a girlie girl. I smile and thank them, wondering what their response would be if they knew what might be going on with Em. Have they even heard the word *transgender*? I hadn't until just a short time ago.

A few more minutes and the games start, to my relief, followed by prizes for everyone. They come in pretty little gift bags, and as the kids start pulling out princess-themed toys, my heart is in my throat. Lindsay looks over at Em's sullen face and dashes off into one of the bedrooms. When she comes back, she's got a gift bag with a pirate ship on it that she hands to Em. Inside is a Captain Hook doll. "I thought you might like this." Em's face lights up. I look at Lindsay and she mouths, *Is this okay?* I nod vigorously and mouth back, *Thank you,* placing my hands on my heart. Then I walk casually, not so fast as to draw attention, to the bathroom, where I lean against the sink and gasp for breath, trying to force the tears back, focusing on the cheerful shower-curtain print, the soap dispenser, even pinching my arm hard to stop myself from losing it here.

Soon it's that time of year when we start thinking of Christmas gifts. Joe's cousin, Em's Aunt Zoe, asks me, "What would the girls like? What about those popular Flutterbye Fairies?" My response: "Ella would probably love it, but Em wouldn't touch it! Em would probably want something in a boy superhero . . . is there a flying Batman?"

Nevertheless, even I keep trying to quietly push things "girl" on Em. I buy most of her pants and a few of her shirts in the girls' section still. There are those subtle details, a heart sewn into a hem or a slight cinch in the sleeve, that I hope to get away with. I feel ashamed that I'm so worried about what others think of us, but I am. I don't want the probing questions about why my kid looks so odd or why I indulge this whim. And so I carefully choose clothes that I think won't elicit attention.

I'm walking around Target thinking about gift ideas when I see the Katniss Everdeen articulated doll with a red clearance tag. *Bingo.* One look at Katniss and you know she's *tough.* With a dark braid down her back, wearing black-and-khaki soldier's gear and combat boots and packing a shoulder sling of arrows, Katniss, the heroine of dystopian teen-fiction series Hunger Games, is the anti-princess. She is clearly a *badass.* Perfect. I place the doll in my cart.

This year Em's class, the Star Room, is holding an extra day of parent-teacher conferences, a quick update to let parents know how the first month and a half of school has gone for their kids. Since there are no long report cards to go through at these meetings, school is held as usual that day, and after I drop Ella and Em off, I head downstairs with Lucia to wait my turn for Mrs. Shea, who is seeing parents in the downstairs auditorium.

Mrs. Shea beckons me over, clipboard in hand. She has a few pieces of Em's schoolwork with her and she points to how Em's letters are starting to develop (lovely, nice straight lines!) and informs me that she is really enjoying Em in the class this year. "What a character! So different from Ella!" "Night and day," I agree.

Then she looks at me, her eyes narrowing, and I can see that she is trying to figure out how to tell me something, something she's not sure if she should even say. I wait, attempting to appear encouraging.

"Mrs. Lemay . . ." She hesitates, then pulls out one more piece of preschool artwork from the bottom of her pile. There are several stick figures drawn in thick black marker. "Sometimes, when we ask Em to write her name — because that's the rule, we always label our work — she does it, but then . . ." Again, she stops. Maybe it's the temperature in the wide empty auditorium, but I feel a sudden chill, the hairs on my skin standing up. She points to a part of the sheet I hadn't noticed, an angry black scribble underneath which you can clearly see in a child's handwriting *Em.* "What I've seen her do then . . . is that . . . well, after she writes her name like we require, she goes back and . . . she crosses it out."

Crosses her name out.

Something tugs on my consciousness, a thread of memory, long buried.

It is so difficult to eradicate M.

"Do you think, Mrs. Lemay . . ." Mrs. Shea asks, her face pinched with concern, and suddenly, I want her to stop talking *right now;* something has my insides in a vise grip and I cannot breathe. "Mrs. Lemay, has it ever occurred to you, is it *possible,* that Em may *actually believe* she is a boy?"

21

The Kallah

And I passed over thee, and saw thee wallowing in
    thy blood.
And I said to thee: In thy blood thou shalt live!
Yea, and I said to thee, in thy blood thou shalt live.

— EZEKIEL 16:6

DAYS AFTER I TURNED TWENTY IN AUGUST 1996, I TOOK
off for Ireland to be a part-time au pair and tutor for the chief
rabbi's family as well as a schoolteacher at Dublin's only Jewish
day school.

I was soon occupied running after rowdy little boys and com-
posing engaging lessons for my class of world-weary fifteen-year-
olds. Fall in Dublin was spectacular, and I had the advantage of
admiring it from the environs of Rathgar, a leafy green inlet with
stately brick homes and verdant, manicured parks secluded from
the bustle of the main metropolis. I was busy enough, for the most
part, to keep the shadows at bay.

One Sunday afternoon, in the precious moments of solitude I
had between baths and dinner, my mother called. "Well, I have
some news . . ." she began coyly. A current of excitement followed
her voice down the wire.

I waited patiently.

"Daddy and I . . . may have found a young man for you!"

Before I could interject, her words spilled over, the clauses ping-ponging off each other in excitement. The next minute unfolded something like this: "The *shadchonis*" — matchmaker — "is very reputable! She found a groom for the Gruenbaum girl! Do you remember her? He was from Manchester? No, Belgium! Do you remember that family . . . no? They remember you. Mind you, it wasn't easy, she had a congenital condition. Heart — no, legs! Not life-threatening but still. The parents nearly despaired — she was almost twenty-four! You know who I mean . . . the second cousin was married to a Steinhaus . . . no, a Nussbaum! Do you remember her? Shaindel? She met you at Shavuos. She found you *fascinating*. She said to me: 'Your daughter is *fascinating!*'"

I cut her off. "Tell me about *him!*"

I had been feeling ambivalent about the dating process and was glad to have the time away in Dublin to think of other things, but I found myself intrigued nonetheless. It couldn't hurt to hear her out, right?

His name was Robbie, but in the yeshiva, he went by Avram, his chosen Hebrew name. He was a twenty-two-year-old Aussie from Sydney, the son of assimilated Jewish parents, and he had, at the tender age of thirteen, become a *ba'al teshuva,* returnee to the faith, under the wing of a local rabbi. He was now learning at Mir, the premier Torah institution in Israel for young men. I perked up immediately when I heard that he was not religious from birth. Perhaps this young man was . . . different, like me?

"Supposedly, he is *brilliant!*" my mother chirruped. "The *shadchonis* assures me that he has the makings of a real Torah scholar!" When I heard that, I became skeptical, remembering the first *shidduch* that had been suggested for me over a year earlier, an American Israeli whose mother had pulled the plug when she learned I didn't come with a monthly endowment and an apartment in Jerusalem for her brilliant son. Frequently, becoming engaged to the next budding Torah scholar came at the cost of financing his studies indefinitely.

"Maybe," I said. "What does he look like?" It was superficial, I knew, but the emphasis on Torah study from a very young age at the expense of all else tended to make the young men in our community look, well, a little pale and hunched, like people who had emerged from a cave after years of captivity.

"Tall *and* handsome!" she exclaimed triumphantly. "Okay," I said, agreeing to meet him, my heart fluttering with a thrill of excitement.

No expense was spared for a ticket home and a trip to Fenwick's department store in Newcastle, where I purchased several tasteful outfits and some subdued makeup for the occasion of my date.

The night before Robbie and I were scheduled to meet, Ephraim and my mother drove to Newcastle airport to greet the young man, and when they returned, my mother was in a state of ecstasy. "He is *a prince!*" she gushed. "A prince among men!" She grabbed me by the shoulders and danced me awkwardly past the kitchen table. I allowed myself to be jerked about, even giving in to the moment with embarrassed laughter. My stepfather averted his eyes from the physicality, but even he was smiling broadly, his cheeks creased and his eyes backlit with pleasure. Not for the first time, I felt sympathy for the difficulty of his position, having opened his home up to an adult "daughter" whom he was now obliged to marry off.

When the doorbell rang shortly after six p.m. the next day, I was pacing my room at the top of the stairs. My stepfather took Robbie into the dining room and subjected him to a series of questions, the last hurdle of the vetting process before we would be allowed to meet face-to-face. Time passed interminably until finally, the dining-room door swung open and I was called downstairs. Heart pounding in fear and excitement, I slowly entered the room.

The boy who sat in the dusky blue velvet chair by the window rose quickly to greet me. He had red hair and almost translucent pale skin. His lanky limbs took a moment to compose themselves into the concerted act of rising, and when he did, I noted that, indeed, he was tall, approximately six feet. Because we were forbidden to touch before marriage, neither of us offered a hand. I did, however, briefly study his face. I took in the neatly trimmed beard and bright blue eyes behind wire-frame glasses. While he wasn't a conventionally handsome man, his features soft, not strong, he was attractive enough.

I sat myself across from Robbie and folded my trembling hands in my lap. I discovered to my consternation that I could not access the words to begin a real conversation. The last time I had spoken unguardedly with a man who was not my brother or stepfather had been in the ninth grade, during my rebellious phase, when I had for a time enjoyed the scandalous attention (and eventual chaste peck on the cheek) of my friend Alisa's cousin. Thankfully, Robbie broke the ice by asking about my job in Dublin. I then asked what he had been learning at yeshiva recently. He shared something from the week's Torah portion.

I took a deep breath. *This is the test,* I thought. I offered several interpretations of the passage he had been discussing, talking about a *machlokes,* controversy, on the application of the words. Robbie's eyes widened as he stared at me. My stomach dropped in disappointment. *Oh, ugh. He's one of them.* I thought about getting up and walking out of the room, pleading a headache, indicating that the date was over.

It had been only five months or so since Rav Miller's parting lesson, and the wound still felt fresh. He had sat at the dais above us drawing links between Satan; Jacob's evil twin, Esau; and the creation of woman, coolly explaining that all these were designed by God solely for the service of the Jewish man, either as a snare that he must avoid or a tool, like a ladder, that he must use to climb to great heights. That is the reason, he went on, that the holy sages abjured man to avoid speaking "in excess" with any woman, even his own wife. A woman's duty was not only to care, feed, encourage, obey, and fulfill a man's every physical need; she must also sacrifice the intimacy of time spent together, to urge her husband away from her and back to his studies. Otherwise, like Satan, she would lead the man to his downfall.

During that lecture, I had sat staring, stone-faced, ahead of me, my pen down on the desk, the tape recorder hidden inside of it making the faintest whirring sound. "Don't worry," he had concluded, his voice heavy with sarcastic disdain for those of us with the following concerns: "Your husband will still *love* you just as much even if you chase him out of the home to study Torah."

Rav Miller must have seen something disagreeable in my face. "Nu," he had said then, speaking in my direction, "these things need to be taken with a degree of *eidelkeit,* some *humility.*"

I searched Robbie's face now for signs of contempt for or discomfort with my boldness. At least on the surface, I did not see any. He was still staring, but if anything, he looked . . . pleased. When he opened his mouth and spoke, my heart leaped with joy: "I've always wanted to find a wife to share my learning with." The few girls he had been paired with in the past, he confessed, did not seem to enjoy complex discussions about learning. "I do!" I said happily.

Please, God, I prayed, *let him be the one.*

Several hours flew by. When my mother and stepfather popped through the door, flushed with excitement, we were surprised to discover it was close to midnight. We arranged — I through my mother, Robbie through his hosts — to meet again the very next day.

Our courtship was a whirlwind. We met once in the lobby of a large hotel in Newcastle, where we sat and sipped bottles of Coke, then at the aquarium, where we stood several feet apart, for modesty, admiring a floor-to-ceiling tank that included several species of sharks. We discovered more things that we had in common. In those years when neither of us had been as strictly religious, we had fallen in love with the Star Wars movies. It was then that I asked, half teasingly: "So, do you have a dark side?"

Robbie went quiet. A shadow passed over his formerly animated features. I worried that I had crossed the line, somehow offended him. "You know," I hurriedly explained, "like *t'a'vah* or *ga'avah,*" I said, referring to the sinful traits of lust and arrogance. "I am more drawn to arrogance," I ventured timidly. His jaw relaxed. "For me it is more about desire," he confessed.

Our ability to be open and honest with each other about our flaws was the deciding factor for me. He too declared that he was more than satisfied. Within two weeks of meeting for the first time, we were officially betrothed, and I assumed a new and exciting identity: the future Mrs. Avram "Robbie" Gold.

The day of my *vort* arrived. It was a chilly afternoon in December, not as cold as the Northeast American winters of my youth, but markedly grayer. I stood in the hallway outside the dining room where we had first met just a month back, trying to pick Robbie's Australian accent out of the babble of tongues within. The men were enthusiastically engaged in the exchange of Torah insights, quips, and anecdotes, laughter punctuating their remarks along with the clink of our small silver schnapps glasses filled to the brim.

I could barely believe my good fortune. Once unofficially engaged, I had begun to set aside my ambivalence about becoming the wife of a Torah scholar, as Robbie had openly enthused about the role he saw for me as a teacher of women. We would work as a *team,* bringing wayward secular Jews back into the fold.

I felt immeasurably blessed. Soon, I would be ushered inside the circle of belonging — by choice. For the first time in my life, I would find myself an insider, a participant in the joys of normal family life and community.

I remembered Rivka Malka, my first study partner, who had come back to sem from her first summer break glowing with joy and adorned with the jewelry of a bride, *kallah,* from her *choson,* bridegroom. She was barely seventeen years old when we sent her off, dancing a *mitzvah tanz* in her honor one evening after the Sabbath. We had strung together dozens of white cloth napkins to form jump ropes, and as we danced and clapped and sang, she skipped between the ropes, double Dutch–style, from childhood to womanhood, through the double helix formed by the rapidly moving, intersecting lines. I had secretly wished I could be like her, finding a soulmate so quickly and easily. I did not know then if I could ever find my *bashert,* as my own soul remained incomprehensible to me.

And yet, miraculously, here I was, standing behind a door that would shortly open, invited to partake of the bounty within: a husband, children, a home, all strong ropes to tether me to this world, rendering me impervious to the buffeting of internal winds. I arranged and rearranged my navy and gold braided headband, tucking stray hairs behind my ears, admiring the way my sparkly new diamond caught the light, casting arcs of rainbow confetti on the hallway wall. I pressed my hand to my stomach as a grumbling noise escaped. I had been too nervous to eat much that day.

Ear to the door, I listened to the toasts that my seminary *rabbonim* gave. They said things that made me blush and glow with pride, heaping praise on me for my kind nature, modesty, and strong values. It was the standard engagement trope, but today I didn't care.

As master of ceremonies, Ephraim gave the final toast. Part of me was sad that my father was not there, but overall, I was relieved. I had not seen him since the start of seminary. My handsome, dark-skinned father with too-long hair, always dapper in his light-colored suits, would have been a spectacle in this sea of black-hatted, bearded men whose pale, papery skin and bowed backs spoke of lifetimes of spiritual devotion. Not unlike these men, my father revered his books, crowing like a pirate over treasure as he described finding rare manuscripts in the ancient catacombs beneath the Vatican or in some remote Iranian village. He would be invited to the wedding, but only if he respected our rules.

The door swung inward, interrupting my thoughts, and to cries of "The *kallah!* Bring in the *kallah,*" I was ushered in. The men parted in haste, stepping back to keep the prescribed distance from a woman. I advanced as I was directed to the object wrapped in a white handkerchief that lay on the carpet.

The plate chosen for the ritual breaking of the plate had not been my first choice. I had hankered after a Villeroy & Boch platter, a harlequin pattern in a riot of bright colors on a black base; however, due to the exigencies of time, I had settled on a simple piece of white china with a spray of delicate pink, blue, and lavender lilies. Everything would have to be settled quickly, my dress and wig purchased, the hall booked, invitations sent, as my wedding was just two months away. The time between a betrothal and wedding was rife with temptation and so, by custom, it was kept brief. The very next week my *kallah* classes would commence; if I hadn't been so exposed to the world in my youth, this was where I would have learned what my intimate duties to my husband were and found out, for the first time, how those many children I planned to have would be made.

I approached the wrapped plate, steadied my foot above it, then slammed it down quickly.

Crack! The delicate porcelain gave way under the crushing weight of my heel.

"*Mazel tov!*"

The room erupted with noise as hands were shaken, backs slapped, and conversations unstoppered, along with another bottle of sweet liquor. I searched briefly among the men for Robbie's eyes, but he was engulfed in the embrace of a large man whose ur-sine appearance was underscored by the wide fur *shtreimel* on his head and the black knee-length *kapota* that he wore. I turned and quietly left the room, joining the women in the kitchen to accept their effusive congratulations and embraces.

Late that evening, sitting in the vinyl recliner in our kitchen, I was too excited for sleep. The white handkerchief that had cov-ered the broken plate lay open in my lap as I sorted through the shards. Most of the salvageable pieces I would give away, lucky to-kens for as-yet-unwedded girls. Even fourteen-year-old Roselyn, who had taken to sulking at the recent attention paid me, would receive a piece.

I fetched my diary and began planning my wedding. *A Win-ter Garden!* I wrote, inspired. *The mechitzah* — modesty divider *— covered with white curls of ribboned snow and crisscrossed with delicate ivy leaves!* My bouquet would be *lush red and white roses with dark green ferns. A snow-white wedding! A princess wedding! All potential, waiting for the spring's golden touch to "spring" into life.*

To me, the decorations I chose would mirror my soul's revival. *It's like* The Secret Garden, I noted, *a life spent having to hide all that potential, to have your joy locked within you — to be brought to life because you've found love. That's us.* One can just hear my contented sigh.

I came across a shard shaped like a shark's tooth, and, recalling with pleasure our date to the aquarium, I wrapped up the piece of broken plate in white tissue paper and set it aside for myself.

The first sensation that broke through my fugue was muted and thin, like a premature bud attempting to claw its way out of un-yielding earth.

I am sad. Why am I sad?

I fell back into a drug-induced torpor and slipped away.

When I awoke next, the anguish was there to greet me, bright and pulsing, and so was my memory.

How could he do this to me?

I shook the bottle of Valium that Dr. Rutenberg, Ephraim's evening study partner, had prescribed for me, but it was empty. For over a week it had kept me away from reality as I had floated from day to night. The mattress that my mother had dragged into my room so she could sleep by my side the night she and my stepfather broke off my engagement stood upright against my closet.

When reality returned, so did the questions.

How could such a thing happen?

How could I not know or suspect what kind of person he was?

The phone call that had begun my descent came after a two-week spell of troubling silence from Robbie. It was a little over a month until our wedding, and we had previously been in frequent communication. "Are you okay?" I asked when he finally returned my call, phoning from Jerusalem. His answer, a simple, dull "No," had sent chills down my spine. Then, as I stood there, he had removed the floor from under my feet, knocking me down with his words, his confession.

"I made a terrible mistake." "I am not worthy of you." "Can you ever forgive me?"

The answer, of course, was no. I could not forgive his betrayal — not only of me, but of the values I thought we both held dear. The fact that his betrayal was with the wife of a rabbi, a mother of six, made what he had done revolting beyond endurance. But I could not speak, so instead, I dropped the phone in its cradle.

I must have stumbled in to my mother and Ephraim with the news, because the next thing I knew, they had left me in the recliner by the kitchen and gone off to ask for a *da'as Torah,* a rabbinical ruling. Whatever the rabbi said would be binding, having the weight of law. When they returned, I looked dully at their faces, at the masks of pity they wore. When they told me my engagement had ended, I wondered numbly: *Why are they so sad? I am a stone girl.*

But unfortunately, I was not a stone girl, or not for long, anyway. I was human, and I cared, enough to be racked with pain, to require Valium so that I could stop reliving the nightmare, to require that my mother drag a mattress into my room and sleep by my side for that first night. Once the narcotic settled into my bloodstream, I floated somewhere above the pain but below real life. The stone girl returned. I welcomed her.

Now, almost two weeks later, I was at the bottom of my pill bottle, and the pain was back. My mother and Ephraim were upstairs sleeping peacefully. Life had gone on for them, closing itself around their daughter's wound once more, as if it had never happened. The house was quiet and still.

It was silly for me to question why, I knew that.

I had known why from the moment my future fell apart. Had I truly imagined that my arrogance would go unpunished? I had told God Himself that I refused His offer, that I would not walk with Him because *He* had not chosen *me*. This now was the logical consequence to my words. Had I really thought it could end any other way, fool that I was? And for my stamping my foot like an impetuous child I had been cast out farther than I had been before. With a broken engagement, unable to tell people why because of the strict rules that prohibited needlessly speaking ill of others, I would be a source of quiet speculation, of stigma; an indelible stain would accrue to my character for years to come. It would affect my eligibility and, in all likelihood, the entire course of my future.

Blistering anger tore at my gut.

I dug my fingers into the arms of the chair, hoisted myself up, and went upstairs to my bedroom, where I shut the door behind me. I sank to my knees in front of my closet, located the brown shoebox nestled among the black and navy pumps and penny loafers, lifted its lid with steady fingers, and shifted the contents with purpose until I found the small object wrapped in tissue paper. I examined the shard of engagement plate, shaped like a shark's tooth, turning it over and over in my hands.

After rolling up the sleeve of my green satin housecoat, I pressed the broken shard of plate against the soft skin of my upper arm.

Slowly, with care, I drew the shard down from biceps to crook of elbow, watching as tiny crimson beads sprang to the surface, pooling on exposed flesh. I gave an involuntary hiss as the pain swelled, sharp and bright. The hair on my arms stood up as what felt like an electric current passed from my head to my toes. I gave a shuddering sigh.

Again, and then once more, I pierced my flesh until narrow tributaries of blood ran into each other, expelled with each heartbeat, singing out, it seemed, that I lived, that I *might yet* live, that my life was *mine* to live . . . or not. I couldn't stay a stone girl forever.

Wrapping my arms around myself, I stroked the goose bumps on my skin, inhaling the copper scent of blood. Baring my teeth, I whispered to myself through them: "*I* still love you." I imagined the words taking on life above me in the dark room, ready to tear the flesh from those who would harm me.

"*I* will never leave you," I vowed, nonsensically, and then the dam splintered and broke.

It would be one year, seven months, and thirteen days before I would leave my home for good, the place that nearly claimed my soul. But the night I shed my blood to save my life — that was the beginning of the end. That was my first step toward freedom.

• 22 •

Paradise Lost

She went sifting through my hands, impalpable
as shadows are, and wavering like a dream.

— HOMER, *The Odyssey*

*M*RS. LEMAY, HAS IT EVER OCCURRED TO YOU, IS IT POSSIBLE, *that Em may* actually believe *she is a boy?*

The truths that I have strenuously kept at bay, those things that I have shoveled under a heap of excuses, pour over me, a deluge of connections that I can no longer ignore.

For Em this is reality. This is no game to her. There is *no pretend.* It is we, her parents, who have been pretending that this is all a game. And with that realization comes gut-wrenching fear.

Not my baby girl. No, no, no. *Anything but this.*

I am helpless against the tears, unable to catch them all as I swipe at them with the back of my hand. "I'm sorry, I'm sorry!" I repeat. Mrs. Shea holds on to my arm and pulls me toward her for a brief hug. "I just don't know what to do," I say, my voice wobbling all over the place.

"You're a good mother," she says soothingly, giving me a little shake. "You'll get through this too." I nod but I am not listening to her; instead, I am tasting the devastation in my mouth, acrid, ashy. My breakfast presses against the wall of my stomach.

"Maybe you can bring her to see someone? A psychologist?" she suggests. "Yes, I'll do that," I manage to say, and she's looking at me sadly as I back away, wiping the snot and tears with my coat sleeve like a child. "It'll be okay," she calls out after me. But she doesn't know that; she can't know that. It's quite possible that it's never going to be okay ever again.

I pass another mom on my way out; she's clutching the hand of a little girl with blond pigtails. The child looks up at me curiously, taking in my wet cheeks, and I feel a wave of bitterness. I'll never be that mom again. Her with her *normal* kid. I get to the car and lay my head down on the steering wheel and cry.

I dial with trembling fingers and leave a message for Joe. I tell him what Mrs. Shea said, how serious this is. He texts me back in a bit. He's sympathetic but busy, late, in between meetings; he's working a full-time job while trying to start his own company. He promises me time that evening to talk.

When the key turns in the lock, I jump up and grab the door before Joe can open it. "Hey, hey, are you okay?" he asks, alarmed because my face is swollen from crying. "The meeting. Mrs. Shea," I remind him, and I can't believe he's been able to push it to the back of his head all day. *How does he do that?* I think for the hundredth time.

I start to tear up again, and he wraps his arms around me a little stiffly, uncomfortable, I know, with my sadness. It hasn't been often that I've cried over the years; I can probably count the times on the fingers of one hand — until recently, that is — and I feel a flicker of annoyance. He says now, "If it truly is what it appears to be, then we can't do anything to change it," displaying the stoicism that has been both a blessing and a curse to us over the years. "You need your emotional energy." And just like that, I feel both supported and incredibly, awfully alone.

We sit uneasily on the couch together, become immersed in

some television show, sharing the space but sitting apart. Suddenly he swipes at me gently with his hand, then once again, a little gesture of reconciliation, a teasing move that I have come to know. It means: *I'm not up to this emotional shit right now, but can you love me anyway?* I move into the space that he's created for me with his outstretched arm. "We'll get through this," he says. "Yes, we will," I reply. *I hope.*

I'm still weighed down by sadness, but when I retire to bed that night, I fall asleep almost instantly because I'm also exhausted. I dream.

We are on a high floor in some hotel in a city . . . maybe New York? Ella and Em are exploring the suite while I am unpacking the bags on the bed. They are younger than they are now, perhaps two and three. The French doors are open to the hotel balcony, letting in a nice breeze. Em is heading to the doors, toddling toward the railings. I feel a momentary clutch of anxiety, but I assure myself, the railings are sturdy and safe. I keep unpacking, one eye on her. She is looking back at me, smiling, when she slips one chubby leg into the space between two railings, dangling it twenty stories above the street. I realize, with a sickening lurch, that the railings are too far apart. "Em, *stop!*" I scream, dropping the clothes and beginning to run. As I reach my hand out to grab her, she slips the other leg and then the rest of her body through. My hand closes on empty air. "No! No! *No!*" I shriek over and over, collapsing against the balcony, wailing. I cannot look down; I do not want to see her tiny body on the pavement below. I swing my own leg over the railing, determined to join her. Joe grabs me from behind and I kick and scream, fighting to break free. "Let me go," I wail. "No, you can't go," he implores. "It's over for her now. You have to stay."

When I wake up with a heave, my bed is wet from sweat and I am shivering. There are even tears on my face, something I've never experienced before from a dream. I take a few deep breaths, ready to comfort myself. That's when the events of the previous day come back to me with a wallop and the nightmare comes to life. I am losing my daughter. She is asleep, breathing peacefully in the room next door, but she is also slipping away, one foot dangling over a void. I cover my face with my hands and weep as quietly as I can.

Oh, my love. Oh, my heart. Oh, my Em.

A small sound escapes, and Joe stirs. I turn the other way and lie still as he gets up and heads to the bathroom. When he is back and quiet once more, I allow my grief out again, but this time I cover my face with the pillow and bite down on it to muffle any sounds.

It is hard to breathe under the pillow and for one wild moment, I wonder if I *should* die this way, so that I will never lose her. I can't leave, though. I am Mama, and Mama, I have long known, is not just a word but a promise.

I drag myself out of bed and into the shower, where I let the water scald my body, carry away the stink of bad dreams.

After breakfast and before dance class, I text my friend Andrea about Em. Can she give me some advice? I think we need to see someone specifically about Em's gender issues. Andrea is a friend in our town with two little girls but she's also a social worker and a school guidance counselor. We arrange an emergency playdate for that afternoon, and until the hour comes, I am anxious, distracted, and weepy.

"Mommy doesn't feel well," I tell Ella when she asks plaintively why I'm not listening to her. "Lie down, Mama!" Ella orders and she and Em make a big deal of getting me pillows and blankets and a plate of "medicine," which consists of a few Ritz crackers, a black olive, a strawberry, and, after some scurrying and the sounds of the fridge door opening, a disgusting blob of mustard on top. I thank them profusely.

When everyone is down for quiet time after lunch I sit at the table and open my laptop. I Google the words *transgender child* this time, then *transgender preschooler,* but few articles of relevance show up and nothing at all with practical advice about what to do with kids Em's age.

Before I know it, it's time for our playdate. I buckle the kids into the car and we head to the Family Room, a co-op play area. Andrea buzzes me in and we struggle up the three flights of stairs to the carpeted play space where there's enough fun stuff to occupy the kids for a week.

Andrea and I sit down on a battered sofa to talk, but with the kids hovering around us, eager to show off toys they've found, we must resort to speaking in code. There's also another mom there, so we give up on the topic for a while. When the room is finally cleared, the kids are hungry, so we move to the snack area, where there's a well-stocked cabinet, and soon we're doling out goldfish crackers and pretzels in paper Dixie cups.

"She is young, but it's possible." Gender is something that develops earlier than sexuality, Andrea explains, and the two traits develop distinctly from each other. "But what will that mean for her?" I ask. "How will she . . . live her life?" "Normally!" Andrea answers, and I am grateful, at least, for the confidence in her voice. "When parents and family are supportive, transgender kids can thrive. That's really important," she adds, her voice low, "otherwise . . . the outcomes for these kids are . . . not so good." She winces, her eyes sad. "I don't mean to frighten you," she goes on, "but studies have shown that forty-one percent of transgender people have" — she hesitates, but there is no way to soften the blow of what comes next — "attempted suicide at least once."

Suicide. *Forty-one-freaking-percent.* Nearly half. Almost one in two. There is no way that I can compute this to make the number anything less than the nightmare that it is.

Oh God. No, please.

What would make so many people want to die? Will Em want

to die? Suddenly, all my bright dreams for her hit a brick wall. There will be no high-school dances, no first loves, no prom, no college graduation, no watching her walk down the aisle.

The dreams of my motherhood have collapsed to a single intent: keeping my child alive. There is nothing else.

Andrea must see the raw fear in my eyes. "It's going to be different for Em," she says quickly. "When families are supportive, the risks go down *substantially*." "How substantially?" I ask, but she can't tell me. The truth is, and I know it, no one can tell me what to do now. The little I have read makes me realize that our particular path isn't one that too many people have been on before. Damn Dr. Spock and his stupid book. There is no manual for *this*.

"Keep in mind," she says, "there's a good chance that Em may outgrow this. Just a small percentage of young kids who are gender-nonconforming, only around twenty percent, I think, end up identifying as transgender past puberty. She may discover later that she is just gay."

And why didn't you lead with this? I think, a little annoyed. Just gay would be wonderful. I would put that on a bumper sticker, get it tattooed on my skin: *My Daughter Is* Just *Gay.*

I do the math in my mind. So, if only 20 percent of young kids who are gender-nonconforming are really transgender, and 41 percent of those try to take their own lives, that means Em has only a roughly 10 percent chance of hating her life enough to try to end it. Horribly, that sounds better. I can't believe that we are here, that I'm calculating my baby's suicide risk with elementary-school math.

I look at Em, and it all suddenly seems so incongruous that I think: *This is insane.* She's been taking advantage of my distraction to pound down fistfuls of goldfish. The crumbs are guiltily lining her fat cheeks, cascading down the front of her shirt and onto the table.

"Em, that's enough," I say woodenly. "You've had too much.

Finish what's in your hand and then you're done." But I'm thinking, *What are the parenting norms anyway when you learn your kid's chances of reaching middle age have rolled down a cliff?*

"It's going to be okay," Andrea says again as I tear up. *Why do people keep saying that? They can't possibly know.*

The playdate wraps up and I leave with the phone number of the gender-management clinic at Boston Children's Hospital and the beginning of a solid migraine. Joe agrees to put the kids to bed that night and I go lie down, but I can hear them outside the bedroom. My light is off, my earplugs are in, and I've taken four ibuprofen. I'm trying to create a sensory-deprivation tank to halt the saw that's cutting into my skull, but I can still hear them, the rhythm of their nighttime rituals. Bathing, pajamas, toothbrushing, that moment when Joe threatens to read the instruction pamphlet for our jazzy new humidifier in lieu of a bedtime story ("'Silverclean technology — what is it?'") and the girls start screaming in mock distress. Sounds that are so wonderful in their ordinariness.

I *paid* for this ordinariness with my blood and my tears, I think as a fiery hatred consumes my pain.

You still can't have me, You sick bastard, I tell God.

And You will never have them. Never.

• 23 •

The Firebrand

Enough — I have been tried enough —
My wandering — long wandering.
Yet I have found nowhere
To leave my misery.
I am a girl who speaks to you,
But horns are on my head.

— AESCHYLUS (ATTRIBUTED), *Prometheus Bound*

ND SHE LEFT, AND SHE SETTLED IN A FAR-OFF LAND, and she began life anew.

Except that between my broken engagement and the day I left Gateshead for good, there were twenty months, one for every year that had shackled me to *this* life, *this* world, *this* framework of being. And for a long time, no one, least of all myself, knew that leaving was as necessary to my continued existence as drawing air into my lungs.

In the months following the shock of Robbie's betrayal, there were moments of spiritual adrenaline, times that I felt better off for having endured this trial. I was, in the words of the Prophets, a "firebrand plucked from the flames." Tempered by tragedy, I felt myself to be impervious to anything that could cause further trauma or pain.

When the burst of adrenaline slowly ebbed away, I was left with an interminable dull ache, a feeling of hopelessness about my future, and, always, the rebellious heart that I believed had caused all this trouble to begin with.

What I thought of as my third option, that which I had entertained since my last days of seminary, began to seem more attractive, though as impossible as ever to implement. Suicide would not bring me relief from myself, I knew. It would only compound my eternal alienation from God. I expressed in my diary these dark thoughts that were more pressing by the day. I asked God to take my life, to relieve me of a body that I no longer wished to inhabit. I didn't know how much longer I could hold on.

As spring approached, I found it difficult to leave the house and do "useful" things, as my mother had ordered. Day and night had slowly reversed on me. I would sleep until ten in the morning and stay up until two a.m. Even taking the bus into Newcastle felt like a challenge. My heart would pound from anxiety as we crossed the Tyne Bridge, as I imagined the guardrail breaking suddenly and the vehicle plummeting into the water. I could no longer enjoy the view in the evening when the bridge lamps would cast streaks of golden light on the water that I had dubbed "the Procession of Spirits" because of the way the lights danced with the waves. My nerves felt raw; fears bloomed in my mind like weeds. Outwardly, to others, I maintained the cheerful façade at which I was adept, but once home, alone with my mother, I expressed my feelings of bitterness and despair. Coupled with her feelings of bitterness, our conversations became increasingly toxic.

My mother, at her wits' end about what to do with me, berated me for giving in to my feelings, for not rising to conquer the challenges God had presented to me. She saw me throwing my life away out of spite. I *was* angry, for certain. The anger grew like a tumor in my gut until it seemed to be powering my existence. But there was something else happening. Perhaps it had always been present, if less intrusive. I had read articles in the past about this condition called depression. My mother hated the word and refused to apply it to me. I was not depressed, she maintained, even if such a thing really existed. What I needed was to take myself in hand with self-discipline and prayer. I needed to ask God to grant me my purpose, bringing me my *bashert,* so that my life could be fulfilling. Above all, I needed to change my increasingly sour attitude about our community and my marriage prospects; these were what stood in the way of happiness.

When I suggested that I see a doctor to talk about my sadness, she replied sharply: "Nonsense!" My mother was deeply suspicious of mental-health professionals. Psychiatrists, she claimed, had all been taught to find fault in religion, having absorbed in their training attitudes of contempt for people of faith. If she allowed me to see one, he or she would certainly try to convince me that it was our way of life that was to blame for any depression. Besides, if it were discovered that I was seeing a doctor for this reason, I could bid farewell to my chances at a good *shidduch.* Any form of mental illness was an indelible stigma in our world. Moods were something that good *middos* (character) could fix.

I persisted with the idea of seeing a doctor. My mother finally threw her hands up and allowed me to speak to our general practitioner. I was prescribed a low dose of an antidepressant, but it only served, I felt, to make me feel hollow, emptier than before. I ceased to be able to cry, but my anger did not dissolve with my grief. About four months after the date of my would-be wedding, my mother put her foot down and demanded that I leave the house each day and do something "useful."

It was by this time summer in Gateshead, and there were few forms of acceptable work for an unmarried girl in our world.

When our community travel agent advertised for an assistant,

I promptly gave her a call. "I'd love to have you," she said. "But you're too pretty, my dear. You'd be a *michshal*" — a stumbling block — "for the yeshiva boys that come to our office." The only options that remained were teaching in the local schools or becoming a seamstress or a *sheitel macher,* a wig hairdresser. There were no teaching spots open, so I began sewing lessons but soon discovered that I had little passion for the craft.

With my opportunities dwindling, I looked into hairdressing. Gateshead College, less than a mile away, had a yearlong course that provided some sort of hairdressing license. I signed up for lessons. One day during a break between clients, I took a walk through the halls and found myself in the campus library. Between the librarian's desk and the bookshelves there were several rows of boxy white computers with access to the internet, something we did not have in our home.

I shyly asked a librarian to show me how to navigate online. She asked me what I was looking for; an article for a research paper, perhaps? "Can I look up the *New York Times*?" I asked, remembering with nostalgia the newspaper dressed in a blue plastic sleeve that I had eagerly picked up from our driveway each morning in Monsey, a universe that now seemed light years away.

With a click of the mouse, I was in. I discovered that while I had been sequestered these five years in the seminary and in my new home, the most remarkable things had been going on in the world outside my cocoon. I had to drag myself away that day to return to class. I began to spend more time in the library reading news articles, eventually skipping my coursework altogether. If I found a topic that interested me, I printed out articles and brought them home to read in the evenings.

Above all, I loved the *Sunday New York Times* op-eds.

The perspectives of the articulate, impassioned contributors on matters of politics, justice, and human and, more narrowly, women's rights shattered the restricted lens through which I had been viewing reality. I had long been aware that the modern woman believed herself to be "emancipated" but it had been impressed upon me that this was a source of great unhappiness and lack of fulfillment for her. Now I heard the voices of accomplished women who seemed blithely unconcerned about the sense of purpose they had allegedly forfeited in order to set about revolutionizing the world around them in significant ways.

What if?

An idea took root. What if I *did* go to college like I had planned to all those years ago? Not for some practical vocation, something that I could one day do from my home, like bookkeeping, but rather in a field that required a high level of both expertise and engagement in the world?

Rabbi Miller had warned the sem girls about the dangers that college would pose. During our last days in seminary, in funereal tones, he had related the tale of a former, exceptionally devout sem girl, a South African from a good family, who had *insisted* on going to university. She had *promised* Rabbi Miller she would be able to maintain her *frumkeit* (religious observance) at college. Several years later, Rabbi Miller had learned that she had married a man who would keep the Sabbath *only* if *she* asked him to! We'd all been horror-struck at this story. The pain that the loss of this girl's pure *neshama,* "soul," had caused Rabbi Miller brought tears to our eyes.

But surely my neshama *is not thriving now?*

My mother immediately and forcefully vetoed the idea of college. No one would touch me after that, she was sure, not with a ten-foot pole. Was I really so spiteful that I was willing to ruin my own life to seek revenge on her and our community for not providing me with immediate gratification? Did I seek to ruin her life too? If I left Gateshead, then surely she must follow me to provide a home wherever I went, which would end her marriage and force her to live out the rest of her days in destitution, alone. Perhaps this was what I had wanted all along, she suggested. When she had calmed down, she implored me to employ patience. She acknowledged that this time was difficult and painful, but it would soon be over; much rested on my attitude. She promised to redouble her efforts to find me a mate — quickly. Once I was married, she maintained, I would be fulfilled and, therefore, happy.

The fall and winter of 1997 brought several punishing dates with boys who, I was assured, were "brilliant," "the next great Torah leader," or a "perfect match" for me, only for me to discover that they possessed average intellects, lackluster personalities, and aggravatingly insecure mannerisms.

Gateshead, 9 March 1998

I think about all that life has planned for me, or at least what my mother does. I think about going into those living rooms where those scrubbed and polished little boys sit in their new black suits and brushed hats, and think to themselves that I may be the one, and I want to laugh or be sick or run out of the room, out of my life, and never look back.

Had I not opened Bracha's letter, I might never have left.

Bracha Zuber had been my best friend during my years in Boston. She had lived in a brownstone up the road from ours with her large family of eight or so children. I had envied her pale, almost translucent, blue-veined skin and the tight curls that she wore braided down her back. She shared my love of books, but Bracha did not read books so much as *consume* them. By the time I had read through half of a Ruth Chew chapter book, she had finished and tossed aside two thick volumes by L. M. Montgomery or even a C. S. Lewis. We spent hours in play pretending to be adventurous heroines from our favorite stories.

When I moved to Monsey in the summer before fifth grade, Bracha and I vowed to remain friends forever and visit whenever possible. Though our lives diverged, we had kept in touch over the years, mostly through letters. I had congratulated her on her marriage and subsequent move to Israel. Every few months, I received one of Bracha's handwritten letters, the rows packed tightly with her minuscule script, which, when a page filled up, would track up and down the margins, making it a challenge to follow her already digressive stories.

Bracha's latest letter sat buried in a pile of papers in my room for several months before I finally opened it. Frankly, I hadn't wanted to hear the contented patter about her married life. One morning in early January, almost a year to the day of my broken engagement, I opened the overstuffed envelope. I read distractedly about her job as a housecleaner (she'd finally quit it); I read about her pregnancy (in its late stages) and about the *kollel,* the institution of learning for married men, that her husband attended. *Good for her,* I thought.

On the top of the last page, I read the words *I have some sad news to share,* and I immediately felt a sinking in my stomach. Before I moved on, I knew in my heart what had happened. Bracha had lost her baby. *She looked like she was sleeping,* Bracha wrote about the little girl that had been delivered stillborn.

As I sat on my bed with Bracha's letter in my hands, I began to weep. It had been months since I had last shed a tear, but now I found myself bawling, shaking with deep grief for Bracha and her baby. And because I was crying for her, I cried for myself too, for the child I was beginning to realize I might never have and for the hopeful child I had once been.

I went to sleep that night with a heavy heart.

It is not fully dark, but that in-between twilight time, where the sky is bruised purple dotted with the first stars. I am running down a deserted street in a residential neighborhood I do not recognize. *I cannot find the baby,* I think desperately. *Where did I leave him?* Fear and confusion make my heart race. What does he even look like? Suddenly a bus lumbers into view. I wave my hands wildly to flag it down. The door opens; the driver beckons me into the dark space within. I climb aboard. Suddenly, I have an image in my mind of where the baby is.

"I'm looking for a park," I tell the driver, a man whose features I can't quite make out in the dimness. "What stop is it?" he asks. I don't know. All I can see in my mind is a swing set in a park on a dark landscape.

I start to cry because how can I get to the baby if I don't know what park he is in or even what his name is? "But you do," says the old woman with gray curls and strange light eyes who appears beside me. "You *do* know his name, dear," she says gently, insistently. "Yes," I say, remembering. "His name is Rosh Chodesh."

This is odd, I know, because Rosh Chodesh is not a name but a term for the new moon, the day that begins a lunar month in our Jewish calendar. When I say his name, the silent passengers around us stir to life. I look at them with growing horror as they advance upon me, their faces empty of humanity, murderous in intent. They surround me, grabbing my arms and legs, pinning me down to the floor of the bus. Just as I lose hope, the old woman reaches her hand through the pile of bodies, and when I grasp it, she pulls me out of the fray. Together we fight our way through the mob, scratching, clawing, kicking until we have broken free of the bus. I find myself alone again, this time in a quiet field, where I can see, in the distance, the shadowy A-frame of a swing set. Though logic dictates I am too far from it, I can hear the swing as it moves back and forth, its rusty chains groaning. I begin to run toward the structure, praying that the baby is still there. I must save the baby. Everything depends on it. The whole world depends on it.

I woke up with my heart pounding. *What a dream,* I thought, laden with symbols that so clearly reflected my friend's loss. I tossed and turned for nearly an hour, finding it hard to return to sleep. After a restless night, I rose early in the morning. I knew what I needed to do.

When I could hear my mother moving about and after my step-father had left for his morning prayers, I entered the kitchen and closed the door behind me. My mother stood at the sink, rinsing the breakfast dishes.

"I need to leave." I spoke calmly and clearly.

She did not ask me what I meant; she did not need to.

"I am going to apply to college," I continued, "in the United States."

She sighed. "We've discussed this, Miriam," she responded with studied casualness. "Do you want a coffee? There's just one cup of hot water left in the kettle." She turned back to the counter.

"I am *dying* here, Mom."

It was only after I said these words that I realized how deeply true they were. I *was* dying here, and only partly because of the thin scars that were accumulating like ladder rungs under my long sleeves, emblems of those moments when anger and self-loathing became unbearable. Something essential inside me was dying, a thing that today I found myself determined to save.

"Nonsense," my mother said, backing up against the counter. "This drama is of your own creation."

She was ready, as I knew she would be, with the words that would wear my resolve and test my determination — her will against my will. "We need to discuss this, but now is not the time. You are not in control of your emotions —"

I cut her off. "Then when *is* the right time? Tell me!"

I could no longer hold back frustrated tears. It was already too late, I knew, to pull together an application for most colleges for the coming year. But I would not survive intact another year here, I was sure of it. It was now or never. Tomorrow, I might lose my resolve. Tomorrow, I might meet a young man who was "good enough."

My mother, it appeared, had already moved on. She began to bustle about the kitchen once more, laying out the cans of tuna fish and crackers to prepare Ephraim's lunch, feigning calm. I moved to stand in her path, blocking her from resuming her day, a day that would be like the one before it and the one after it, like every single one in a graveyard of days. Finally, she turned to me, meeting my eyes reluctantly.

"I am going." I enunciated each word carefully, my voice shaking ever so slightly but with resolve, not fear. "And the *only* question you need to ask yourself is if you'll be part of my life or not. If you don't let me go, I am going anyway, and I swear to God, *you will not see me again.*"

Swearing in vain was forbidden. I wanted her to know how truly serious I was.

The chink in my mother's armor appeared in the form of a distinct sigh. She looked suddenly sad and tired, and because I loved her, I was sad too. But I could not move or signal empathy. If I did, surely all would be lost. A long moment passed in silence.

"And how do you intend to pay for this, may I ask?" she asked reproachfully. My heart skipped a beat. "I don't know," I answered candidly. "I'll apply for scholarships, and I'll get a job, I suppose."

"You will not get a job!" she said sharply, shaking her head with vigor, and I realized then, in a surge of joyful disbelief, that *I had her.* "I won't have you spending half your days doing who knows what instead of focusing on completing your studies. It would take twice as long. That's not the way to do it."

She was thinking hard now, caught up with the idea. Could she be, I wondered, hoping beyond hope, even remotely *excited* for me?

"We have to think about this more, of course," she went on.

"But if you want my help applying, and you're going to need it, there is only one place I can think of that will respect our values and our way of life."

My mother, after spending the rest of that day and the next in thought and after talking to my stepfather, begrudgingly offered to help me apply to the University Professors Program, a small program at Boston University, where she had earned her PhD. This was my only shot, she made clear. It was this or nothing. I happily agreed to her terms.

"Sue." My mother was on the phone with the dean's administrative secretary, an old BU phone book in her hand. "This is Judith Pinnick, previously Netzer." I hovered outside the office door. When it opened several minutes later, she addressed me: "They're putting an application packet in the mail tomorrow. It's not too late to apply for September, Sue said. In fact, she encourages you to. Apparently, you would be the very first legacy student in the program."

The University Professors Program had been founded in the seventies and accepted a small group of students who wished to design cross-disciplinary or unique majors. My mother believed that the small size and elite quality of the program would provide a "better environment" for the requirements of my faith.

But first I had to contend with the daunting task of piecing together a robust application in less than a month; transcripts, essays, letters of recommendation had to be sought and gathered, and I had to find some way to take the U.S. college entrance exam, the SAT, despite living in England. The test presented quite a challenge, as I had not taken a math or English class since my junior year at Bat Torah.

It was too late to order test-review guides, but the very next day I paid a trip to Newcastle's largest bookstore, Waterstones, and picked up a series of standard high-school math textbooks. For the next two weeks I sat in our kitchen recliner for hours on end, reading through the material, memorizing formulas, and allowing myself a problem set per chapter. If I got it right, I moved on. There was simply no time to review any English or grammar material.

Two weeks later, on a day in late January, I took a train down to a U.S. military base outside London and sat in a room guarded by a soldier armed with an automatic weapon (so that I wouldn't wander about the base, I imagined) taking my exam. Afterward, having a few hours before my train ride home, I took the Underground to Selfridges, a gargantuan department store with a large food hall, and attempted to drown my sorrows in a tub of imported kosher Ben and Jerry's frozen yogurt. I was sure that I had performed miserably on the math section of the test. My heart sank at the thought of losing my one chance to go to college.

When my scores arrived in the mail several weeks later, I was elated to discover that I had performed quite respectably on the math and had managed, miraculously, a perfect 800 on the verbal section. *This might actually happen,* I thought, giddy with joy.

Getting transcripts sent from the seminary was no easy task. I had to sit through meetings with Rabbis Kohn and Miller and excuse my decision to go to college. They weren't thrilled and were generous with their warnings, but what could they do? I had my mother's reluctant approval and the transcripts were by rights mine. I promised them I would leave college as soon as I found my *bashert,* though I instructed my mother, "No arranging dates while I'm away!"

I finally had my full application package in the mail to Sue, who promised us an expedited review. Three weeks later a fat envelope was dropped through the mail slot at our front door. It was a Sabbath and that meant, by Jewish law, I was unable to open the envelope, even touch it, until nightfall. I spent the next few hours in exquisite torture, and the moment that three stars became visible in the night sky, indicating that Sabbath was over, I tore the envelope open and spilled its contents on the table. I found several glossy pamphlets and a letter on official Boston University stationery inviting me, Miss Miriam Netzer, to join the class of 2002. Included with the letter was an award of a scholarship — full room and board.

I left Gateshead on August 26, 1998, bound for Boston, Massachusetts, by way of London, England. I was twenty-two years old, a newly minted college freshman, a virgin in every sense of the word, and completely unprepared for the wider world.

• 24 •

The Theory of Status Quo

A garden enclosed is my sister . . . a spring shut up, a
fountain sealed.   — SONG OF SONGS 4:12

WHEN JENNIFER HORTON, LICSW, ANSWERS THE PHONE,
her voice is warm and strong. "Tell me what's going on with
Em," she says.

We're on the clock but I have no urge to rush. If I can keep this
woman on the phone for days, I will. My words, when they come
out, are all over the place. I describe the obsessions, the clothes-
changing and Doggy Sweater; the pretend play; the new urgency
in her voice when she declared, "I *am* a boy, *not* pitending." The
way she swats at us when we try to touch her, flying off the handle at the smallest provocation. The bruises, physical and emotional, when she slams her fists and her head into us, the walls, the
floor.

"I don't know exactly what's going on, but I know *something*
is going on," I say. "And I don't know if" — *Say the word* — "she
could" — *Say it, but don't lose it* — "be . . . transgender or if this is
just some weird OCD phase, but right now it's getting impossible.
She's miserable. Heck, we're all miserable. She says she hates God
for making her a girl." My voice begins to wobble. "I don't want

her to hate anyone. I don't want her to hate herself." To my acute embarrassment I am crying once more.

"First of all, I want to tell you what a great job you're doing." Jennifer's voice is calm and sympathetic, coming over the phone like a soothing balm. "I have seen parents who have a much harder time accepting their kids and you are clearly doing all the right things: You are listening to your child and learning everything you can. That's the best thing you can do for now. Listen and learn." I nod vigorously, although I know she can't see me. "Okay . . ." Breathe in. "Okay . . ." Breathe out.

"Also, she *is* very young, not even four," Jennifer continues. "Kids typically do explore gender-nonconforming behavior at this age, and many *do* outgrow it. Children, being fairly rigid in their thinking about what is or is not an acceptable preference for a boy or a girl, may say they are one or the other because they prefer masculine or feminine toys or dress. That's a matter of *expression*, which is different than *identity*. A transgender identity is a deeply held, usually permanent identification with a gender that is different than the one you were assigned at birth based on your sex. Transgender youth are *persistent, insistent,* and *consistent* in their identities. Em hasn't had too much time yet to persist."

"So that study is correct, the one that says that only twenty percent of young kids who say they're transgender actually end up that way?" I ask hopefully. "Not quite," she tells me. "That study was misleading. The sample group had kids from the entire gender spectrum, including those who showed only some mild form of gender-nonconforming behavior; being a tomboy, for example. These kids wouldn't fall into the category of transgender to begin with." "Oh," I say, my hopes falling a little. "What about the kids who consistently identify with a different gender than their assigned sex at birth?" I ask. "We don't have the data yet," she answers, "but anecdotally, far fewer move back from their transgender identity.

"I know it's hard as a parent to not have clear answers," she says gently. "But we may not know for a while about Em, therefore the best thing you can do is keep things fluid as long as possible. Keep the door open and *keep listening.*"

Keeping it fluid. That meant avoiding any big changes while allowing for superficial ones. Let her wear the clothes she wants. The pixie haircut is okay. Keep using the name Em outside the house if she'll allow it. Let her have a boy or gender-neutral name at home. No pronoun changes unless she's adamant on it. If she is, reevaluate. If not, stay the course.

When I hang up the phone, I feel ten pounds lighter. This is something we can live with. This is clear. Here lies hope. Em's got a good chance of outgrowing this obsession; this is my takeaway. She's always thrown 100 percent into whatever she's obsessed with at a given moment, like the clothes-changing and the Doggy Sweater. True, we are now going on a year and several months of this being-a-boy thing, and that's at least three times longer than any other obsession, but she's also not insisting on changing her name and pronouns outside our home. Maybe we just needed to ride this storm out.

Joe too is relieved when I discuss the conversation with Jennifer. He holds me tight to his chest, presses his cheek into the crown of my head. I've even got the name of a book to buy now: *The Transgender Child* by Stephanie Brill and Rachel Pepper. It has a foreword by Dr. Norman Spack, the doctor who founded the Boston gender clinic that referred me to Jennifer.

The next day I tell Kristie Colwell, the director at the Purpose School, what Jennifer advised, and she nods. "Something I've been meaning to tell you," she says. "Em isn't as outgoing as Ella. It's possible she's uncomfortable playing with the girls, who are all about relationships and emotions. The boys are much more straightforward at this age. She may feel more drawn to the boys and think that this must mean she's a boy." "It's possible," I respond. I am so happy, I hug her. This is one more piece to stack on the pile of "just a phase." For the first time in weeks, I feel hopeful again. Winter break is around the corner and I am ready to celebrate.

Joe and I sit down to talk to Em about where we are as a family regarding her claims. We're sitting on the couch in the living room. Our babysitter and honorary older sister Kasey has taken Lucia and Ella out for a walk. While they collect leaves, we tell Em about Jennifer and some of what we discussed. "There are kids who have a brain and heart that thinks and feels they are different than what the rest of their body looks like, and if . . . that's who you are, we will still always love you just as much," Joe says. "I'm a *boy*," Em says wearily. "I'm a boy *everywhere*."

"I understand, love," I say, "but for now, let's pick a name together for home, maybe similar to Em, to use instead of all the other names we've been switching between."

"A boy name?" she asks. "*Yes,* but . . . maybe one that can be both?" I say. "Jackson!" she states emphatically. "Honey, it needs to sound like yours so we don't get confused." Joe and I exchange glances. "Jackson!" Her eyes pool with tears as she begins to clench and unclench her fists.

Joe stands up. "Em, that's not an option," he says. "Let's pick something that works for all of us." "There are plenty of M names that are very cool," I say, trying to think of ones that are gender-neutral. "Mackenzie? Morgan?" We know girls by these names, so Em vetoes these suggestions out of hand. "What about Mica?" I suggest. "I thought that was a boy's name," Joe says. "Listen, we don't need to decide now," we conclude.

Later that day Grammy calls. We discuss our dilemma. "What about the name Mica but pronounced 'Meeka'?" she says. "That's a girl's name, I'm sure of it. I heard it somewhere recently." I look it up, and yes, Mica, pronounced "Meeka," is a girl's name, from the Latin *amica,* friend. But Em is stubborn. *"My*-cah!" she says. Then adds, "Maybe." *How does she know "Meeka" is a girl's name, damn it?* This seems to be the best we can get out of her today. *Mica, maybe.*

"Mica is a kind of shiny rock," Joe remarks to our treasure-loving child. Now even Em has a ghost of a smile on her face. She tries it out: "My name is Mica." Then she grins. "Hello, my name is Mica! Hello, my name is Mica!" When Kasey returns, I pull her aside for a minute to explain. "Sure," she says, shrugging her shoulders and agreeing to use the name for Em. Not for the first time I admire the unflappable, accepting attitude that has made her such a great babysitter.

The Transgender Child arrives in a few days and I eagerly start to flip through it. It seems to echo a lot of what Jennifer said. Consistency is key for diagnosing young kids with gender dysphoria, which essentially means they are painfully at odds with the gender to which they were assigned. The book also states that kids this young, while having a sense of gender, might not feel fixed in this identity until at least four or five.

The chapter that interests me most is titled "Transition Decisions: When Should I Let My Child Live as Their Preferred Gender?" I come to a paragraph that reads: "The younger the child when they assert their cross-gender nature and request to live in accordance with their inner gender identity, the longer the parents can wait. That is, the longer the child can get by with a more ambiguous gender state."

Keeping things fluid. Amen to ambiguity.

Things are looking up. Everyone notices an improvement in Em's behavior once we start using the name Mica at home. I'm able to throw myself with renewed vigor into Christmas preparations this year. I even get Em into the same red velvet ruffled coat-dress as her sisters (modified to jacket length by a tailor) by calling it a "pirate coat" and she smiles and poses on Santa's lap. Her list that year is caricature boy: Superhero stuff! Animal stuff! Sports stuff! *No dolls.*

"No pink, please," I warn the relatives when they ask what the girls want this year. Joe and I discuss how Em appears more relaxed. We are giddy with relief. "That therapist is worth her weight in *gold!*" Kathy declares. Even she can see the difference in Em on her weekly visits. Em is less moody and more flexible, which means she's still thinner-skinned and more temperamental than most kids her age, but she's something approaching the norm.

Christmas Eve arrives, and we head to Lowell for a holiday dinner with Joe's family. I'm nervous. I hadn't wanted to press the matter of presents, but I wonder if the message got through to everyone. Dinner is wonderful, Greek food, representative of Joe's half-Greek cousins. I love the spanakopita, grape leaves with seasoned ground lamb, the white yogurt dip, the lemony potatoes. There's even a traditional ham and fixings, so everyone's appetite is sated.

After dinner the call goes out and the kids race to the Christmas tree. Lucia, at a year and a half, lets out a shriek of excitement, and everyone laughs. The kids are told to sit on the floor while the adults hand presents out. Eager hands rip into the paper, calls go out for help in freeing items from Fort Knox–worthy security measures. The first present that goes to Em is a winner — her aunt has come through with a *Jake and the Never Land Pirates* ship. Em's grin is immense and gratifying. There are other presents, however, that are more feminine, and I can feel her stiffen. A Doc McStuffins coloring book, a pink and purple school supply set, and a black puffer vest with large foil gold stars garner a gloomy look. I hold my breath for the test of our instructions about being gracious. When she drops the vest on the floor, I swiftly bend down and meet her eye. "Say thank you," I whisper, and my voice has an edge to it, a warning that, pretty soon, I'm

not going to ask so nicely and someone won't be getting her bak-
lava. She looks up at me for a long moment and I think, *Oh God,
she's going to pitch a fit,* but then she mumbles to the room at large,
devoid of sincerity, "Thank you." It doesn't matter because at this
point no one is listening anyway.

Christmas morning at our house comes early with excited
shrieks: *"Santa came! He came!"* He had, in spades. There are
dozens of boxes wrapped in thick cream-and-gold-striped paper
flowing out from under our tree to the far walls of the sunroom.
I catch Joe's eye. "Some of these are regifts from birthdays," I
whisper, "or stuff I had in the attic for years." He shakes his head.
I am compensating for the emotional chaos in our lives, and it's
evident. Still, this is Christmas morning and sacred, so we all turn
our attention to the children, who are screaming with excitement
and pulling wrapping paper in fistfuls off their loot. The sounds
of ripping and the yelps of joy are magical. I close my eyes for a
few seconds just to take it in. One by one, the Lego sets, dolls and
superheroes, board games and sports equipment are revealed. Everyone seems delighted. "Santa just *knew* I wanted a Lalaloopsy
doll!" Ella sighs, full of faith and love for the bearded demigod.

I'm impatient. There is a gift hidden among all the others that
will be performing double duty. "Here!" I finally pull the Katniss
Everdeen doll out of the pile closest to the tree. "Here's another
one for you, Mica," I say, pointing to the large tag with a gold *M*
on it and placing it casually in her arms. She accepts the box and
begins to unwrap it. When she sees the doll, she drops the box
like a hot coal. "Why did Santa get me *this?*" she says, and the disdain is written across her features. It's the same twisted lip of disappointment in the universe, in the powers that be, that she had
when she had looked up to me from the toilet seat several months
ago and queried, "Why did God make me like this? Is He stupid?" Then, I had been flummoxed. What had she been told, and
by whom? God wasn't a big topic in our house. Was this coming
from a kid in school? "God isn't stupid, honey," I had answered

rather lamely. "If you believe in God, then believe He made you special and unique." The look on her face was clear: she did not agree with me. I didn't blame her.

Now, I widened my eyes in pretended joy and awe. "OMG! Mica! Is that . . . is that a *Katniss Everdeen* action figure? Those are *so rare.* Santa must have really appreciated you to get this for you!" "Who *is* that?" Em asks suspiciously. "Only the coolest, baddest, strongest warrior *ever,*" Joe chips in. Even my mother-in-law acts thrilled for Em. Ella asks plaintively, "Why didn't I get the Kap-niss doll?"

"You can have it." Em picks up the doll and hands it to her sister, ending the charade.

Flip-Falls

If you live in the dark a long time and the sun comes out,
you do not cross into it whistling.   — MARY KARR, *Lit*

WHEN I ARRIVED IN BOSTON FOR THE SECOND TIME IN
my life and moved into the all-girls residence on Bay State
Road, a leafy street lined with brownstones, I had no intention of
leaving my religious practice behind. It had been intrinsic to my
core identity since I could first form thought, as much a part of me
as skin and bone and just as inseparable. There I sat at my matric-
ulation ceremony, a carefully pressed, twenty-two-year-old freshman in a midcalf-length navy skirt with a modesty kick pleat and
a handmade yellow blouse buttoned up to the neck. I was a living
anachronism amid the sea of shorts and T-shirts on that sweltering August day.

My mother had been right; my classmates and professors at the
University Professors Program (or UNI, as we called it) did respect my different way of life, though they were at times curious
enough about it to ask questions. It was also true that my seminary education, the *pilpul* style of learning, equipped me with a
good set of analytical tools for my courses, especially those that
involved textual analysis.

I recoiled, however, the first time I heard the Old Testament, as the Torah was called here, receive the same treatment as Homer's *Odyssey.* That the tenets of one's faith could be laid out on a slab and dissected like an anthropological artifact or a piece of literature shook me. However, the more I read, especially the books of other faiths, the more I realized that my people did not have a monopoly on truth or, in fact, on spiritual greatness.

Lynn Davidman, in her book *Becoming Un-Orthodox,* notes that all the ex–Hasidic Jews she has interviewed have a first-transgression story, a moment when they initially broke the halacha, Judaic law, tearing a hole in the sacred canopy of their faith and community. She also describes a stage she calls "passing," in which individuals change their outward appearance to be able to blend into the non-Orthodox world. For me, both moments came together the evening I wore jeans outside for the first time.

It was a Saturday night a month or so into my first semester. I was standing on the sidewalk on Bay State Road waiting for a cab to take me and my friend Becca to the studio apartment we had found through campus housing farther down Commonwealth Avenue. Becca was my first friend at BU, a Modern Orthodox Jewish girl from Ohio, bookish with a caustic wit, whose rebellion was secretly practicing Wicca alongside her Jewish faith. The jeans were a purchase I had made at Filene's Basement and had yet to wear outside the girls' dorm. They were comfortable, stretchy, a fashionable bootcut. I wore them as I was packing up our belongings for the move, and they felt a damn sight more practical than my long skirts. Once we'd taped up the last box, I realized I did not want to take this magical garb off. So when we headed outside with our boxes to wait for a cab, I wore them. The moment I crossed the threshold wearing the illicit garment was both thrilling and frightening. Surely I would be caught. *By whom?* My logical mind prevailed.

It was a warm, blustery evening. The sensation of the soft, thick fabric encasing my calves and thighs, the wind that blew in the forbidden empty space between my legs, all these were delicious and unforgettable. Better yet was the joy of blending in, of looking just like any of the hundreds of coeds milling about, enjoying their Saturday evening, heading out to dinner or a party. As we waited, I danced up and down on the sidewalk with the leaves, shifting from one leg to another and pirouetting. Becca laughed at me good-naturedly. She still wore long skirts and didn't seem tempted to do otherwise.

From that moment, it was just a matter of time before I shed most of the cornucopia of rules that had regulated my life. I reveled in each new experience. I set out to discover my taste in music, now that all music was available to me, and find out what I enjoyed eating, now that most things were on the table (although it took me a while to try bacon). I felt like a child again.

With all the liberation of my *frei* life, there came an equally pervasive anxiety. Some experiences challenged me because they required information I did not possess. What was the appropriate attire for a party or a baseball game? How did I know a boy was genuinely interested in me? What did I do to signal interest back? When did I pay for food at a restaurant — before the meal or after? Should I get a credit card and how did it work?

Some things drained me on a deeper level; leaving behind my Orthodox practice required nothing less than a deconstruction of all strata of my life. In my previous existence, all waking moments were occupied with meaningful rituals, ways to plug into a higher purpose. Now my activities, though titillating initially in the freedom they conferred, felt aimless and *thin*. I had not found a replacement yet for the *tachlis,* purpose, that had driven my old life. For meaning, I now had to look to myself. The challenge was that I had never been told to trust my heart for anything. Such an idea was anathema to our culture. One didn't trust one's heart. One looked to the Torah, and in cases where the answer was not specified, one asked a rabbi.

And most difficult of all, I never had that moment when I "lost my faith," which, despite what Rav Miller had said, was not rooted in my intellect but deeply heartfelt. No amount of exposure to books of philosophy or science could remove what had already been grafted at my most elemental level of being. I *felt* that God existed, and not having any other God but the one of my youth, I continued to believe in Him, which put me and my rebellion outside of the circle of His grace. In some fashion I had adopted the hedonist's creed of "Eat, drink, and be merry, for tomorrow we die," except the death I anticipated was my heavenly comeuppance. There would be a price for my freedom, of this I was certain. Perhaps there would be someone to intercede on my behalf one day, like Rabbi Meir with Acher. But even if there would not be, I could not live the life God had ordained for me, I knew, no matter the cost.

One evening, as I was sitting on the trolley with Becca, returning from a movie, I heard a voice say: "Can I ask you something?" I looked up into the hazel eyes of a fellow passenger, possibly a grad student, judging by his age, handsome, with close-cropped brown hair. He dropped his eyes to the open book on my lap, a guide to paganism that Becca had lent me. "How does it work? Do you believe in spells and stuff?" "It's not my belief," I answered solicitously, "but it's interesting." The young man introduced himself as a fellow BU student in the air force ROTC program, and we chatted for a few minutes until the trolley rounded the corner of Commonwealth Avenue and gave its customary ear-splitting screech. I got up to leave. The young man, whose name was Eric, hastily jotted down his phone number and passed it to me, sticking out his hand to shake: "If you're interested, we're having an ROTC party later tonight, and I'd love for you to come. Your friend can come too, of course."

Becca put her foot down. She would not go with me, no matter how I begged. She didn't think attending a party with drunken cadets was a promising idea, and besides, she had no interest in dating non-Jews. I went without her.

I ended up having a wonderful evening. Yes, the drunken cadets were loud and occasionally obnoxious (mainly to one another) but Eric and I managed to hear each other well enough over the din to discover that we had both lived in Europe for several years, and as a result, we had arrived at college later than our cohorts. At the end of the evening we made plans to meet again.

I found Eric funny, levelheaded, and sweet, but as we saw more of each other, my lack of experience became a source of deep anxiety to me. I had experimented with kissing during my first weeks at college, but I was fearful of further physical intimacy. I confessed to Eric that any hesitation came from my dearth of experience in this area and he offered to let me take the lead.

Up to this point, anything I had done was *reversible* in my mind. No one from my old life knew me here at Boston University and I could still run back to Gateshead, tail between my legs, if things didn't work out. Not that I wanted to. However, once I lost my virginity, those ties would be cut forever. An unmarried woman who had been sexually active in relatively liberal Monsey was referred to as a *zona,* prostitute. Life in even more stringent Gateshead would surely never be a possibility again.

After a few more weeks had passed, I decided I was ready. After I'd fortified myself with several cans of liquid courage, we fell into bed. I began to tremble from fear halfway through the act of making love and pulled away. It took me two nights to consummate our intimacy. Afterward, standing in front of the bathroom mirror, I examined my countenance for the signs of this radical shift. I had done it. I had actually done *it.* There was no turning back now. Remembering my mother's story of Caesar crossing the Rubicon, I whispered to the girl in the bathroom mirror: *"Alea iacta est."* The die is cast. The girl in the mirror smiled back.

I woke up the next morning feeling ebullient. Eric cooked me an omelet while amusing me with stories of his time abroad and teaching me how to swear in Italian. When he took off for class, I decided to skip mine. The day felt like a holiday to me.

I walked from Kenmore Square to Boylston Street, practically skipping at times. As strangers passed, walking quickly in the brisk November chill, I felt a new sense of kinship; *I am one of you now.* I was just a slightly-older-than-average college student with a boyfriend, wearing jeans and a clingy sweater, who read Dostoyevsky in her spare time and had just rediscovered Cyndi Lauper. I felt so *ordinary.* It was priceless.

A light drizzle began to thicken as I found myself in front of a Lord & Taylor department store. Bright holiday displays had been out for weeks and in their glass cages, mannequins draped in expensive winter garb, their limbs entwined in newly suggestive poses, languidly ignored passersby. On a whim, I headed in, noting with pleasure the sounds of holiday caroling being piped through the store's loudspeakers.

When I was a child, catching the strains of Christmas carols had been the guilty pleasure of each and every winter as far back as I could remember. In the mall or on the street as I passed those peaked houses of prayer, I would linger longer than necessary, dragging my feet to catch more of the ethereal melodies that lifted my spirits.

One winter break when I was in eighth grade, my mother and I took the bus into the city to visit the Metropolitan Museum of Art, where we eventually found ourselves in a gallery dedicated to medieval paintings, tapestries, and triptychs. Gregorian chanting accompanied our viewing over the loudspeakers, underscoring the extremities of emotion displayed, the agony and ecstasy strangely enticing. As the sounds washed over me, I experienced a painful joy that brought with it tears. The joy was shortly succeeded by a clamoring guilt. These were false gods and admiration of them or their sacramental music was a serious transgression, idolatry, one of Judaism's three cardinal sins.

After that day, however, I continued to secretly indulge my vice, listening to homemade bootleg cassettes of *St. Matthew Passion* by Bach or Monteverdi's *Magnificat,* headphones on and volume low, under my blankets at night.

Now I had committed another cardinal sin: illicit sexual relations. I was really knocking them all down, I thought wryly. I decided to buy my very first Christmas item that day at Lord & Taylor: a snow globe that housed a golden angel holding aloft a trumpet. I turned the silver dial underneath and the tinny strains of "Hark! The Herald Angels Sing" began to play. I might have need of this angel, I thought wistfully, now that I had cut myself off from my community.

Eric and I dated until his graduation in the late spring, when he earned the second lieutenant stripes that I proudly pinned on him. That summer, we flew to Tacoma, Washington, where we spent two bucolic weeks on his mother's farm. I learned to pack cheese, milk cows, and even, with mixed results, fish (I actually caught an old shoe). I gained several happy pounds and a lasting friendship while feasting on his mother's homemade strawberry shortcake, coated with thick, fresh cream and hand-picked fruit. When our time was up, we hit the road in Eric's lovingly retooled 1975 AMC Hornet, heading back along I-90 to crate up his belongings for shipment down to his first assignment at an air force base near Panama City, Florida.

Our trip home itself was memorable; we took a detour to Yosemite, passed up and through the Dakotas, and wound our way down and across the exotic lands of Tennessee and Mississippi. Most nights we slept in the car or in a tent, and we bathed and washed our clothes in streams. Even today, the scent of Doc Bronner's Peppermint Castile Soap evokes the feeling of freedom and memories of the open road.

When we arrived back in Boston, I helped Eric pack his belongings and bade him a sad farewell. We both knew that our relationship would not stand the rigors of separation. We respected
each other and enjoyed each other's company, but our affection
wasn't the love that either of us had set to find out in life. It was
time to move on.

At the start of my sophomore year, sans Eric, I felt the full force
of my solitary existence for the first time. I was once again visited by that feeling of otherness, the chasm that seemed to separate me from others. The students I lived with at the dorm were
eighteen or nineteen years old and more comfortable in their skin
than I had ever been. Attempting to make conversations about
their unfamiliar universe exhausted me, and despite my positive
experience with Eric, I did not feel comfortable with men and the
dating rituals of the world.

It was then that I discovered Hapkido. An acquaintance of
mine, hearing that I was interested in taking a martial art, recommended this Korean form, even finding me a *dojang* to sign up for
instruction in Quincy, Massachusetts, about a half hour south of
the university by trolley. Within a short time, I was hooked.

What a feeling of power there was in tossing someone in the air,
in maneuvering my body to fend off attacks. I loved the dance-
like movements: the airborne seconds during a flip-fall, the grace
and power of a well-executed spin kick. And of course, there was
the knowledge that no one had ever done anything remotely like
this in the history of Gateshead Sem; of this I was certain. With
Hapkido also came a set of friends, most older than myself and
settled into their careers as teachers, electricians, or cops. They
were warm, quirky, and safe. Within a short while they began to
invite me to family events and parties outside of classes held at
the *dojang*. I went trick-or-treating for the first time in my life
with one classmate and his kids.

My instructor, Hal, a former Green Beret and now a middle-aged electrician who could spin a yarn better than he could a kick, became a father figure of sorts to me. "Here we're family," he would say, and feeling a dearth of family in my life, I welcomed it.

Though I continued to return to Gateshead several times a year, each visit was increasingly hard to sustain emotionally. Crossing the threshold into the foyer in my stepfather's home gave me the sensation of reentering captivity with all the attendant feelings.

After arriving in Boston, I had begun a new chapter in my life with my own father as well. I had visited him in California for the first time the summer before my sophomore year, spending two weeks in the Westwood area of Los Angeles, near the UCLA campus where he taught. We took long walks and met friends of his for meals. I had known little of his work or his personal life before. It filled me with pride to witness the unabashed reverence he received from the Persian Jewish community for whom he had resurrected a rich twenty-five-hundred-year history from manuscripts scattered across the globe.

Much as I wished to, however, I found that I could not slip into the empty space created by the years lost between us. I felt a longing, witnessing his laughter and easy banter with the daughters of his close friend Nahid, whom he had seen regularly since their infancy. I did not even speak Farsi, though I had taken classes. I had a sense of being a celebrated stranger those times I went to visit my father. The relationship that had never been with us was, quite likely, irretrievable. It was up to me to create a different one, more equal, if less intimate.

By the time I began my junior year at Boston University, I had moved to Quincy in order to be closer to the *dojang* where I was spending most of my evenings.

My time as a martial artist became instructional not only in the scores of joint locks and throws that I practiced but also in teaching me the limits of friendship — and my own capacity for it. There was a fox in the henhouse. An instructor from another *dojang,* a former student of my master, had begun turning his attention from one to another of the single women in the class. After having a one-night stand with a fellow classmate, who subsequently felt humiliated, he set his sights on me. Feeding me a whitewashed version of what had transpired between them, he had coaxed me to intercede on his behalf with my classmate and friend. The blast of vituperation with which she met me shook me to my core — and threw me into his arms.

The atmosphere in the *dojang* was slowly poisoned, and what was once a congenial haven became a place of rivalries and internecine fighting. I slowly withdrew from many of the social events of our group, particularly after my former friend introduced me to the trials of slut-shaming, but continued to faithfully attend each lesson. I had invested so much of my time here and so little elsewhere that I couldn't bring myself to give it up. I decided, however, to take a — temporary — vow of celibacy. No more dating for me. My faith in my own judgment had been severely compromised. Men, I decided, were indecipherable creatures, full of tricks and machinations. It was best to keep away.

I threw myself into my studies, my Hapkido lessons, and a part-time job at our college bookstore. "You will be okay," I promised myself daily. Even if the rest of my life was solitary, I was free. This mattered above all.

26

Dearest <Child>

Children climb the walls and fall down the wells and run the razor's edge of possibility until sometimes, just sometimes, the possible surrenders and shows them the way to go home.

— SEANAN MCGUIRE, *Beneath the Sugar Sky*

February 24, 2014

Dearest Child,

Happy fourth birthday, love.

What a year we've had. You've grown so much, and in wonderful ways. You're tall, barely an inch shy of your sister! You can recite your numbers up to a hundred (okay, so you skip a few here and there, quite cute) and you've started connecting sounds with most of your letters. Pretty impressive!

You're a wonderful sibling. You and Ella have the greatest adventures, and you are quite creative together. The other day you each made a robot head out of paper bags. We go through a lot of Scotch tape in our house! It's a good thing Santa brought you about twenty packages!

Lucia adores you and follows you around like a puppy; the

other day you gave her a ride on your back and she was squealing with delight.

You climbed up the tallest rock at Breakheart Reservation with your dad, and when you got to the top, you stretched out your fist in triumph and hollered. I thought this captured your spirit perfectly.

You love superheroes, and I love when you create your own zany costumes and parade around the house "saving us." In your own way, you are my hero. I have heard it said that bravery is not being unafraid; rather, it is being afraid and doing something anyway.

I know it doesn't always feel easy for you but you're doing okay. I want you to know that there are lots of people in your corner.

You are the light in my heart. Think about that when life gets you down, okay? Don't ever forget that you are deeply treasured. Life is surprising and sometimes it's hard, but it's *always* worthwhile. Be open to adventure, and be true to yourself, always. You never know what the future might bring.

I hope this year brings you much happiness. After all, you are *my* happiness.

Love,
Mama

27

A Different Source Code

Daughters of Jerusalem, I charge you
by the gazelles and by the does of the field:
Do not arouse or awaken love
until it so desires.

— SONG OF SONGS 2:7

SEPTEMBER 2, 2001, STARTED OUT AS SUMMER BUT BY late afternoon blew a crisp dry air, electric with the promise of a kaleidoscopic New England autumn. Five o'clock found me in my usual spot, perched behind a huge oak counter, an island in the midst of a sea of bookshelves and college bric-a-brac, ringing up customers.

The Barnes & Noble Boston University Bookstore at Kenmore Square, located directly beneath the brightly lit landmark of the Citgo sign, was a five-story hive of activity as students, recently returned from summer vacation, dropped in to stock up on the semester's required reading and school supplies.

I loved my job as a bookseller, though it supported little more than a book-buying habit. I was a dilettante when it came to reading. For pleasure I gravitated toward more exotic material, topics like snake-handling churches in Appalachia and Southern gothic true crime. My academic interests ran to the drier stuff: entrenched conflicts and complex histories between nations, particularly in what is known as the Middle East.

To that end, earlier in the year I had picked up a book on a little-known Saudi cleric, Osama bin Laden. The book was well written but less exciting than rattlesnakes for Jesus, so I hardly cracked it that summer, and it had made the transatlantic flight to England and back again with a nearly virgin spine. With books, as with other things in my life, I was reluctant to engage and rapid in retreat. I could not have known that this was about to change for me. That things would change everywhere.

"Did you find what you were looking for?" I asked the young man who placed his books down on the counter. "I think so," he said, smiling at me.

I didn't recognize Joe Lemay from a visit he had paid to the bookstore in the early spring of that year, even though he would later claim we had a conversation about the book he bought then, a volume of the *Collected Works of Edgar Allan Poe.*

Joe maintained that our paths intersected with a trick of light. As he walked into the bookstore back in April, I was descending the escalator from the second floor. Light bouncing off the glass revolving doors threw a prism of light onto my head, reminding him of the halo on the stained-glass Madonna in the church of his youth. This was particularly funny to us later because I am not a Catholic and I am most certainly no saint, besides which, I teased Joe, the image for him, as a lapsed Catholic, should have sent him running in the opposite direction.

Instead, he was determined to find out more about me. When I rang up his purchase then, he considered asking for my number but decided to come back the next day instead, as he was dressed in sweaty gym clothes. He returned the following day, and the next, but was disappointed to find that the "bookseller girl," as he came to think of me, was not there. I had cut back on work hours to prepare for my last belt test before black belt.

Joe had not seen me again until that day in early September when he'd walked into the bookstore for a magazine and spotted me behind the counter. This time, covering all his bases, he picked up a volume by Charles Bukowski and one by Charles Dickens: "I figured I had a shot with at least one of them."

When the young man with the light brown hair and bright cerulean eyes asked me if I'd like to grab a coffee sometime and would it be okay if he took my number, I hesitated. I didn't know him at all, and I wasn't feeling ready to date anyone yet, having recently settled into my self-imposed celibacy.

I studied him carefully for the first time, though, noting that he was of medium height and build, handsome in a comforting way, with a strong face and direct eyes, dressed for work in khakis and a blue button-down shirt. I suspected he was in his early twenties, like myself, though the guileless expression in his blue eyes made him appear younger.

I knew better than to trust my first impression. How, then, to get rid of him without being rude? "This is my e-mail address," I said, writing it down in lieu of a number. "I'll be busy until early November, though," I cautioned him. "I'm going to Korea next month with my *dojang* and then taking the GREs." It was a brush-off, but it wasn't. I was pleased with my handling of the situation. I assumed that the young man would forget about me after two months and that I could emerge, perhaps, given sufficient time, as someone more capable.

The interim, as it transpired, brought about events that should have made us both forget this exchange. Overnight, the little-known Saudi cleric in my book had emerged as the evil mastermind of the horrific 9/11 terrorist attacks, and I had gained a more vivid sense of purpose in my studies.

I was surprised, therefore, to open up my e-mail the first week of November to find a missive waiting for me from Joe, the young man from the bookstore. He asked if he could take me up on that coffee. I was dubiously impressed with his polite persistence. Sighing, I agreed. What could it hurt? I could meet him right at the bookstore after work that Sunday without much wasted time or effort.

I nervously scanned the small crowd at the bookstore café when I got off work on Sunday afternoon. *What if I can't remember what he looks like?* As it turned out, I recognized him immediately — the big blue eyes, the unguarded smile. We grabbed our drinks and sat down at a small table. I found myself awash with a sudden sinking feeling. This couldn't work, but wouldn't it be nice if it could?

We talked about simple, lighthearted topics: what we liked to read and do, where we'd been, my coursework, his job as a software programmer. My initial impression was accurate. Joe had a directness, an unapologetic candor, that, despite myself, I found charming. My heart skipped a beat. About forty-five minutes after we sat down, my date stood up, apologizing that he had to pick up a friend at the airport. *So soon?* I found myself thinking.

"I don't know, but there's just something *real* about him," I confided to Louise, my landlady, that evening. She cautioned me not to be dismissive before I had given him another chance. "You owe it to yourself to see" was how she put it.

We next met up at an Indian restaurant on fashionable Newbury Street, where we spent several hours immersed in conversation, and Joe made me laugh so hard that I nearly spit out my drink. Throwing caution to the wind, I called him up the following week and invited him to go see the new Harry Potter movie with me. At Thanksgiving, Joe offered to pick me up and take me to dinner at his family's home. I had planned on joining Louise at her sister's house, but as soon as I got off the phone, she shooed me away: "Go!"

• • •

It wasn't long before Joe and I were a couple, which meant that I had to call my mother and break the news to her. "Is he . . . Jewish?" she asked after a moment of silence. "No," I answered. She sighed, a pained sound. "Is it . . . serious?" "It could be. We just started dating. But . . . I like him, Mom. He's a good person."

"I know, Miriam," she said, pleading in her voice, "but what you don't seem to understand is that . . . this will end up worse for *him* than for you." "How so?" I asked, beginning to feel the heat rise in my neck. "He will be hurt badly when he realizes the *impossibility* of your relationship. He won't be able to understand *why.*"

"Maybe I don't understand!" I said sharply and not quite truthfully. "Explain this to me! Why is it so impossible?" I could have written a book about all the reasons, I had heard them so many times.

"Don't make me say it," she begged, but then she continued anyway: "This can bring you both nothing but suffering. Joe may be a fine person, but he is *meant* for something *different* than you. Let him be. His capacity, his purpose, his fundamental nature, it is for something else."

"I have found his capacity to be more than adequate," I answered, my voice shaking with suppressed rage, and I hung up.

Not for the first time, a part of me wished I could cut my mother out of my life like a gangrenous limb. I almost wished she had done the deed herself when I dropped my religious observance or when I started dating Eric. But she had held on to me, continuing to call several times a week, beginning each conversation with the same cheery greeting, regardless of the way the last one had ended. *She's either in complete denial or a saint,* I had thought more than once. Coming from the religious perspective that I knew her to have, she offered a level of support that was unusually generous. Other ultra-Orthodox parents might have sat shivah, a mourning ritual, for a child who left the path of Judaism, cutting her off.

My mother had even visited me in Boston, bringing Ephraim on one notable occasion. Out of respect for her, I wore a long skirt and long sleeves during the days he was in Boston, though slipping these clothes on made me cringe. They were painful reminders of the girl I no longer was.

I wondered how much Ephraim knew about my life in Boston. My mother had a penchant for rejiggering facts when she relayed information or told stories, something that had both amused and frustrated my brother and me growing up under her roof. I imagined there was a heavy filter through which most information about me passed to Ephraim, my stepbrothers and stepsister, and other community members. "It's my private life," my mother responded to the query one day. "I don't have to satisfy anyone's curiosity!" "By *private,* you mean 'shameful,'" I had said accusingly.

I knew there were no pictures of me hanging in the hallway or on the fridge with the dozens of photos of the stepchildren and grandchildren. I thought then about Kathy, Joe's mother, who had shown evident pride in her son's girlfriend. Why couldn't my mother be proud of me like that? What an upside-down world she lived in that my perfectly good life was her dirty little secret.

While it was unfair for me, I at least understood the ideas that underlay her perspective. But I felt guilty for Joe, a young man whom any mother should have been happy to have for her daughter. My mother believed, and probably always would, I realized, that Joe and I had fundamentally different source codes, souls programmed for disparate purposes.

There were times that I worried that those beliefs had imprinted on me subconsciously. Coming to college, meeting people from all walks of life, I had more than enough reason to dismiss the spiritual hierarchies embedded in her dogmatic faith, the ones that had been used to divide and subjugate. But what, I feared, if they really *had* become my source code by virtue of the formative level at which they had been introduced?

Joe, with all his wonderful qualities, *did* appear unconcerned about his interior life. He was intelligent, lighthearted, enjoying a variety of interests and hobbies. The sheer volume of friends he brought with him and the boisterous parties we attended flattened me with sensory overload. How could so many people be drawn to Joe? I asked myself. My mother's belief had been that the more profound you were, the fewer friends you had. Was Joe, according to this heuristic, a shallow person?

One evening, a while after we began dating, Joe and I were in the car, en route to a friend's house for dinner, when he noticed I had gone quiet. "Are you okay?" he asked. "I don't know," I answered honestly, then blurted out: "I love being with you, but . . . I worry about having an ordinary life. I don't want a white picket fence. I don't know if I could be happy with that."

When I turned to look at him, his face was stiff, his eyes wide with hurt. I was confused. Had I said something so terrible? "What's wrong?" I said. "Aren't you breaking up with me?" he asked. "No!" I cried, horrified when I realized the reason for his sadness. "No! That's not what I'm doing at all."

I tried to explain then what my words had meant, the curse of never being satisfied with an "ordinary" life. "Ordinary sounds boring to me too," he had said then, the lighthearted tone back in his voice. "Hate those white pickets. If we get a house with one, we'll tear it down." I laughed, apologizing: "My upbringing was kind of fucked up." I'd told him a little about my childhood. Our relationship was still young, and I didn't want to burden it with my history. "We're all fucked up in some way," he had answered.

As the dinner party wound down, we headed to the kitchen to help our hosts with the washing and drying of dishes. When he finished stacking some plates on a high shelf, Joe came up behind me and slung his arms over my shoulders. I leaned my head back and nestled into the scent of his neck. *This is good,* I thought. *If this is ordinary, then ordinary could be quite nice.*

• • •

Winter break of 2001 was the last time for nearly two decades that I crossed the threshold of my former home in Gateshead. I had left for a two-week stay in England after spending Christmas Eve with Joe's parents, Kathy and Paul, in Lowell. Joe and I had stayed up until dawn talking and when he put me in a cab headed for the airport, I found myself fighting back tears. With each leg of the journey that brought me back to my home, I felt a growing sense of dread.

After several days in England I told my mother, "I have to go back. I'm so sorry." The tears would not stop and the feeling of pressure on my chest had returned. I could barely eat without gagging. To her credit, my mother acquiesced, allowing me to change my ticket to leave early. After taking a last look at the place that was no longer home, I headed back across the Atlantic. Boston was my home now, I realized with joy as the plane taxied down the runway at Logan. Perhaps even Joe was my home.

Our differences never resolved themselves completely; they just became less consequential over time. Joe would pull me gently into his foreign, lively world, and when I tired of it, I would beg off to be by myself for a while. As months gave way to years, many of his friends became my dear friends too, and I noticed that I didn't feel quite so uncomfortable or tired with others.

So this is how it works! I marveled to myself. You stay in one spot. You see the same people again and again, and each interaction added to the last thickens the bonds between you.

There would continue to be times that my mother's warnings would creep into my thoughts, melding with my own fears. *He can't be right for you,* an insidious voice would whisper. *This life is insipid, you'll wake up when you're forty and realize you've done nothing of spiritual significance and it will be too late, you'll be trapped.* I could usually shake these thoughts off, but it was harder to rid myself of the fear that God, biding His time, would one day take back from me the joys that I had stolen.

These thoughts surfaced as a little moth's wing of fear that arose each time I said goodbye to Joe on my doorstep. If I chased them away by day, they would return to me at night, in dreams where Joe would die. I learned to live with the anxiety. I suspected it might always be this way, with love and fear sharing the same space.

One lazy summer weekend in 2003, two years after we met, Joe surprised me by slipping a delicate, intricately carved white gold and diamond ring, an heirloom from his Irish grandmother, on my right ring finger. "This is a promise," he said, "that I intend to ask you to marry me with an engagement ring within a year. I know it will be difficult to make peace with your family, and I want to do this *right*." We had a year to bring my mother around to the idea of her daughter marrying a goy. *Oh, sweetie,* I thought. *You don't understand.* She might acquiesce, but what he wanted, for her to celebrate our union, might well be impossible.

When I explained our intentions to my mother, she again sighed heavily. "As far as I'm concerned, you're as married now as you'll ever be." Though I had expected some form of resistance, her words stung me deeply. "Do you have any idea how horrible it is to imply that our actual marriage one day will be meaningless?" I had spat out, choking with anger. "Nonsense," she returned stiffly. "Joe would understand me. *He* appreciates our faith. He's not poisoned by hatred like you."

"She can go fuck herself," Joe said, red in the face, that evening as I described our exchange. "If she feels that way she doesn't need to come to our wedding." In a moment, however, he had calmed down, as I knew he would. Joe couldn't hold anger in his heart, not like I could.

• 28 •

Prince Charming

A dream is a wish your heart makes . . .

—"A Dream Is a Wish Your Heart Makes"
(from *Cinderella*)

I T'S PITCH-DARK WHEN THE ALARM GOES OFF, BUT I JUMP
out of bed as if I've had a solid eight hours of sleep instead of the
two that have passed since I zipped up our last suitcase. Today's
the day! While the kiddos are still asleep, I wash my face, brush
my teeth, and put on a pot of coffee, though I've already got the
jitters from excitement. Then I head back upstairs to wake them.

"Elll-a, Miiii-ca, Looo-sia!" I sing. Nothing. I head to Em's bed
because she's the closest and I plant a kiss on her cheek, rubbing
her shoulder. "Wake up, love, it's time to go to Disney!"

"Disney!" "Disney!" Sleep-tousled heads emerge from under
blankets like groundhogs in early spring.

Dad is the hardest to rouse. I send the kids into the master bedroom to pile on him with firm instructions not to allow him to fall
back to sleep. His howls are good-natured as they poke and prod
him, and soon, his joins the chorus of excited voices.

I pack a breakfast of bagels for the airport as I run through a mental last-minute to-do list: Licenses, tickets, credit cards, two adults, three kids. Check.

The cab pulls up silently at a few minutes of five and we bundle in, bulky and shivering in our layers of winter clothes.

When the cab drops us off at the airport, Grammy is there to greet us. If it's possible, she seems more excited than the kids. This trip has been her idea and is largely her treat. "I've been dreaming of this since Ella was born!" she says. I'm a little nervous flying with the kids and spending a week with the six of us crammed into a one-bedroom cabin but Joe tells me not to worry, it will be worth it. It's *Disney,* after all!

Once the novelty of being on a plane wears off, things go south. No one wants to stay in her seat. When the bulky carry-on bag loaded with snacks and toys runs out, we are left with three grumpy, sleep-deprived kids and a changeover in another airport. Blessedly, in the last hour of the last leg of our journey, Lucia and Em fall fast asleep and Ella is contentedly making lists of the princesses and others she hopes to meet at Disney. I poke at Joe in the seat in front of me and point, grinning, to the page where she has laboriously written the following in what her teachers have encouraged us to call "brave spelling": *Aryil, Sindrila, Mekee Mose . . .*

We arrive in hot and muggy Orlando before noon, and immediately shed our jackets as we board the shuttle. On arrival at our cabin, I start to unpack and the kids explore the woods outside. "There are so many pinecones!" marvels Ella. After we all have a quick nap, we're ready to hit the parks. On the bus ride to our ferry, Ella sits down next to a garrulous little boy from Arkansas with a thick bluegrass twang and the two hit it off right away. "What's your brother's name?" he asks her. Ella thinks for a moment, then answers, "Em," and then, after another awkward pause, says, "She's my sister." Em's looking out the window but I know she hears the exchange because I see the flinch. It's a rubber-band snap that shows in the lower left corner of her mouth. When we disembark, I walk Ella up ahead of the rest of our party and when everyone's distracted, I bend and whisper in her ear: "Honey, maybe we don't need to point out that Em's your sister?" To my relief she seems to digest this and nods. "Yes, that's true. I don't *need* to say that, do I?" I realize at this moment that we are in an unprecedented situation. No one knows us here. Em can be anyone she wants to be with very little explaining.

Magic Kingdom is our first stop. Eyes bigger than our heads, we wander the candy-colored streets and fabricated squares where brightly costumed characters mingle with quaintly dressed street vendors. In the distance rises the magnificent Gothic fairy-tale castle: buttresses, spires, pennants, and all: *Cinderella's Castle!*

Within minutes the kids have scored a Mickey and a Goofy in their little red autograph books, and we've stopped for some ice cream to check out our maps and make plans. Ella and Em are actually hugging each other and dancing for joy, pulling at our clothes and pointing at the splendor that surrounds us. Lucia, in the stroller, is looking around as well, mouth agape. No one is fighting, and no one is frowning. I feel a sense of relaxed anticipation despite the heat, despite the difficulty of keeping everyone together and on time for our chosen FastPass activities. Is this the magic that is unfolding?

The next day starts bright and early. Rides, sights, the heat; it's all a little overwhelming but the kids are doing good, even Em is dealing unusually well with the sensory overload.

By day three we have a routine down: Early afternoon we retreat to our cabin just before the meltdowns, if there are any, then head out to a special dinner event. Today, Kathy, unable to nap and recovering from an ear infection, begs a night off, so we leave Lucia, zombie-like with sleepiness, and take the older kids to a late dinner at Disney's Akershus Hall, a Scandinavian-style château that promises the somewhat dubious-sounding "tastes of Norway."

The kids have dressed to the nines for the occasion in antici-pation of meeting their first princesses. Ella is in a pink satin and gauze Sleeping Beauty dress with light-up pink glittery sneakers. Her hair is half up and there's a chintzy plastic tiara on her head (earlier this year I had asked her what her favorite color was, and after giving it serious consideration, she had replied: "Sparkle. *Sparkle* is my favorite color"). Em is likewise looking outstand-ing in the Prince Charming costume I bought her online. I'm sur-prised as we walk about that I don't see more of these. Plenty of Buzz Lightyears and Woodys from *Toy Story,* but nary a Prince Charming. Apparently, these royal sightings are rare indeed, be-cause once the princesses get a load of Em they begin to swoon.

"Oh, Prince Charming!" squeals Cinderella. "I didn't know you were going to be here tonight!" She's got Em's little face in a white-gloved hand, and, impressively, she's acting genuinely smit-ten, curtsying and giggling, touching her blond bouffant. With Em's short pixie cut and dressed the way she is, I realize with a start that there is no way anyone could take her for a girl. At home, I've always assumed people knew, but we're in a whole new world now.

"What name do you go by when you're not being a prince?" asks Cinderella, smiling down at Em. Em looks uncertain for a moment, glancing over to me, and I nod encouragingly, though my breath catches in my throat. "Mica," she says, looking down at the table. I examine Cinderella's face, trying to decipher her expression. Has she figured out that something is different about this child? If she senses something, she doesn't show it. She con-tinues to fawn over Em, holding her hand, and for once, Em seems to be enjoying the physical affection. I let go of the breath I am holding, but my heart is still racing. It's time for the princess to move to the next table, and with a sigh, a blown kiss, and a back-ward glance, she does so.

A trumpet announces the arrival of the next princess, the beauteous redheaded Ariel, sans mermaid tail, dressed in a glittery blue gown with enormous puff sleeves. Ella is agog with excitement and when Ariel reaches our table, Ella twirls, showing off her costume and peppering the princess with questions about life under the water. How do you breathe? Where does your tail go when you leave? After Ariel signs Ella's autograph book, she turns to Prince Charming and holds out a delicate regal hand. "May I have the honor of this dance, Prince?"

A space clears to the side of the room and guests begin to gather to watch the unfolding scene: Princess Ariel, tall, majestic, red locks cascading down her back, miles of glistening fabric, waltzes with a pintsize Prince Charming who barely reaches above her waist and is trying desperately not to step on her toes as he gazes upward with a look of sheer wonder.

Em seems to have grown three inches but then I realize that she's standing on her tiptoes. The guests begin to clap as the music winds down. When a new song begins, Ella cuts in and asks to dance with the princess and soon other children have joined, little princesses in yellow, blue, or pink dresses, some boys with shorts and T-shirts. One Prince Charming ducks out of the crowd to reclaim his place at the dinner table.

Em looks so happy that I feel a tug on my heart. Why can't she be this happy always? She looks up at me with a wide grin: "Can I get dessert now, Mama?" "Yes, you most certainly *can,* Prince Mica!" I say in my best courtly manner, holding out my arm with a flourish and a bow. As we walk to the dessert buffet, I steal a glance down at her. She still seems taller though she is no longer on tiptoes.

That evening after the kids have passed out in their beds, I take the Prince Charming jacket to the sink and wash out a chocolate stain with some dish soap. Joe comes up behind me and rests his chin on my shoulder. "What an evening," he says. "Did you notice how she didn't mind being the center of attention?" I ask. "I did," he says. "And no tantrums today," I say. "Yes." "It's interesting," I say. "Something to think about," he responds. We leave it at that.

The next day's a scorcher and I'm constantly spraying the kids with a water bottle. Thankfully we're at Animal Kingdom, which has water rides. After getting soaked on a ride, Em emerges wailing, fat tears rolling down her cheeks, but as soon as she can muster a breath, she gasps and says: "Can I go again?" Unable to help it, Joe and I burst out laughing, joined by Grammy and Ella and even little Lucia, and after a moment, Em begins to laugh at herself. *Remember this,* I tell myself as I look at us cracking up together. *Tuck this one away for a rainy day.*

Our last night at Disney arrives. Tonight, we will venture up to the castle for a royal banquet, the highlight of our trip before we head home tomorrow. I had woken up early in the morning exactly half a year before our trip to secure this coveted meal option, and it had cost an arm and a leg. *Hope it's worth it,* I think.

We get gussied up. Ella's got her floor-length Cinderella gown on, and Lucia has a shorter version of the same, two small pigtails sprouting from the sides of her head. Em dons her Prince Charming costume again, and as we walk up toward the castle, Ella and Em waltz, holding hands, drawing the attention of several tourists who stop and remark at how cute they look together.

"Brother and sister? Are they twins?" "Not twins, seventeen months apart," I answer. "Ah, the boys always grow faster." One woman nods knowingly. "That they do," I say, stealing a glance at Joe, who grins.

The food at the dinner isn't the best, but what we're paying for, I know, is the princesses and the grandeur of eating high up in the turrets where the view is truly spectacular. Cinderella herself shows up with an adult-size Prince Charming in tow, which leads to some good-natured ribbing directed at Em, most of which goes over her head.

Everyone continues to assume Em is a boy. "Ooh! What a handsome little man!" squeals one lady. "Your son, he's so adorable!" says another. I smile and thank them. Sometimes Ella looks like she wants to say something, but I give her a glance, and she settles back down.

That evening, Em just glows. She's animated in a way I can't remember seeing, at least not in the past year, maybe longer. She's been given a plastic sword as a favor that she's jousting at her dad with, and her sisters are twirling around with new Fairy Godmother wands, turning everyone at our table into a pumpkin.

After dessert it's time for us to head back to our cabin. We check under the table for toys, binkies, any and all paraphernalia. Ella announces she has to go the bathroom again, so Grammy takes her back down the long, winding staircase and Joe heads down with Lucia. I turn to call Em and observe her standing by one of the turret's tall, latticed windows gazing down at the early-evening strollers in the castle square. The look on her face is dreamy and distracted. Although I'm supposed to be corralling her, I drop my bag and dig out my camera instead. What an iconic photo, I think, a prince surveying his kingdom from the castle tower. "Come." I gently place a hand on one epaulet. "Time to go." And just like that, the spell is broken.

The next morning, we wake up all business. We pack our pajamas and toiletries, check and recheck our tickets, last-minute stuff. We take the shuttle to the monorail to another shuttle to the airport to yet another monorail to a plane and one more plane and suddenly we are on our doorstep, having had our fill of adventure, back in the land of obligations, school days, dance lessons, and cold spring mornings where we have to *rush, rush, rush.* The magic has ended, though perhaps a glass slipper's worth remains, just an idea, a whisper of a hint of a suggestion that Joe and I discuss late in the evenings after the kids have gone to bed and early in the morning before they wake up.

What if . . .

The Redaction

We are so accustomed to disguise ourselves to others that in the end we become disguised to ourselves.

— FRANÇOIS DE LA ROCHEFOUCAULD

IT WAS A PROMISING SIGN, I THOUGHT, THAT MY MOTHER was planning another trip to Boston with Ephraim for the spring of 2004. I had not seen my stepfather since his first visit, during my freshman year at BU, and I was now in my last semester of a master's program at the Fletcher School of Law and Diplomacy at Tufts University. I assumed that he was coming to meet Joe, my — as I referred to him privately — "*pre*-ancé."

"Why don't Joe and I pick you and Ephraim up at the airport and then we can have dinner at Rubin's, the kosher deli in Brookline?" I suggested a week before they were scheduled to arrive. "Maybe even Kathy and Paul can meet us there?"

"It would be better," my mother said after a weighty pause, "if this trip was more about us seeing you and where you are living and studying. We'll be there for too short a time. Daddy can meet Joe on a later trip."

"You didn't *tell him* we plan to become engaged?" I cried. "Does he even know Joe *exists?*" "I will tell him when I'm ready," she said uncomfortably. "I can't spring this on him suddenly; it would break his heart." "So, you want more time?" I continued, dumbfounded. "More than the three-plus years we've been together?"

"It's okay," Joe said later that day. "I don't care." But he did, I was sure. How could he not? How unfair for him to be nothing more than bad news to be broken to a man who was not even my real father. Even if Joe could overlook this demeaning treatment, I could not. I informed my mother that if she did not tell Ephraim about Joe prior to next week's visit, I intended to.

The remainder of the week went by and I didn't hear from her. I called and left messages, but they went unanswered. It was on Friday, an hour before the Sabbath for my mother, when she finally picked up the phone. I was standing in Austin Hall at Harvard Law School for a class I had cross-registered for on Islamic law, gazing up at the high red stone arches that lined the hallway, when her voice came over the wire. The professor had started the lecture already and I hated being late for anything, but this was my last chance to reach my mother before the Sabbath, and she was scheduled to fly in with Ephraim on Monday.

"Did you tell him?" I asked after our greeting. At first there was silence, during which my heart sank, but then she said slowly that yes, she had. *Phew,* I thought, and thanked her. Living life in the open was important to me but difficult for my mother. I waited to hear more. There was another protracted pause, followed by a weak sigh. Finally, she spoke again: "Daddy and I will not be coming to visit you Monday."

Feeling the skin on the back of my skull tighten, I pressed the end-call button and sat down, suddenly out of breath, on the stairs under the arches. I swallowed several times, blinking back tears of anger, and then I stuffed my phone in my school bag and slipped into class. I began to feel oddly frozen, almost detached. *I'm never going to speak to her again,* I thought, and with this thought came a sense of relief. Now could I finally be free? She had made a choice, and it wasn't her daughter. Perhaps I had the right to choose myself over her.

I shouldn't have been surprised, I reminded myself as I pulled out my notebook and pen and the week's reading materials. Whether it had been for faith or, as I at times suspected, for self-interest, she had frequently chosen . . . not me.

It was hard to forget the day, shortly after I moved to Boston, when I had innocently inquired if we would be instituting an emergency "phone code" for the Sabbath like we had when my grandfather, living in Florida, had suffered his first stroke. If he was in trouble, his nurse would call us and let the phone ring twice, then three times, then twice again, and we would know to pick up, despite it being a holy day.

"Miriam, we can't do that anymore," my mother had explained to me when I asked for the code. "That was then, this is now." I was incredulous. "What if I'm in the hospital?" I asked. "Not even then," she replied calmly. "What if I'm dying? You would let me die alone?" "You wouldn't be alone," she had replied. "God would be with you." I had wanted so badly to be furious, so the pity, when it arose, was unwelcome. It was one of those moments when I understood how *really real* her faith was to her and how she was incapable of seeing me or anyone else outside of its lens. This time, however, I felt no pity. Sheltering Ephraim from the reality that his stepdaughter was marrying a goy was not a commandment but a copout.

I had difficulty focusing during Professor Vogel's class that day, though the lecture was uncannily relevant to what had transpired on the steps of the hall before it. "In the tenth century," the professor read to us from a source, "the gates of *ijtihad,* interpretation, were closed." He went on to describe a pivotal era in the history of Sunni Islam when the religion's authoritative scholars declared future legal rulings closed to the application of independent interpretations. Moving forward, in most cases, only *taqlid,* imitative or precedential, rulings would be permitted.

Why do we do this? I had asked myself that day, still reeling from my mother's decision. *Why do we close ourselves off this way?* I was thinking mostly of my own faith and the similar manner we had barricaded ourselves against the possibility of change, how the farther back one went in the *mesorah,* the exegetical chain of custody, the more infallible and therefore immutable the words of the rabbis were regarded to be.

It was nearly a month before I spoke to my mother again. It was Joe, my gentile boyfriend, who interceded on her behalf, asking me to consider forgiving her or, at least, resuming conversation. "It's not her I'm worried about ultimately, it's you," he had said. He wanted me to come to a place of peace in my heart toward my mother. Not for the first time, I was envious of his ability to forgive, to move past and onward, whereas I seemed irretrievably stuck.

It was at his behest that I agreed eventually to speak to my mother again. I was able to do so because Joe and I were happy — not perfectly, not always blissfully, but deeply, satisfyingly happy. With each year that had passed since leaving Gateshead, I found myself growing in confidence and the capacity to love. The shadows had retreated farther and farther into their places in my history each new day that I spent in the light.

It was graduation weekend. Joe and I, amid all the commencement activities at Tufts, were also moving my belongings piecemeal into his postage-stamp-size condo in East Cambridge, on a windy corner that seemed to pile every leaf for miles into our driveway and would force us, in the coldest of winter nights, to sleep, coats and boots on, huddled together for warmth on the living-room couch.

Joe had just been accepted into business school at MIT, a ten-minute walk from the condo. I considered a move to DC, where all the national security jobs that I wanted were, but the separation was too daunting. Until I found something more suitable, I would be taking a job at Kathy's nursing home, helping to run a program for certified nursing assistants. It wasn't exciting, but it had an emotionally satisfying component, and I loved the Sisters of Notre Dame, the nuns that spearheaded the program at this Catholic nursing home. Unlike the malevolent nuns in my childhood stories, hellbent on kidnapping Jewish children to convert them, the real-life nuns were endearing sources of genuine inspiration. They were quietly doing good works and bringing about social change under the auspices of, and sometimes in spite of, the patriarchy of the Church.

My father had flown in from Israel en route to LA to attend my graduation, meeting Kathy and Paul for the first time and participating with evident enjoyment in the activities we had planned. The day after graduation and the day before my dad was scheduled to depart, Joe asked if he could take a walk with him. When they returned, both men were smiling broadly, my father nearly giddy. Joe had formally requested my hand in marriage, something that, while not necessary, he thought my dad might appreciate, and he had.

The admiration between Joe and my dad was mutual. In many ways they couldn't be less alike. Joe, a software engineer and now an MBA candidate, navigated a world of concrete data, speaking in a language of zeros and ones. He had a facility with the realm of now that left my academician father's head spinning. My father was at home in the dusty trails of history, tracking the passage of languages and people, speaking over twenty tongues — none of which included back slashes or space bars. To my surprise, my dad had praised his future son-in-law for having his feet planted firmly on the ground.

I accompanied my dad to the airport the following day, and we made a detour to Faneuil Hall marketplace for lunch. It was graduation weekend, and the touristy area was mobbed. Luckily we found a table at a restaurant called the Rustic Kitchen, where, after ordering our food, we tucked into a basket of fresh-baked cranberry rolls. That was when my father asked me how my mother was doing. The embedded question was clear: *How is your mother dealing with your decision to marry a gentile?* I hesitated, distractedly picking out the cranberries from my roll and popping them in my mouth. "She's fine," I said. "But . . . I'm not sure if she'll come to the wedding." My father's green eyes widened. "It would surprise me much," he said, "if Judith decided not to attend the wedding because Joe is a Catholic. Especially given her history."

"What history?" I asked.

"Sit down," I ordered Joe.

We were back in our Cambridge apartment, surrounded by packing boxes, and I had grabbed his hand and pulled him over to the couch. "Why? What's up?" he asked. "Trust me, you're going to need to be sitting for this." Once he was, I plopped down next to him and repeated what my father had told me at the restaurant.

"She . . . *what?*" His mouth hung open. He clapped his hands to his cheeks.

"You heard me," I answered, and because it was so ludicrous, so outlandish, so completely fucking surreal, I had to repeat it.

"My mother was a nun."

"Excuse me?" I had spluttered at my dad, the pockmarked cranberry roll dropping from my fingers. "*What* did you say?"

"She didn't tell you?" he asked. It was his turn to be taken aback. "No!" I practically yelled. "Abba, you're joking, right?" I pleaded.

"No . . ." he said slowly, shaking his head, his eyes still wide. "This is the truth. Judith lived in a convent for a long while before I knew her," he answered, his voice faltering. "I thought she told you. I thought you *must* know."

I felt lightheaded. Everything around me, the bustling restaurant, the white tablecloth, the cranberry roll on my plate, all seemed overly real and highly dubious at the same time. As a jovial person, my father had a keen sense of humor, but his jokes were not of this kind — this would have been in practical-joke territory, too tasteless for him. Also, I knew in a way that what he said was true. It made sense, and furthermore, it made a lot of *other things* make sense: her PhD focusing on Saint Thomas Aquinas, the time we had gone to visit her friend Lucy at a convent in Jerusalem, Saint John of the Cross's poetry, the fact that she knew more than anyone else I knew, more than my Catholic in-laws, about the Christian faith, the fact that she hardly ever spoke about her past.

I could count on two hands the things I knew about my mother's formative years, and then there was the big nothing, the blank space from the day she started college to the day she had met my father, a handsome young associate professor at the University of Illinois, where she had taken courses. Growing up, I suppose that the self-centered preoccupation of youth never made me consider my mother as a real person with a history. Now that I was nearing thirty myself, I realized there *must* have been more to her life. Why had I never pestered her for details or, rather, how had I let her get away with providing such insubstantial answers to the questions I had asked? I suddenly felt incredibly naive, and with that feeling came a sense of betrayal. Why would she not tell me this monumental thing about her life, and who else *had* she told? Did my stepfather even know? My mind was buzzing. I had soon exhausted my father's supply of information; he told me she had taken vows with first one Catholic order, then another, Benedictine and Dominican, he believed, and he urged me to ask my mother for more detail. We wrapped up our lunch, and, with an embrace, he took off for the airport.

On my trolley ride home, I thought of nothing else but the enormous secret that my mother had kept from me. I remembered being in eighth grade and working on a family history project for school. My mother had lent me a photograph of my grandmother as a young woman, but not before she had taken a Sharpie pen and drawn in sleeves on my grandmother's bare arms. I had been offended at this redaction. "Why did you do this?" I complained. "You've ruined her picture!" Even though I was only thirteen, this act felt uncomfortably disrespectful. "It would be disrespectful for me to leave her uncovered" was my mother's rejoinder. "She would be turning in her grave knowing that she was being seen this way." Now I realized just how deep my mother's redaction of her own history had gone. What else had she taken a Sharpie to? Were any of the stories true?

"Huh," said Joe once he had gotten past the initial shock. "It's kind of ironic that she has objections to you marrying me." He was right. *What chutzpah,* I thought.

"Are you going to tell her you know?" Joe asked as we were preparing dinner that night. My mother was due to arrive for her own visit in a few days.

In the end I decided to be up-front. That was *my* way of dealing with things. I also had many pressing questions to ask. Why the conversion to another faith when her own clearly meant so much to her? I didn't even think of asking why, once she'd converted, she took the extreme step of becoming a nun. My mother would never do something for faith that did not require complete devotion, body and mind. That evening I looked up everything I could about the process of becoming a nun, and it was fascinating. I tried to imagine my mother taking her spiritual wedding vows to Christ, perhaps receiving a ring to mark her as his metaphorical bride. I fingered the gold filigree ring on my own finger. "Does this make me, like, Jesus's redheaded stepchild?" I asked Joe. "I don't know," he said, shaking his head.

"He promised me he wouldn't tell!"

My mother was as furious as I had ever seen her. I stammered, "I d-don't think he realized I didn't know, Mom, that you hadn't told me." I tried to pacify her, but she wouldn't hear it. "No, he knew *exactly* what he was doing! And all those years I kept his secrets too! That his father died in a mental institution in Iran! Oh *yes!*" she said, and her eyes gleamed in an unpleasant way: "Abba says he was killed in a car accident! That was a lie!" *Oh, brother.* I buried my face in my hands.

"Maybe," I said, "just *maybe* he didn't want me to go into my wedding feeling guilty that I was marrying a Christian." She ignored me, muttering: "He had *no right.*"

What I tried to articulate to my mother was that my father's revelation might actually have been a good thing — for the two of us. For the first time in years, I was feeling a longing for a greater connection to my mother, a sense of wonder and curiosity for why a brilliant, bookish girl from an upwardly mobile assimilated New York Jewish family had rebelled so starkly against her upbringing to undertake this, for want of a better word, crazy spiritual quest. The story of my mother's awakening at the age of four was now, I realized, but the first chapter in a fascinating pilgrimage. I wanted the rest of the book.

"I didn't know that Jews still *believed* anymore," my mother said once she had calmed down enough to consider answering my questions. "My parents and their friends didn't really." I had been skeptical. "You lived in Queens, New York, and you didn't know there were religious Jews?" "You don't understand, Miriam," she replied. "Grandma and Grandpa made sure we didn't know that side of our faith. They had long abandoned any meaningful practice."

When my mother had entered Swarthmore, a liberal arts college in Pennsylvania, she had shifted course away from the sciences to study philosophy and religion. It was there that she had discovered what she felt was a living faith that practiced genuine devotion and sacrifice. She converted to Catholicism at the age of twenty and entered an order of sisters. She was not forthcoming with many details about her cloistered life except that the name she took for her new life was Sister Mary. I understood that she now believed her choices had been mistaken, that she regretted losing her family for a decade, as they would not communicate with her while she was in the convent. I felt both empathy and a new sense of respect for her. She had sacrificed so much for her convictions. My father had been right. In some ways, she was a saint.

"Why did you decide to leave the convent?" I asked. "What brought you back to Judaism?"

"It was the Six-Day War — or rather," she amended, "its outcome."

In the convent, only the Mother Superior and a few of the senior nuns had access to newspapers and the outside world. The news of impending conflict between Israel and her far larger, more powerful neighbors, Egypt and Syria, had gotten around. When the war commenced, it was generally thought that Israel was doomed. For my mother, in some way, that also meant the end of Jewry. One morning she overheard someone declare, "It's over!" less than a week after the war had begun, and my mother's heart sank. She realized at that moment how deeply she felt for the Jewish people. The nun went on, incredulous: "Israel won!" The relief and gratitude that my mother experienced came with an epiphany: "God is still with the Jews! He has not abandoned them." She returned to her faith, determined to find a meaningful practice.

I tried to picture my mother at the age of thirty or so leaving the cloistered life and assimilating back into the modern world of the mid-1960s. Women's liberation, the sexual revolution, civil rights; what had she made of her new world? Those changes must have been even harder than the ones that I had experienced leaving Gateshead. "How did you manage?" I asked. "Not easily," she admitted. She hadn't known how to shop for things, pay bills, use public transportation. I couldn't imagine how difficult it must have been making friends or even considering dating. I wondered if my father had been the first man my mother had dated in her adult life. She had always radiated a distracted, otherworldly air and had long disdained superficiality. It was hard to say if her cloistered years had created these traits or just exacerbated them. I suspected the latter. "I love you," I said impulsively, reaching for her, but she stiffened in my arms, not ready to forgive my intrusion into her private history.

Joe proposed in the early summer of my twenty-eighth year, and despite the fact that I knew it was coming in a general way, the actual moment took me by surprise. We had gone up to his family's small oceanfront house at Seabrook, New Hampshire, for the weekend and after unpacking our bags, we had taken to the dunes to watch the sun go down. Dropping to one knee silently, he held out a small red ring box. I cannot remember the actual words he said, only the sound of the blood rushing in my ears and the waves hitting the shore, but I know that I answered "Yes" with great enthusiasm. *Yes* to it all.

   Yes to the real world, gritty and uncertain.
   Yes to the long haul, often ordinary.
   Yes to vulnerability, the price of love.

• 30 •

Open/Shut, Boy/Girl

I am invisible, understand, simply because people refuse
to see me.　　　　　— RALPH ELLISON, *Invisible Man*

W HAT IF," I BEGIN AS I TUCK EM INTO BED THE NIGHT
before her first post-Disney day of school, "we asked Mrs.
Shea and Mrs. Zipper to call you Mica at school?" She frowns,
silent for a moment, then slowly shakes her head. "So Em's still
okay?" My heart is fluttering because this would be a great sign,
another beacon to the way back. "No," she says emphatically.
"Em is stupid." "Then, what *do* you want them to call you?" I ask.
She looks up at me, her large brown eyes opaque, indecipherable.
"Tell them to call me nothing," she says. For a second I think she's
got to be joking, but she remains silent as she stares at me. *Oh,
baby.* My hand hovers over her for a moment, then gently lowers
to touch her shoulder. "Sweetie, they can't call you nothing. You
need a name." She shrugs my hand away, scrunches around under
the covers for a minute, then lies still.

I'm surprised and a little relieved. I probably shouldn't even
have asked her this question, given our current directive to keep
things as fluid as possible, but something had felt *wrong* about returning to the status quo after her evident joy those times she had
been taken for a boy at Disney. And despite recent improvements,

there were those moments when I caught Em flinching when she heard her name called. It was almost as if the sound of her name was too loud, disrupting a pleasant daydream.

I wanted her to know that she *had* choices, that we would be willing to go to bat for her if that's what it came to. Joe and I had discussed this and concluded that if she had given us an exuberant, clear yes, we would do what it took to make this happen. But she hadn't.

Why?

Uncannily, her voice floats out softly from under the covers, as if she's plucked the question out of my head: "If I have a boy name, the kids would think I'm funny." I swallow hard and look away. What do I say now? It's true, after all. They will think she's "funny." And if she wasn't ambivalent on some level, wouldn't she insist on a new name? Persistent, consistent, *insistent.*

"Kids can act mean sometimes," I say sympathetically. "It's not right for people to make fun of others, and if they did that, you could tell the teacher or Mommy and we'd talk to them." "No" is her firm answer. "Okay," I say, rubbing her back. "Just tell us if you change your mind." She wriggles away again, leaving my hand dangling over an empty space.

It's Ella who provides some insight into the social repercussions Em is already suffering due to her clothing choices. "We need to have a talk, Mommy," she announces solemnly one day, "in *private.*" I'm amused and delighted. I love that Ella, at five, is getting so mature that she requires *conversations,* not just spontaneous interactions. I close the bedroom door and seat her on my lap on the heirloom rocking chair that Kathy reupholstered for us as a Christmas gift. "What's up, buttercup?"

"Mommy," she says sternly, "you need to start *making* Em wear dresses."

I'm taken aback. For a moment I just study her face. "Why?" I ask. This seems uncharacteristic of Ella, who has been one of

Em's biggest supporters these past months. I even overheard her defend Em at dance class when she showed up for the first time wearing black bike shorts and a white V-neck T-shirt, what I imagined a male ballet dancer would wear. "Just *because* you *should,*" Ella answers and she looks angry and uncomfortable, tears brimming on her eyelashes. "Honey," I say, calmly but firmly, "*why* do you think we need to make Em wear dresses? You need to give me a reason. You know she's not comfortable in them. Shouldn't we all be allowed to wear what makes us happy?" *"No!"* answers Ella firmly. "Make her put on a dress, Mommy!"

"Ella, that's just not nice of you," I say, disappointed. "What if we forced you to wear the clothes that Em likes every day? What if I told you that you couldn't wear a dress again? I'm surprised at you." Now the tears are rolling down her cheeks. I can see that something is eating at her, so I soften my tone. "Ella, please. Tell me why you think this."

"*Because,* Mommy," she cries, her face crumpling, "*because* that way, people will be nicer to her." My heart sinks. I ask her for examples of what kids are doing that is not nice to Em, but she won't give me specifics, only says that this is happening.

"Listen, love," I say slowly. "I don't think making Em wear dresses is the answer." How do I explain to a five-year-old that what we wear intimately reflects how we think of ourselves? Surely she remembers the tantrums that accompanied those times when Em was required to wear a dress — Easter, last year's dance recital? Finally, I settle again on what we've been saying for months and what seems to resonate with my ordinarily empathetic child: "What you are in your mind and your heart is more important than what you are in your body, and Em's mind seems to be telling her she's a boy, so dresses feel wrong for her.

"Sometimes, Ella," I continue, "people feel uncomfortable when they see someone doing something that is different or *unexpected.* That might mean that *they* need to learn to be okay with it, not that Em needs to change who she is." Ella is listening intently and when I finish, she takes a deep breath, nods, and squeezes me in a hug. "Yes. They do," she says resolutely, and the face she gifts to me — the knitted brow, the jutting jaw, the flinty, squinted eyes — lifts my heart. This resolve is what's remarkable about Ella. It's been a part of her makeup from her earliest days, constituting what we've come to know as the Essential Ella. I recall a brief period, around age three, when Ella had begun to stutter. "Mama, why c-can't I g-get the w-w-words out?" She had stamped in frustration. "I'm not sure," I answered, "but it's possible you need to slow down your words and *think* about each one as it comes out." She looked at me then with the same expression and said slowly, with effort and evident concentration: "Okay . . . Mama . . . I . . . will . . . do . . . that." She never stuttered again.

Seeing this resolve surface, I feel a surge of hope. *She's going to be okay; we all are.*

Spring has finally sprung by early May. As brutal as the winter has been, the delivery from it is just as heavenly. A spate of birthday parties appear on our calendar, kicked off by Lucia's second birthday, on the first of May. Even Em gets an invitation to a party, one of the few she's gotten this year. The birthday girl is Katherine, Em's sole friend from the Beginnings Room but now, because she made the age cutoff, Katherine is also Ella's pre-K friend and classmate. She's generously invited both siblings to her party at a gymnastics center.

The day of the party, June 3, is warm and sticky. Ella is dressed in her sparkly pink and purple spandex leotard and Em has on dark shorts and a T-shirt. I ask if she'd like to put some bobby pins in her shortish brown hair because there's a piece that always flops into her eyes, but she says no.

After an hour of flipping and swinging into a pit filled with big foam blocks, the kids come back upstairs to greet us on the observation deck for cake and ice cream. After we sing "Happy Birthday" and tuck into the treats, the party starts to disband. It's a large group, and kids are milling about, running around the small room. The birthday girl is handing out large handmade hair bows with red, white, and blue ribbon, perfect for upcoming Fourth of July festivities. I'm starting to pack up my diaper bag, checking to see that I've got all the water bottles, when I feel a tug on my sleeve. I look up to see a pixie-faced girl with a shoulder-length caramel-colored bob.

"Excuse me!" she says, and I bend down. "Yes, hon?" Pointing at Em, the girl says: "What is that?" I look to see what Em is holding, but her hands are empty. "What do you mean, love?" I ask, but I see something in her face that arrests my smile, something that might or might not be a preschool version of mean girl, a self-assurance laced with contempt. "What is *that?*" she repeats loudly, pointing at my kid, "Is *that* a *boy* or is *that* a *girl?*"

I look at her grimly, taking a deep breath. "*That,*" I say, "is Em. Em may seem like a girl in some ways but she's a boy in her heart. So I guess she's a little bit of both." As the five-year-old socialite frowns at me, I wonder if this is the moment where I get quietly banned from future parties, and I decide that I don't care. In my best "And this ends the matter" mommy voice, I smile broadly at the girl and tell her, "And . . . I think she's *awesome.*" The girl turns on her heel and stalks off. *Is this how it starts?* I think.

My heart is heavy that afternoon and evening. At least, I tell myself, Ella and Em weren't witness to our conversation.

It's the last week of school and the day of Ella's preschool graduation.

Kathy, Joe, Em, Lucia, and I wait on the steps outside the church adjacent to the Purpose School, where graduation ceremonies will be held. I have mixed feelings today, as do the other moms. We congratulate and commiserate. It's wonderful that our kids have reached this milestone, but their growing up means our letting go, and we know this well. Those moms whose youngest kids are graduating today are in tears already. I'm saving my tears for the actual processional, but I'm handing out tissues.

"You'll be doing this next year!" Kathy smiles at Em, who is standing on the stone steps, hands thrust into the pockets of her jeans, kicking the step with her sneakers. She's wearing a tie for the occasion; it's hanging askew over a T-shirt. She pulls off the look quite nicely, I think. What she hasn't managed yet today is a smile, though I've warned her that when it's her sister's turn to walk down the aisle, it had better be there, no ifs, ands, or buts. Lucia is dressed identically to Ella, in a blue kimono-style dress with fuchsia flowers. There's another one in the attic in Em's size, gathering dust on its clear cellophane wrapper.

When the door to the church opens, we find a pew together and take our seats. There's a small painted wooden bridge on the altar up front. Finally, the moment arrives when the music begins and the door to the back of the church opens. Each little graduate, crowned with a blue felt cap, walks down the aisle to waves and cheers. Ella appears proud and confident. We blow her kisses and clap as she walks by. After the kids take seats up on the altar, Kristie begins her speech. I am moved by how she describes this rite of passage, what the kids have learned, how much this school has loved and appreciated them. She tells us not to worry too much. She realizes this is a big moment, but we need to trust that our kids are ready for it, even if we're not. Then, one by one, the graduates are called up to cross the bridge to receive a certificate of completion with a handshake and a hug from the teachers and Kristie.

Afterward, relatives flood to the front of the church to pick up their graduates. Kids pose for photos in clusters of three or four best friends and family members. Joe hands Ella a bouquet of flowers and we snap a few pictures. Em manages a genuine smile and I'm grateful for it. I had glanced down at Em during the procession, taking in her slumped posture, her eyes dark, flat, and indecipherable, and I wished, for the thousandth time, that things were easier for her.

We head back to the classrooms, where thick manila envelopes with artwork and classwork are bequeathed to us along with thank-you notes for end-of-year gifts and each child's progress report. On paper, I note with a quick glance, Em has been do-ing well. She's even started using the toilet independently as of a few weeks ago, writes Mrs. Zipper in her neat round script. The notes also mention that Em will join the others to do activities — *if asked*. It's a small but revealing modifier.

Mrs. Shea stops me in the hall on my way out the door. "I want you to know," she says, and her eyes suddenly fill with tears, "Em came over and hugged me today. She's never done that before. I think she's getting more comfortable." I know that Mrs. Shea loves Em, and I tell her now how grateful I've been for that, for everything.

The next day, Friday, brings us to the last day of school. We'll be back on school grounds other times, but only for a day camp, offered for a week or so. I pick the kids up and all three of us head to Papa Gino's pizzeria, where Sue, one of the class moms from the Star Room, has gathered us to celebrate. By the time we get there, most of the kids have seated themselves in booths already. I plop my bag down near a table occupied by several moms and go fetch Lucia a high chair. Ella runs off to sit with some of the older siblings, her friends.

When I come back, Em is standing in the aisle looking at a booth that is filled to the max with boys. The table next to it has an empty space, but it's all girls. Before I can say something, one of the moms asks the girls to squeeze over more to make room for Em. Wordlessly, she shuffles into the spot and there's an awkward lull in the conversation until the girls start to chatter again.

I can tell Em is uncomfortable, but what can I do? "Want to sit with me?" I ask her. She shrugs and stays put.

Soon I'm caught up talking to the moms about summer plans

and whose kid will be in what classroom next year. I'm proud of the way I've been ahead of things in organizing our summer. I've got several camps lined up, and everything's labeled and printed out on a calendar: zoo camp, theater camp, soccer camp, and several weeks at a camp run by our own town's public-school district, which seemed like the perfect way to get Ella introduced to her future kindergarten classmates, few of whom attended the Purpose School, one town over from ours.

When the pizza arrives, I walk a slice over to Ella, then to Em, who quietly accepts it and starts eating. The girls at her table are laughing and jostling one another, their bodies in constant movement. All except Em, who might as well be projecting an invisible force field judging from the empty space that surrounds her. I swallow hard. "Hey, Em." I bend, whispering in her ear: "Whaddya say we take our pizza and skedaddle? We can eat it while we're watching *Jake and the Never Land Pirates*!" "No, Mama," she rumbles softly. "It's okay. I want to eat here."

When I return to my table, I find I can't focus on the conversation anymore. When the pizza's all gobbled up, the kids start to spill out of their booths. A group of boys have spotted a jar of lollipops stationed at the far end of the restaurant on a small table near the condiments. They discuss a race to the lollipops. "Come on! Let's go!" They egg one another on with easy familiarity. As the boys begin to pelt across the restaurant, their moms spring to attention, reining them in with calls: "Come back here *right* now!"

At that moment my eye falls on Em, who is also looking after the boys and the chaos they have created. Her chin is resting on her hand and her lips are parted in a soft smile. When I search her eyes, the look of longing I see in them stabs my heart. *She's lost,* I suddenly realize. She's stranded. She doesn't belong with the girls, but the boys don't want her either. She knows it too.

I feel the urgent need to leave before the tears start, so I make a pretense of checking the time and begin to gather my kids. I am in such a rush to leave that I forget Em's backpack and will have to retrieve it from Sue later.

Once we're all buckled in the car, I feel calmer, but my mind is still stuck on this painful epiphany. Em is lost in some no-man's-land. There are no maps or guidebooks for where she stands, at the crossroads. *Maybe* we *need to show her the way,* I think. *But what is the right way? How can we be sure? What if we send her down the wrong path?*

I'm distracted by these thoughts. I wait in the intersection for a car to pass, then press on the gas and drive forward. That's when I see a second car, one that I hadn't noticed, coming up behind the first one, barreling toward the left side of our minivan, the side that holds my four-year-old strapped into her car seat. It's going way too fast for this busy street with schools and moms in cars that contain their whole universe. I have just enough time to think, *It's going to hit us,* as I slam the gas pedal down to the floor.

• 31 •

The Luckiest

My beloved spoke, and said to me, "Rise up, my love, my
fair one, and come away. For lo, the winter's past, the rain
is over and gone."   — SONG OF SONGS 2:10–11

W E WERE MARRIED ONE CLOUDY AFTERNOON IN LATE
August 2005 in Newburyport, a picturesque seaside destination on the northern coast of Massachusetts. "It won't rain," I
said with certainty, though the sky was pendent. Joe, fearing me
overly optimistic, had sent his groomsmen in search of umbrellas
for our guests, "just in case." My prediction was borne out; the
sky remained cloudy, but dry.

We stood, holding hands, on a stone dais overlooking the pier.
In the distance, children ran up and down the park's walkways;
dogs leaped to catch Frisbees; the smell of freshly cut grass wafted
up from the ground, where picnic blankets had been laid out. Behind us was the ocean, tall masts of sailboats standing like church
spires.

Above stretched a length of white tulle, fluttering in the strong
breeze. This was our makeshift chuppah, the Jewish wedding canopy, draped over bamboo poles planted in large flowerpots and
festooned with white impatiens. Joe and I had wanted our cer-

emony to reflect both our families' heritages. The details of the ceremony itself had been enthusiastically and creatively sorted out by our officiants, Deacon John, representing the Catholic Church, and Rabbi Karen, from a Reconstructionist Jewish denomination. Not for a moment did I imagine that the ceremony would satisfy my mother's religious standards. I looked out over the sea of faces; she was not there for a rite that to her was meaningless.

She was, however, in Newburyport. After receiving permission from her rabbi, she had agreed to come to the reception, which we had moved to late evening for her sake, after the Sabbath. She had spent the day, I assumed, at her bed-and-breakfast, having made exacting arrangements with the owner regarding her Sabbath needs.

I shook off any lingering sadness. I was surrounded by people who cared for me and who genuinely rejoiced in this moment.

My father, upright, proud, walking a little too fast, had accompanied me down the aisle. He had looked so handsome, his silver mane smoothed back, dapper in a black tuxedo and bow tie. Joe's father, Paul, had not waited with his son on the dais. He had been diagnosed with pancreatic cancer four months earlier and had died less than two months before our wedding. The shock and grief had accompanied us right up to the day of the wedding, making this day, if possible, even more poignant and meaningful.

This moment felt at the same time both huge and intimate. Once under the canopy, Joe and I were the only ones who existed. When I looked into his eyes and smiled, the smile felt like it was coming from every part of me.

We had both written our vows that very morning, arriving at them in the characteristic last-minuteness that we'd brought to most elements of wedding planning (to Kathy's chagrin). Now it was my turn to recite them. I vowed to view with appreciation each day that we spent together and to take life's adventures together wherever they may lead. Joe vowed to cherish what he referred to as my *Mimi-ness,* the unique spirit that he saw and loved in me. Few things could have made the moment, and the day, more perfect. Even the rain held off, beginning to descend only minutes after the ceremony, once the last picture was taken.

"I don't see her." I turned to Joe. His face tightened, the promise of a storm. We were waiting in the vestibule of the reception hall, and the time had come and gone for the newly minted Mr. and Mrs. Lemay to be introduced for their first dance. My mother was supposed to partake in this part of the celebration, to walk in with one of the groomsmen, but she was not here.

She bailed on me, I thought, my heart dropping. She had been too sad, too overwhelmed. I imagined her sitting in her room in tears, unable to bring herself to come yet distraught over missing my wedding. I knew that she must feel like she had lost me. *I am not lost, Mom,* I wanted to shout. *I am finally found.*

I stood straight and adjusted the layers of my dress. Focus on today, I told myself. This day, this moment, that is all we have. In a minute, I would be dancing with Joe to the song that had been our first and only choice. "The Luckiest," by Ben Folds, had been emblematic of our love since the beginning: "Now I know all the wrong turns, the stumbles, and falls brought me here." I couldn't hear the song without tearing up, thinking about the turns in the road that had seemed like misfortunes at the time but had ultimately brought us together. That is what we were celebrating tonight. I couldn't let my mother take this moment from me.

Suddenly, the door to the vestibule opened, admitting a powerful gust of wind and flecks of summer rain. She stood there looking momentarily confused, her face a skein of tangled lines, the smile she had mastered, the grief she had subdued. She had been caught in the rain that held off until our ceremony was done, and her jacket and wig were dripping. My mother looked at that moment old and defeated. I felt the tug on my heart. I wanted to embrace her, to thank her for changing her mind. For being here, for this acknowledgment, for what it was worth. Before I could approach her, the groomsman gave the word and the sound of trumpets heralded our grand entrance. I was swept forward into the hall.

Two Roads Diverged

"Night comes on, Aeneas. We waste our time with tears.
This is the place where the road divides in two."

— VIRGIL, *The Aeneid*

I HEAR THE HORN FIRST. IT IS ONE LONG, UNWAVERING RE-
buke. Next, the screech of brakes, a scream of desperation. Inside the minivan, all is quiet except the low growl of the engine
pressed to its limit and the sharp intake of my breath. I have time
to think, *Please,* and then, with inches to spare, I pull through the
intersection. The driver of the car that plunges through the va-
cated space is still pressing the horn, but the sound, Doppler-like,
fades into nothingness, as does the vehicle, now far down the road.

"What happened, Mommy?" asks Ella, aware that this is not
the normal course of events for a drive home. "Ooh, that was
scary," I say as I do a quick check in the rearview mirror and
inquire if my passengers are okay. "Okay, Mama," say Ella and
Em reassuringly. Lucia seems fine too, at a glance, though she's
straining at her buckles to look around the car, where objects —
small toys, crayons, and half-empty snack bags — have been dis-
placed. I assure myself that we are intact, that all that's *actually*
happened, to answer Ella's question, is that we have one fairly

shook-up mom and the splayed contents of the diaper bag on the floor. Today will not be a world-ending day.

As I proceed, chastened into extra caution the rest of the route home, I find my mind stuck in an odd loop. It seems caught in a replay of the near collision but with alternate endings, second cuts, where *almost* becomes *did.* In my mind's eye, the left side of our car takes the brunt of the impact, steel door caving inward, glass flying; Em's body is flung against an unyielding mass of metal and she is killed instantly. I can see myself picking up her lifeless body, screaming for her to wake up, to breathe, to come back from wherever she has gone. *Stop it, damn it, stop it,* I will myself, wiping my eyes with my sleeve. I am what Kathy calls "awfulizing," and I need to rein myself in. But as soon as I drag my thoughts away, they turn back.

Now I am at her grave. A small coffin is lowered into the freshly dug earth. I fall on top of it, determined that today, I will be buried here too, under the headstone with her name.

What name?

What should be a simple question is deeply troubling.

What name?

Surely not Em, I realize. If I were to bury my child today, it could not be as Em. It would be an unforgivable betrayal of who she was, of who she fought so valiantly to be.

If you couldn't bury her as Em, why force her to live this way?

The clarity I have sought for so long arrives with a stunning clap.

I know what to do now.

Today my child is with me; tomorrow she may cross that narrow bridge. What would I have wanted to do for her if this were her last day on earth? For whom must she live in shame and suffering, torn in two by internal conflict? Joe and I have vacillated, I can see this now. We have wheedled and engineered this compromise, and in so doing we have forfeited her wholeness and her trust.

Are we too late, though? I worry. Could she still believe in the possibility of a life where she is one person, whole of body and mind?

I hustle the kids out of the car, noting with relief that Joe's car is parked on the street.

Though it's taken me so long to awaken, I feel that I can no longer wait to act.

I stand for some moments at the bottom of the stairs gazing up toward his office, trying to formulate the words I need to say. "Be direct" has been Joe's consistent recommendation. I knock.

"Joe." He turns in his chair, looking up at me inquiringly.

"I think we need to let Em transition — now."

He's silent for a moment, and then he stands up, putting his hands in his pockets. He nods. "Okay."

I'm not expecting this simple agreement. I ask, a hint of suspicion: "What do you mean, okay?"

"I mean, I agree. I think we should let her transition now."

I stare at him.

He lifts a pile of mail off a folding chair and I sit. He tells me the things that have been running through his mind. "You know how the consensus is that somehow it's safer or less risky to wait as long as possible before allowing a kid to transition?" I nod. I have discovered that this idea has a name, watchful waiting. It's analogous to "keeping things fluid."

"I think the reality is exactly the opposite. Think about it." He leans forward. "What's the risk of socially transitioning a kid at the age of four?"

"They could change their mind?"

"Exactly! What's the worst-case scenario if they do?"

"Ugh. I think we'd be known as the crazy parents forever. I guess it would be pretty embarrassing."

"Totally," he says. "Maybe even bad enough that we have to move to another town. But . . . think about it . . . what's the risk if we *wait* another year?"

I nod. I know where he is going with this. It's an excellent articulation of the direction my thoughts have been leading.

"In my view," he continues, "the real risk is in waiting, in forcing her to endure another year of shame and self-loathing. You can't walk that back so easily. That's permanent damage that can lead down a dangerous path.

"With all we know about the risks," Joe concludes, "we can't afford to wait if a transition is what we believe she needs to be happy."

Yes, I think, *this.* If we move now, we risk having to reverse everything — name, pronoun, hair, clothes — back again in the indeterminate future. If we do not move now, we risk a growing darkness, a tragically worn path that has already claimed too many lives.

I reach out my arms for him and we stand, wrapped in each other and in thoughts of the monumental task ahead of us. Then I say what I probably haven't said enough, or at least not sincerely enough, in the past few years: "I am so grateful for you, love. I am so lucky that you are their dad." Today I'm indebted to Joe's infuriatingly level head and his annoying habit of running the numbers on everything.

Now that we can see the path, what's left is the question of how to clear the way so that Em is free to make her own choice — not the one we think is best for her but the one that her heart directs.

"What about that video?" Joe says now. "What if we show her that Ryland kid?"

The messages had been trickling in for a few weeks now; *I saw this and thought of you* is how most of them begin. Even Kathy forwards me the YouTube video of six-year-old Ryland Whittington. *Thought you'd be interested,* she writes, *however difficult . . . but inspiring.*

The first time I watched the video, a homemade slide show depicting one family's journey with the young child who they initially believed was their daughter but who had ended up being their son, I had to pause halfway for a long, full cry. Ryland's parents had explained in the most moving but simple words why they had allowed their kindergartner to transition at the age of five. This was the first case that had come to my attention of a child near Em's age transitioning, and the transformation was profound. Ryland went from an unhappy, lackluster little "girl" with golden ringlets to a radiantly happy, confident boy with a buzzcut.

Joe and I pause in our discussion as my mother, here for her thrice-yearly visit, summons us from downstairs. The time for Friday-night Kiddush is upon us; are we ready for it? I look at Joe and we sigh together. This would be a complicating factor, my mother's presence. How would she deal with a transition? Not well, I suspected. She's raised an eyebrow at Em's shorter hair and our use of the name Mica at home. Em, a keen observer of human nature, had told us on the first day of my mother's visit that she specifically did *not* want her to use the name Mica. My mother, probably relieved, never offered. I had, however, relayed to her what Jennifer Horton said and explained what being transgender meant, to which my mother had speculated that gender confusion no doubt came from the trauma that immodest parents inflicted on their children by walking about the house naked. I hadn't known whether to laugh or scream. I had settled on "First of all, Joe is far more modest than I am, and second, that's a load of crap." No, my mother insisted, offended, there was research. *Everybody* knew.

"Should we wait until she leaves in a few weeks?" I asked Joe now. "No," he answered firmly. "If this is what Em needs, then this is what we'll do. Your mom will just have to fall in line."

Friday-night meals during my mother's visits are hard for me in the ordinary course of things. The kids love the Kiddush and the candles, the smell of freshly baked challah, and the way our house gets an extra once-over. For me, the rituals provoke a sinking sensation, a reminder of a time when my life was squeezed between the words *thou shalt* and *thou shalt not*. This night is no different.

I watch Em during the meal, the way she tucks into her soup, the way she tears chunks off the challah and squeezes them into balls before stuffing them in her mouth, and I can't believe we are at this crossing. But we are, and to hold out for some different future would be at best futile and at worst potentially deadly. There is no tomorrow, I remind myself. There is only today. And these are our choices today.

A week goes by. Ella and Em enjoy the camp that the Purpose School runs for kids during the week and a half before the public schools let out. We think about what we are about to do, the hugeness of it, and we watch for signs that we should reverse course. But none appear.

It is Friday night once more. The Kiddush dinner is nearly over. Joe and I glance at each other across the table. I nod.

"Mica," Joe starts, "Mama and Daddy have something we'd like to show you. Can you come with us to the office?"

Em is practically swallowed up by the big black leather swivel chair in Joe's office. Her feet are barely peeking a few inches over the side of the seat, and I feel a catch in my throat as I see her this way, diminutive in appearance yet so fierce in her demands to be heard. *You really are remarkable,* I think. No matter how long and difficult this struggle has been for us, it is nothing, I realize, compared to how it has felt for her.

Joe's laptop is open on the desk and the video of Ryland is paused on the screen. I glance at the desktop, littered with envelopes and notebooks full of diagrams and jotted ideas. My eyes fall on the Popsicle-stick pencil holder with the glued-on letters and sequins that spell DADDY that is signed by each kid (with a handprint for Lucia). On a shelf above it is the little wooden house

I picked up at the craft store that the kids have painted in a riot of colors, adding blobs of clay to represent each member of our family. There's a mom and a dad standing on the front stoop in the middle holding a roughly baby-shaped object. On either side of the house is a door out of which a figure bursts. One figure has long hair and is wearing a pink dress; the other wears dark shorts and a blue shirt and has shortish (but not short enough, its creator maintains) dark hair. Each figure has tiny painted specks for eyes. *What will happen to these keepsakes?* I wonder briefly.

Joe presses Play and we both hang back while I read Em the words that come across the screen. Em stares, betraying little emotion, as the story begins with the birth of a baby girl. When I reach the words *As soon as Ryland could speak, she would scream, "I am a boy!,"* my voice thickens with tears, but Em is still as a stone and just as emotionless, though her eyes are locked on the screen.

I hear her voice again after we view a short video clip where Ryland, now around three and playing with his sister in the bath, clearly says: "She is my sister, and I am her *brudder.*" "Can you play that again?" Em asks quietly. Joe and I glance at each other. "Sure, buddy," he says, and he plays it again and then, when she insists, once more. Her eyes widen a fraction at the appearance of Ryland as a handsome, smiling boy not much older than Em.

When the video concludes and Joe stops it, the room is quiet. Em lowers her gaze from the laptop to her hands in her lap. When she looks up, my heart sinks, because I can see that the hood is back, the invisible curtain that drops over her expressive eyes, the one that sets down the million-yard stare, that says she's not home for visitors.

"Mica," I say gently, taking her hands in mine. "What do you think about that boy?" I ask, my voice catching. "Would you like . . . to be like that, with everyone knowing you're a boy?" Joe affirms my words. This is a possibility, he tells Em.

The telltale twist drags at Em's mouth as her eyes darken. "I can't," she says dully. "I have to be Em. I can be what I want at home and at the grocery store, but I *have* to be Em at school."

And just like that, she has slipped away, retreating back into the make-believe world we have created for her, where we pull the strings and she dances, satisfying the script that tells her what she is and who she must be regardless of what she *knows* and *experiences.*

I kneel in front of her, my eyes level with hers. "Look at me, baby," I plead. When she does, I can see the curious color of her eyes, the dark greenish brown of the forest floor, almond-shaped like my father's. *God, she is beautiful,* I think, and the beauty, I know, has little to do with eye shape or color.

"*I believe you,*" I say, and the tears start to fall again. "*We believe you.*"

Joe draws close, nodding. "We didn't always understand, and we might not always understand it all, but we believe you." She does not speak, but neither does she look away. I realize I am holding my breath, afraid to break this moment with a sound or a movement.

"There's always going to be people who say you can't do something," Joe continues. "I've been told that plenty of times. So has your mom. But you need to ask yourself what is the right thing for you and forget about what everyone else thinks." *This is his moment,* I think, remembering those early days when I would shut my eyes as he skillfully whirled a laughing toddler in the air. *This is their death spiral and he's got her tight.*

"You have a choice," he says now to the four-year-old who is so still, she appears to be carved from stone. "You can stay at your school and they can call you Em, if that's what you really want, or we can have them call you another name, if that's what you choose. *Or,*" he continues, "we can send you to a *new* school with a new class, where they will only know you as a boy."

I can see the words as they make landfall. When Joe presents the third option, a fresh start, there is a distinct shift. It's her eyes that tell us what is coming next. They are hood-up, open, alive. Then come the words, the ones that change everything, in an instant, for all of us.

"I want to be a boy *always*," he says. "A boy named Jacob."

• 33 •

A Boy Named Jacob

Marvel not that I said unto thee, ye must be born again.

— JOHN 3:7

O KAY," SAYS JOE, GRINNING DOWN AT HIS SON. "OKAY, buddy, that's what we're going to do. *Jacob* . . . I like it." He holds his arms out for Jacob, who hesitates a split second, then comes in for a hug. I move in on them, wrapping my arms around both. *My boys,* I think. The buoyancy of relief and the weight of sadness are a strange combination. *Alea iacta est.*

When Jacob wriggles out, I ask him where he came up with the name Jacob. It's not one he's used before. At first, he shrugs. "School?" he asks. There aren't any Jacobs in his class, but maybe in another? I can't help feeling a twinge of anxiety about this name. Jacob is no Morgan or Dylan; it's a chest-thumping, loin-girding, red-blooded male name. No ambiguity there. Still, I think about the courage it has taken for him to tell us what he wants, and I am afraid to even whisper another suggestion. I know that when I said I believed him, it was not just a statement but a promise.

"You're a brave little boy," I say, and the joy of using this hard-won word, *boy,* that has been denied for so long, the rightness of it, feels good, and from the look on his face, I can see that it feels good for him too. Next steps, I think, trying to corral my thoughts. What do we do next?

"Do you want us to tell your sisters and Bubby about . . . Jacob, or do you want to tell them?" I ask. "You tell them," he says, suddenly frowning again, "but not *yet.*" I glance at Joe over Jacob's head and he shrugs. He doesn't seem perturbed by the unmistakably male name or Jacob's reticence to share it with his grandmother and siblings.

When we come downstairs, Jacob bounces down, two feet at a time, followed by Joe, then myself. Bubby has given the girls (*the girls;* that feels odd now that it refers to a different subset of my children) some soy ice cream bars for dessert and Jacob asks for one as well. He is hopping from one foot to the other and twirling as he waits for the treat. Joe raises an eyebrow and I smile at him. After the snack and teeth-brushing, when we finally wrestle Jacob under the covers, I whisper in his ear, "Good night, *Jacob,*" and he smiles up at me, a thousand kilowatts of four-year-old goodness.

"Why doesn't he want to tell the others about Jacob?" I ask Joe as we huddle downstairs on the couch. "He's scared," Joe answers. "Wouldn't you be?" "Yeah, I guess so." I lean on Joe's shoulder. "Actually, I'm fucking terrified."

"I'm going to miss her," he says, taking the words right out of my mouth. "Me too," I say. "Joe?" I ask a few minutes later, because I can't let it go. "What do you think about the name Jacob?" "I like it," he answers. "It's not my favorite but it's nice." "No," I say, "I mean that it's not unisex . . . that it's all-out *boy.*"

"Do you want him to go with another name?"

"Maybe," I say, frowning. I don't want to give him the impression that we are not fully behind him, but I do want some more wiggle room, I realize. *Here I am, the one with cold feet.* I didn't expect to be the one with cold feet.

And it's possible, I think, given Jacob's request to wait on any announcements, that I'm not the only one.

• • •

Jacob wakes up the next morning earlier than usual. By the time Joe and I are downstairs, he's already hard at work making *something*. There are reels of Scotch tape, Popsicle sticks, and about twelve big red plastic cups out on the floor of the kitchen. For a moment I stop in the doorway to watch. Whatever he's doing, he's concentrating on it intently. "Good morning, love," I say, and he looks up and smiles. "Mama, look, I'm making an invention," he says. "What does it do?" I ask, my heart fluttering because he's still carrying about him this energy, this sense of *presentness*, that I haven't seen before. "Lotsa things," he answers. "Mostly it can fly." Trying to sound casual, I say: "Hey, sweetie, the name Jacob is great, but I thought of a cooler one!" "What?" he asks, his face tightening. "Jonah!" I say. "It's less common than Jacob and that makes it *rare,* and super-cool, and," I assure him, "it's a boy's name." There's a little lie embedded in there, but he can't know that. Sure, it's a boy name in this country, but in Israel, Yonah, meaning "dove," is primarily a girl's name. He shrugs. "Nah." "Just keep an open mind about it, okay, hon? We can talk more later."

That morning, Joe and I call Kathy to tell her the news.

"Wow," she says. She wants to know everything, every detail, and then she says, her voice lowering: "I'm going to miss her. I bet you're going to miss her too." "Of course," I answer, "badly. "But . . ." I grasp for words. "*She* wasn't real. Not the way *he* is. I can see that already."

Joe adds, leaning over the phone, "Yes, he's just . . . so *alive.*"

"You're both very brave," says Kathy. "I want to let you know how proud I am of you." Her voice breaks for a brief moment. "Your dad would have been proud, Joe." Joe laughs. "That is, if he didn't think we were all crazy," he responds, but then adds quietly, "Thanks, Mom. That means a lot. We need you now more than ever."

On Monday, Joe accompanies me to an appointment I made at the Purpose School. Jacob is home with my mother, but first we drop Ella off for one of two days of camp that week. Kristie is in her office doing paperwork and getting ready to close the school for the summer. She moves aside a few boxes and pulls up some chairs. I'm anxious and my stomach is a mess, as it has been for days. Kristie closes the door behind us and says, in a sympathetic tone, "So . . . tell me what's going on."

Joe looks at me. I've been the liaison at school for the past few years, the one who attends PTO meetings and conferences. This one's mine. I nod to him and begin to tell our news, but I have to grab a tissue because of course I'm tearing up. "We had a talk with Em," I start again, "and" — I falter, unsure of what pronoun to use — "she . . . he wants to live as a boy."

That's when Kristie interrupts, and her voice is brisk, on the verge of curt. "I know this is upsetting, but you need to focus on the fact that at least your child is healthy. There are parents out there who can't say that much."

The scolding smarts; I am suddenly ashamed of my tears. Then I remember a conversation I overheard, moms talking about a child at the school being treated for a life-threatening disease. *She must think I'm making such a big deal over this,* I think, *when she's worried for this other kid's life.* "I realize that." I nod, blushing. "But what I'm trying to say is that Em wants to transition, but not at the Purpose School. I don't think we'll be back next year."

It's Kristie's turn to look visibly upset, and she's one of the people I respect most in this world, so I'm feeling steadily worse. "Why don't you wait until the end of the summer to decide?" she asks. She tells me then that she remembers they had a pre-K kid who said he was a girl for a while but that he outgrew it by the end of the first month of kindergarten. What if Em is going through a similar stage? I can tell she's holding something back by the way she bites her lip, but whatever it is, she's not telling us.

That's when Joe cuts in, sensing my distress. "These are all good questions and we've thought about them," he says. "This has been a struggle for us for a long time. We feel that he knows who he is and that we need to support that now. If he changes his mind, then we'll support that too." Kristie nods and says, a little stiffly: "Okay, if that's what you think you need to do. You know we will miss you here." As she's escorting us out of the office, she asks, "What name did she . . . he . . . pick?" "Jacob," I answer. "That's a nice name," she says. I nod and attempt to smile too. She wishes us luck and I know that she's trying to find the right thing to say, but, like me, she's deeply shaken.

Is this the way it's going to be, I think, *even with our closest friends?*

The next morning when I drop Ella off again, Kristie is waiting for me at the door to the school. She looks pale, and her eyes are red. She asks if she can have a minute. She's visibly nervous. I'm nervous too.

Once we're in her office, Kristie closes the door behind her and her eyes fill with tears. "I couldn't sleep last night," she begins. "I was wrong. I'm sorry about the way I reacted . . ." I reach out to hug her, but she's not done. "I was surprised and worried for all of you, and I . . . I think a part of me didn't want *you* to give up on *us,* didn't want to admit that we weren't right for . . . Jacob anymore. You know we love your children, all your children, and we always will." "I know," I say, "and I am so grateful that you care enough about Jacob to feel this way and to express it." Then we're both wiping at our tears and promising to keep in touch often. Kristie and the teachers and staff have been our extended family for the past three years. I think they'll be there for us if we need them again. Kristie confirms this: "Hey, if it doesn't work out in the new school, you *always* have a place here. We will figure something out." I am grateful. I know that this would be difficult, as the school has a waiting list a dozen deep before the start of summer.

After camp that day, I take Ella for a drive to Dunkin' Donuts and get her a cup of Munchkins. When we pull into our driveway, I let the car idle.

I turn to her. "Ella, big, brave, wonderful sister . . ." I begin.

"I'm not going to have a sister anymore?" Her eyes are wide, brimming with tears. "I don't want to lose Em," she says plaintively and the tears fall. "She's not going anywhere," I assure her again, but I'm crying now too, which isn't helping either of us. "She's *always* going to be *yours,* your sibling, we're just going to call her by a new name, and use *he* when we talk about her — I mean him." This pronoun thing is harder than I thought. I hope it will be easier when we don't go back and forth anymore.

"It's not going to be the same," Ella says solemnly, the tears cutting tracks down her face. "No," I say, sighing, "it's not going to be exactly the same. But I think, Ella, I hope, that it's going to be even better. I hope your brother is going to be happier now."

She nods, looking up at me, on the verge of a new round of tears. After taking a shuddering breath she says, "That's good for him but sad for me." "I know," I answer, "and it's okay to feel that way. I feel like that too." It would be impossible not to feel this way. I am so proud of her, I realize. She has handled this with more grace than we could have, or even should have, expected. I pull her out of the car seat and onto my lap and we rock until she picks up her head and gives me a wobbly smile. "Let's go inside and see that Jacob boy, Mama."

That evening Joe is out with friends and I'm relieved for him. He's had a rough couple of months, working double time to get ready to launch his company and dealing with this new stress in parenting. This is the perfect opportunity to have a discussion with my mom about the changes ahead.

When I get downstairs after tucking the kids into bed, I find my mom in our dining room, sitting at the end of the table, reading.

Most of her evenings in our home are spent this way, usually with a book of *mussar,* a morality guide, or the weekly Torah portion. Her routine has been the same for every visit: reading, dinner, reading, upstairs for a shower, and in bed by nine. I've made several successful attempts to break her of her routine, to draw her into the living room with Joe and me, but I can tell she'd prefer her books, so more often than not, I leave her to them.

I take a deep breath, then a deeper sip from the glass of red wine that I have poured for myself. She looks up at me, curiously.

"Mom," I start. "I want to fill you in on some things that are going on now with . . . Em."

She'll never live a normal life.
   You're pushing her down a path of no return.
   This is a social fad and you've fallen for it!
   It's part of an agenda to destroy normal family life.
Some of these are doubts that have plagued me too, so I'm prepared to answer them as calmly as I can. What helps is that I have seen *him,* and I, too, am starting to believe.

I reiterate the things I have learned about transgender kids. They *can* live normal lives, I say, if they are supported and affirmed in their identities, and that's what we intend to do for Jacob. What kind of normal life did my mother think he could have if he were forced to live, day in and day out, as the person he knew himself not to be? And no, Joe and I were not pushing *her* to be or do anything; we had finally, after nearly two years of compromise, cleared the way for our child to make *his* own choice. The door was open now and would remain open. He knew that he could reverse course if he wanted to. We had been clear about this and would continue to be clear.

"You can't make someone transgender or not, just like you can't make someone gay or not," I say, knowing full well that the set of beliefs she ascribes to preach precisely that. About the agenda? I'm not sure to what she's referring, and it turns out neither is she.

When I ask to see evidence of this agenda and where I might read more about it, she is momentarily flummoxed, then she rallies, accusing me angrily of mocking her words. I sigh and mentally prepare to disengage.

That is when she adds: "I'm not calling her anything but Em until she asks me to," and suddenly my vision blurs and I'm shaking with anger, yelling, maybe even loud enough to wake the kids: "Don't you understand *anything?* How *stupid* are you? He's not going to ask *you* to. He *knows* you don't believe him!"

Then I think about "Jonah," and I realize that my faith in my son may also be less than pristine. There may well be nothing in the world that can ameliorate these doubts, I think sadly. I might just need to learn to live with them.

• 34 •

On a Dark Night

The wound is the place where the Light enters you.

— JALAL AD-DIN MUHAMMAD AR-RUMI, *Mathnawi*

LATER IN THE WEEK, JOE PROMISES TO TAKE JACOB FOR a haircut. "As short as I want?" asks Jacob eagerly. "Yes," I answer, and my smile is real, because over the past few days I have watched nothing short of a miracle unfolding.

"It's like a light switch just flipped on," Joe whispers, excitement in his voice, and I concur. "Who knew he could *talk* so much?" Jacob's been chattering nonstop, like he's been saving up his words and now the dam has burst. Suddenly he's noticing the sparrows nesting in the rhododendron bush and the green buds sprouting yellow flowers in the tree outside our living-room window. He wants to know *everything* about *everything,* and he wants to know right now! *What's that, Mommy? Why does this do that?* "Look! Look!" He's wearing us out with his pointing finger but we don't care. We're giddy with joy too. *What cloud were you living under, buddy?* I think at times with sadness, *I wish we had helped you sooner.*

Not everything's been perfect, or simple; far from it. My mom has been avoiding using a name at all for Jacob since we broke the news. She's been referring to him as "this one" or "kid" or "child," as in "Oh, would you look how clever *this one* is!" and "Hey, big kid!"

"This is getting ridiculous," I fume to Joe.

And to my surprise, Ella is having a hard time with the name. We have less than a week left before the start of a new camp but Ella calls her brother Em about six times out of ten, and I'm starting to panic. "I'm sorry!" she says. "I keep forgetting!" "We understand," Joe tells her. "But you need to practice more. We can't send you both to camp next Monday if you're using the wrong name." Joe's upped the ante now, but we're still bumbling about a few days later, and everyone's getting frustrated.

"How will the other kids know to call me Jacob?" asks Jacob. I'm taken aback. He knows we've changed his name on the camp registration. "Oh!" I say, realizing what he means. "You just need to *introduce* yourself as Jacob. Here, let's practice," I say, sticking out my hand. "Hi, my name is Mimi. What's yours?" "Hi, my name is Jacob," he says, taking my hand and adding, without missing a beat, "and I'm a boy."

Ella and Joe have been watching this, and Ella starts to giggle, then laugh uproariously. I'm trying not to laugh, but it's just too funny. "You goofball!" says Joe. "You don't need to *say* that you're a boy. They can tell that just by looking at you!" Jacob beams again. "Okay, ask me now," he demands. Joe obliges, and with a goblin grin, Jacob announces: "Hello, my name is Jacob!" Pause. "And *I'm a boy!*" Then he falls over laughing. What comes out isn't a titter or a giggle but an expansive, gurgling brook of a guffaw, a full-bodied, sidesplitting, tear-inducing howl. *What a beautiful sound,* I think. *I haven't heard this sound before.*

We practice over and over until the laughter peters out, and then somebody farts, and off we go again.

"Seriously, what should Jacob do if Ella calls him Em?" I ask when we've all caught our breath. "Just ignore her?" suggests Joe. "Hmm ... I wish there was some way we could remind her," I muse. Suddenly, I have an idea. "Jacob! Run upstairs and pick two of your favorite T-shirts," I command. "We're going to have your name printed on them! That way Ella can see your name when she's talking to you!" Joe agrees. "That's it!" The kids are excited. Ella wants a shirt too, of course, so they dash up the stairs to pick the T-shirts out while I start checking for local screen-printing shops. I find one a few blocks from the Purpose School that I'm familiar with and determine that they can fill rush orders. Bingo! We're in business!

"What name did you want?" asks the elderly gentleman behind the counter at Ultimate Design Apparel. "Jacob," I answer, "I think." He doesn't seem to catch my hesitation as he helps me fill out the form. For the next few minutes we talk about fonts and thread colors. He tells me they can turn the T-shirts around in a few days.

When I pull up in the driveway, I can hear screams coming from the house. As I open the front door, Jacob bursts out of the sunroom, face red and twisted with furious tears. My mother runs in from the kitchen, ready to intercept him. "She *refuses* to listen," she fumes. *Of course* she *does,* I think with a burst of anger, *because you're refusing to call* him *by his proper name and you're making no effort at all on pronouns.* I manage to broker a détente of sorts, but it leaves both my mother and Jacob sulking.

The phone rings. Relieved, I race upstairs to answer it. It's Jennifer Horton, our therapist. The day that Jacob had chosen his name, I'd phoned and left an emergency message: "Please call as soon as you can. It looks like we're going ahead with a transition." When I thank her for getting back to me, she apologizes for taking so long. She was at a health-care conference focused on transgender topics. "That's okay," I say breathlessly, and I fill her in on all of it: the realization that living in limbo was harming Jacob, the video of Ryland, and Jacob's choice. "I know you said keep things fluid," I conclude, a little nervous, "but Joe and I both felt that the time was now."

When I'm done, Jennifer says, "I'm glad that you reached out to me because I have more concrete information to offer you. There was some groundbreaking new research shared at the conference that sheds light specifically on kids Jacob's age who question their gender." She pauses, then sighs. "It appears that in the past, our profession has done a real disservice to young children presenting as transgender."

Then Jennifer tells me that mental-health professionals across the country have been tracking the appearance of younger and younger kids with signs of genuine gender dysphoria, and researchers were seeing evidence that the strength of gender cognition in these young children equaled that of their cisgender peers — that is, children whose gender identities corresponded with the sex they'd been assigned at birth. In other words, a transgender boy and a cisgender boy identify equally strongly with the male gender. This contradicted the assumption that young children did not have a strong awareness of their own gender and that watchful waiting was the correct response.

"So showing Jacob that you trust him fully is probably the best thing you could have done," Jennifer says. I ask now, exposing my own hesitation, "You know, I guess I do feel ambivalent about something. Not the transition itself, just the name. Jacob is so male. Not a name with any wiggle room. I just don't know what's right." She gives it some thought. "There's merit to each way," she says finally and, I think, not particularly helpfully, though I realize she can't really tell me what to do here. "There's something to be said for showing him your commitment to his choice, but on the other hand, it's reasonable for you to ask for a name that feels safer for you — most kids don't get to choose their own names."

That evening Joe takes my mom out for a long walk. "She's being obstructive at this point," he'd said. They're out for about a half an hour and the sun is starting to go down and I'm getting ner-

vous. She finally comes back alone, distracted and overly cheerful. I text Joe: *What happened?*

She'll call him Jacob, he answers briefly, then he tells me he's
headed out to blow off some steam at the rock-climbing gym. Oh
my.

When we're in bed I ask, "How did you get her to agree?"
"Well, at first, she didn't," Joe admits. "She told me the same
thing about waiting for Jacob to ask her. I explained, like you did,
that we didn't think he was confident enough, and that's when she
gave me all her objections. I tried to be polite and answer them
but in the end, I just gave up and said, 'Look, Judith, if you're going to be visiting with the kids, and we hope you will, you need
to call him Jacob.' She looked at me then and said, 'Well, I need
to obey the man of the house.' And that was it." He rolls his eyes,
then jokes, "Hey, maybe she's onto something; maybe you should
listen to me more. I'm the man of the house!" "Shut up," I say,
swatting him.

The next morning dawns and for the first hour or so, my mother's still using filler names. "Hey, you!" she says teasingly when
Jacob snags a snack off the counter. At the point when my nerves
are frayed, around noon, I overhear her calling her grandson Jacob. I close my eyes in gratitude. I broach the topic gingerly that
evening. "Thanks for using Jacob's name."

"I hope you know what you're doing," she responds, pursing
her lips, and for once, I don't get mad, because I hope so too. I
keep clinging to the reality of what we're seeing, the resurrection
that is unfolding.

Some changes are seismic, others subtle. He's started showing off his knowledge of phonics: "Hey, Mama! That letter makes
a *ha* sound!" He's peppering us with requests to go places and
try new things: Can we go for a hike? Can we go to the store?
Can I try that? What's this for? Suddenly his pockets are ripping,
they're so full of junk, screws, feathers, wild mushrooms, washers,
detritus that I have to catch before they gum up a load of laun-

dry. "Jacob's treasures," we've taken to calling them as each day he lays out his haul. I find myself scanning the ground as I run errands, looking for scraps of anything that might pique his interest. Then there are the changes that we mark by their absence, those odd behaviors that begin to disappear within days of my son's arrival.

Kathy drops in one afternoon and after an hour pulls me aside. "Did you notice he's not *barking* anymore?" In all the tumult of change, it had escaped my notice. When our neighbors Janice and Carolyn come by to take my mother for a walk, a ritual they've developed, he answers their greeting with one of his own, a simple if shy "Hello." The crooked elbow lingers for a week or two, then it, too, evaporates into anecdotal history.

We are nearly a week into the transition the first time Jacob asks an adult to call him Jacob. I give Sensei Kevin a heads-up before Jacob's private karate lesson starts. Kevin's a quiet, slender young man who does a great job with the kids and seems to have an endless supply of patience. I'm almost frustrated when he doesn't ask me follow-up questions, because I'd rather he do that than go off thinking I'm nuts. Nonetheless, I'm delighted when Jacob asks him shyly to call him Jacob and he answers, "Sure thing. Now let's practice our stances," and they go on with the lesson like nothing happened.

But that afternoon, during the lesson, I sneak out to the car, call the embroidery shop, and ask them, if they haven't already completed the order, to put the T-shirts on hold. I feel like a heel, a total jerk, but the anxiety is burning a hole in my gut. I know he's happy, I can see it, but what if this is just temporary relief? What if my mother's right and somehow his being called Jacob will close off an option for return that I can't foresee? What if there's another path that I haven't discovered?

I feel nearly immobilized as the day wears on. I'm losing some of the energy that came with the adrenaline of change. I keep watching him and wondering what to do, picking at a mental scab. Finally, I broach the topic with Jacob directly. I tell him I love the name Jonah and it means a lot to me. I ask him to please, *please* consider it. When he says "Okay, Jonah," unenthusiastically, I'm surprised that I don't feel much relief. Nonetheless, I go to my room and call the embroiderers back again, hoping they haven't closed yet. "Can you please change the name to Jonah?" I ask, and I spell it out. "Oh . . . kayyy," says the woman on the other end, who must be confused about why we wouldn't know what name to put on a size 5 T-shirt from Carter's. "Are you sure?" I feel like tearing my hair out. No, I am not sure. That's the problem. I say, "You know what, I'm so sorry, but can you wait until tomorrow morning? Please?"

After I hang up I notice that Kathy's called to say good night to the kids. I call her back and she remarks that I sound anxious. I tell her I'm sick to my stomach over what to do. I don't want to pull back, but I can't walk forward. I'm stuck.

"Pray," she says simply. This doesn't feel like a constructive answer, but I don't want to be rude. "Okay," I say, but she must sense my insincerity, "*Listen,*" she says, "I can't tell you the number of times I've gone to bed with no clue of how to dig myself out of a hole and woken up with the answer, *clear as the day.* Just pray. The last thing before you go to bed tonight, pray for an answer."

I go to bed that night like I always do — without prayer.

It's not something I can explain to Kathy, but I'm pretty sure I already know any answer God would give, and I'm not interested in hearing it. The God I know doesn't appreciate anyone stepping outside the script when it comes to gender, and He certainly wouldn't approve of me breaking the rules altogether with my son, I was certain. *I'm on my own here,* I think.

I'm running down the narrow hallway connecting the thirteen row houses. My floor-length skirt makes a slapping sound against my legs, occasionally wrapping itself around them — a python binding its prey — and I stumble. There are sem girls clustered in the hall and in doorways. They are slowing me down, so I duck and dodge, ignoring friendly calls. I am nearly at the classroom door. There is a clock on the wall, but I cannot see the time because the face is blurred. *I'm late,* I think.

"You're *late!*" declares the tall reedy girl with the hawk-like nose and a thin, clipped British accent. What is her name? Esti something? She is this term's class representative. With her watery blue eyes and bland attire, she is a paragon of virtue and unappealing plainness.

"The *rav* is almost here!" she continues sharply. "He is halfway up the stairs!" Her words seem to hover in the air, angry. I hang my head and go to my desk. The room is silent as Rabbi Miller enters, old and wizened. With effort he makes his way up the podium and sits down. With scrabbling fingers, he turns the page of the ancient book that is in front of him and says, in a voice full of cracks: "Miss Netzer, would you do us the honor of reading the *posuk*?"

I glance down at the verse, my finger ready on the text. My eyes widen. The words, even the book itself, have vanished, replaced by a single white napkin. Where is the text I am supposed to read? I stammer as I flip the napkin over quickly. On its back is a crossword puzzle of sorts, but with only two words, and the squares are already filled in, the letters written in a classical Hebrew script. The word that marches downward reads *Eh-hieh* — "I will be." Across it, sharing an aleph, the first letter of the alphabet, is *Ai-ekha* — "Where are you?"

Instinctively, I place my hands over the napkin, shielding its message from prying eyes. Has anyone noticed?

I stand up quickly and walk, trying not to draw attention to myself, toward the classroom door. Nonetheless, turned heads and sharp gazes follow me, rustles and murmurs. I am almost out. Just as I reach the row nearest the exit, Esti rises wrathfully to block my passage. She grabs my arm. In a panic, I shove her violently and she hits her head on the door frame with a horrific clap. I open my mouth to apologize, to beg for forgiveness, but then I remember the cocktail napkin balled in my sweaty fist, and I start to run. Arms like coils reach out to hold me back, but, twisting my body and ducking, I escape the room. Back through the hallways I race. Sometimes I leap, weightless, but other times I am dragged down by cumbersome flesh. Was this hallway always so long? Where is the exit? I must leave. I have stayed too long.

When I wake up, heart pounding, my first thought after getting my bearings is *I've had* this *dream before, the one about the crossword puzzle on a napkin.*

Though it's the middle of the night, I suddenly feel wide awake, almost jittery. My subconscious mind is telling me something, I'm sure. It's practically shouting. I decide to locate the notebook with the original dream. (I've been a meticulous recorder of dreams for a good part of my life.) I slip out of bed, grab a hooded sweatshirt, and head up into the chilly attic.

Our attic is indeed a hoarder's paradise, as Joe has lamented. I must shove aside several piles of boxes and big storage bags to make it to the back, where, under the eaves, wire cages hold many of the books I have carted with me from various iterations of my life. My diaries are still packed in a box, and when I pry it open, plumes of dust shoot up, making me sneeze. I turn on a lamp and start to read, quickly skimming the entries.

It's a while before I find it, in a diary covered with a piece of tartan wool that I had glued to the cover for decoration.

October 7, 1997

Had some strange and awesome dreams on Rosh Hashanah. Three, in fact, that I recall. The awesome one — that an iron fell down on a white napkin — and I turned it over, and there, burnt into the reverse, was like a waffle-iron pattern of boxes, the words, intersecting each other like a crossword puzzle (though upside down), were my name spelled in Hebrew characters, *Mimi,* and *Ai-ekha.*

Ai-ekha.
Where are you?
When Adam partakes of the forbidden fruit from the Tree of Knowledge of Good and Evil, God calls to him, "Where are you?" Adam replies, "I heard Your voice in the Garden, and being na-ked, I was afraid, so I hid." According to the commentaries, Adam became aware of the shame of his nakedness only because he'd defied God's command and eaten from the Tree of Knowledge.

I had long believed my own sin to be a similar theft, lusting af-ter knowledge that was not intended for me.

But what about the second phrase in my recent dream? *Ai-ekha* was crossed with *Eh-hieh.* Standing alone, *Eh-hieh* is clearly in the future tense: "I *will* be." However, in the phrase's most sig-nificant usage in the Torah, the rabbis chose to interpret it in the present tense: "I *am.*"

Moses, the prophet, asks God at the Burning Bush, "What name should I give when I tell the people of Israel about You?" The answer had always sounded flippant to me, a brushoff de-signed to shut down further inquiry. *I am that I am,* and . . . stop asking questions.

Suddenly, an idea sings out to me.

Was it possible? Truly, if one were to be pedantic, *Eh-hieh* was in the future tense, Biblical Hebrew not having a present tense for the verb *to be.* One might therefore read the line not as "I *am* that I *am*" but "I *will* be that which I *will* be." Was it possible that God was referring to Himself not as what He was or is but as *what He will become?*

If so, God's message to Israel was "Don't try to pin me down with a name that will define Me, because *I will in the future be a new Self, a different Being than I am today.*"

God evolving? It sounds blasphemous, against everything I have been taught of His immutability, but in the chilly attic surrounded by night, it also sounds beautiful and, somehow, right.

And suddenly, a door that I have slammed and held shut for almost twenty years opens. For the first time in a long while, I feel an urgent need to communicate with the presence that has dogged me since my youth. The mystery that is my son has frozen me in my tracks. I want to move forward but I am afraid. What's at stake feels bigger than anything in my life. It is *my child's* life. For this alone, I decide, for this alone I will ask for a miracle.

What are You trying to tell me?

I pick the small book up off the wire shelves, where I knew it would be. It's nearly as thick as it is wide, and it fits into my palm.

This pocket-size Torah, a parting gift from a seminary friend called Tzirel, long ago lost its hard cover. The first and last pages are now coated with clear contact paper so that on its front the beginning verses of Genesis are visible and on the back the last words of the Book of Chronicles. Wedged between its 1,881 pages are 39 distinct books, 929 chapters, and 23,099 verses. In the Jewish faith, it is one of three legs upon which the world stands, the history of all that ever was and a blueprint to all that ever will be.

I shut my eyes tight and flip the pages back and forth several times like I'm shuffling a deck of cards, the breeze blowing the small hairs that stand on end on my neck. Blinded thus, I might as well be on the edge of a cliff on a dark planet with no sun.

"Show me," I say, stepping off.

And He does.

• 35 •

Nahapochu

A person often meets his destiny on the road he took to
avoid it. — JEAN DE LA FONTAINE, *Fables*

M Y HANDS ARE TREMBLING AS I LIFT THEM FROM THE
book to cover my face. I begin to cry, and the tears are sweet
and cleansing, not sad. The book lies open before me, and I put
my fingers back on the verse they found.

And Isaac said to his son: "How is it that thou hast found it so
quickly, my son?" And he said, "Because the Lord thy God
brought it to me."

Genesis, chapter 27. Isaac, old and blind, his faculties fading,
has been sitting in a tent waiting for his elder son, Esau, to bring
him the game upon which they will feast to bind the birthright
covenant Isaac will bequeath to him. But it is not his elder son
who comes to him now; it is Esau's younger twin, Jacob, disguised
as Esau in his brother's fur cloak and animal skins.

Jacob greets his father, and Isaac pauses, suspicious, confused.
He reaches for his son, touches the cloak and the animal skins. It
feels like the hirsute Esau, but the voice — surely that is Jacob's?

Furthermore, he has just sent Esau out to hunt. How can he have returned so fast with game? He asks, "How is it that thou hast found it so quickly, my son?" Jacob has a response at the ready, but he answers a question that Isaac had not known to ask. His father's heart is as blind as his eyes and he cannot see that God wills his younger son to claim the birthright.

Jacob says simply: "Because the Lord thy God brought it to me."

Indeed, it is God Himself who has engineered this moment, because sometimes parents are blind to the true nature of their children.

Like Isaac, I too have been blind, about many things.

With the gift of a son dressed in the skin of another, I am suddenly aware of the truth of it all. That I, too, am loved. That for my path in life, there was never a need for me to ask forgiveness, only, perhaps, to give thanks, because every step was meant to be just as it was.

Nahapochu — all is reversed.

It is all so simple and clear that I must laugh.

My Jacob, my son, could not have survived the world that I escaped. His light would surely have been diminished or worse, put out.

I *had* to leave.

I was *intended* to leave.

It was my leaving that brought this child to me, not as a punishment but as a most sacred gift. And he has arrived, *not a moment too soon,* not a moment too late, bringing with him my own redemption.

A Brave New World

Eadem mutata resurgo [Though changed, I rise the same]

— EPITAPH ON THE TOMBSTONE OF JAKOB BERNOULLI

I CALL THE EMBROIDERY STORE AS SOON AS IT OPENS AND ask, "Is it too late or can we still go with Jacob?"

"It's not too late. But if you want them by Monday you can't change your mind again." It sounds like the same lady from yesterday evening, and she's justifiably annoyed. When I apologize profusely, she warms up. "That's okay, sweetheart. We want to make sure we get it just right. Now are you *sure?*" she asks one more time. "Yes," I answer, smiling to myself. "I am sure, and I'm sure that I'm sure!"

Today, I have a pretty significant task. I've gotten a response back to the e-mail I sent my friend Jill, whose daughter recently graduated from the large public preschool in our town last year. Jill is what my stepfather would have called a *macher,* someone who knows people and knows how to deal with them too. I had written to her about the transition and asked if she could introduce me to the preschool director, Donna, ASAP. This situation called for some finesse. I had a kid to get into school for September and it was June. When I read through Jill's e-mail again, I started to tear up: *Anything you need, Mike and I are here for you guys.*

I e-mail the director, and my words sound so breezy and confident that I have to grin.

> We are looking to enroll our son in your pre-K program rather late and find ourselves in an unusual predicament. We are very happy in our current preschool . . . yet following two years of seeking advice and biding our time, we have reached the conclusion that our son, who is transgender (born a girl), may very well need a fresh start in order to transition to his genuine gender identity.

Satisfied, I press Send.

I receive a call from Donna within hours. Jill assured me she has a warm heart, and I find this to be the case. "We'll put Jacob on the waiting list," she says. "I'm afraid you'll have to take whatever day/time options are available." "That's fine," I tell her quickly. The very next day I get a confirmation: Jacob has a spot, if we want it, for five days a week from nine to one. That's more hours than I wanted, and it will come with a hefty price tag at a time when Joe is leaving his old employer, but we have no choice. "Yes," I say. "I'll take it."

That afternoon I bring the paperwork over to the school. I sit in my car in the large, curving driveway with the big manila envelope, double-checking to make sure the information is correct.

One line remains blank. I have left it for the very end. It's the space where you fill in your child's name, first, middle, and last.

JACOB JOSEPH LEMAY. The pen wobbles a bit and a small hiccup of pain escapes from me during my next breath. Writing makes it official. Em is gone.

Feeling sure this is right does not mean, I realize, that there is no pain. I dab at my eyes and tell myself sharply, *Keep it together.*

Once I'm positive I won't cry, I check the mirror in my car to make sure I'm not dripping mascara, then head into the school. The woman who lets me in is Lisa, the administrative secretary. She's tall with short curly brown hair and a large smile. I wonder what she knows about Jacob, about us. I pass the manila envelope to her, and she takes out its contents and sets them on her desk. That's when I see the name again:

JACOB JOSEPH LEMAY.

I burst into tears. "I'm sorry," I gasp.

"That's okay," Lisa says, handing me a box of tissues. She knows. She offers me Donna's office to collect myself in because Donna is out. "Take all the time you need." I gratefully disappear into the office. I sit on the edge of a chair, pulling out tissue after tissue. Every time I think I'm done, the tears begin afresh. *She must be wondering what I'm doing already,* I think miserably.

Finally, it's evident that there will be no regaining control. But I can't stay here all day, so I exit. Lisa looks at me sympathetically as, mustering a smile, I tell her that if she needs any more information to please feel free to e-mail me at the address I've provided on the document. She smiles reassuringly. "He'll be okay here," she says. "We'll take good care of him, I promise. He'll be safe."

As the first day of camp approaches, Jacob's anxiety about which bathroom to use escalates. At the Purpose School, there were two unisex bathrooms, but at his new school building, where next week's camp takes place, there are separate boys' and girls' rooms.

Joe explains to Jacob that he can use the boys' room but that the urinal is not for him. That takes a little bit of diagramming and some awkwardness. I've talked to the camp director, a nurse named Mary Beth, who turns out to be both supportive and, to my surprise, knowledgeable about this topic. "Tell him not to worry about the urinals," she says. "The little kids don't use them anyway."

"But what if someone looks under the door?" Jacob asks, his eyes brimming with anxious tears. "They shouldn't," I say firmly. "They can get in trouble for doing that!" He's still worried. *Shouldn't* doesn't always translate into *won't;* he knows this as well as I do. "You can also use the bathroom in the nurse's office," I offer, knowing that this isn't a good solution. What would the other kids think when he didn't line up with them to go to the bathroom? Jacob was already so sensitive about not standing out. I decide to ask Jennifer Horton what to do. We have an appointment in her office for that afternoon.

I've left plenty of time for our drive to Jennifer's office, so Jacob and I have some choices on how to spend the extra time once we get there. He decides it would be best spent getting ice cream and I'm happy to comply; the day is warm, bordering on hot. I regret this decision when the store clerk hands Jacob a large scoop of Death by Chocolate that is probably highly caffeinated and definitely very, very messy. Oh, well.

"You look like a crime scene except with chocolate instead of blood," I tease him. Though we've got to get going, he's discovered a small water fountain on the walk to the car and he insists on walking along the rim. I look at him, balancing on the edge of the fountain, covered in so much chocolate that he reminds me of that *Peanuts* character Pig-Pen and I think, *How did I not notice this energy before? This is a boy, a normal boy.*

But while he's a normal boy, he's also an unusual boy, so we head off to see Jennifer.

I've spoken to Jennifer Horton but never met her, and she turns out to be a petite woman in her thirties with a light brown bob and clear grayish-blue eyes. She welcomes us into her office, and within moments, Jacob has explored it top to bottom and is excitedly planning the crafts he will do during the visit. She's got beads and pipe cleaners and Popsicle sticks and, of course, Scotch tape.

Soon, Jacob is happily gluing materials onto a piece of cardboard while I fill Jennifer in on the events of the past week. Then I go out to the waiting room to let Jacob and Jennifer talk.

"He seems to be doing well," she tells me after Jacob and I have switched places and he is in the chair outside the door. She shows me the pictures that Jacob has drawn for her, one of which is a stick figure with what looks like a short stack of pancakes teetering on its head. I realize with a smile that this is his "faux-hawk" hairdo.

"He's identifying fully as a boy, and he seems happy with the transition," she confirms. We talk about camp coming up and the concerns that Jacob has about the bathroom. Then she asks me how I'm doing. "You know . . ." I say, my voice wobbling as my words trail off. "This is the hardest time," she says. "It does get easier." "I'm looking forward to that," I say shakily.

Before we leave, Jennifer tells me she will write the requested letter to confirm Jacob's diagnosis of gender dysphoria for the school. It's unfortunate that they have asked for it, she adds, and it shouldn't be required. In fact, it's unfortunate that anything associated with being transgender is listed in the *Diagnostic and Statistical Manual* as a mental-health disorder at all, she says, because being transgender might be related to an anomaly in the endocrine system, although it can have psychological repercussions. I've read that before, I realize, in the words of Dr. Spack, the endocrinologist from Boston Children's Hospital.

Science has yet to catch up with this subject, Jennifer continues, and researchers are not fully certain why a person ends up with chromosomes and reproductive organs at odds with the way the brain's gender has developed, but it may have to do with hormones released during fetal development. "But without this diagnosis," she continues, "transgender people wouldn't have access to the life-affirming treatments that they need, including hormone therapy and, if and when needed, gender-confirmation surgery." She hopes that one day it will be better understood and properly classified. Though that's at the bottom of my list of concerns right now, I do too.

When I leave, I feel like we're on solid ground. We're getting the help we need, and we seem to be on the right track. Something, though, isn't sitting comfortably with me and I mull it over on the long ride home. It was something that Jennifer said when praising Joe and me for coming to terms with Jacob's need to transition; more accurately, it was something I saw in her eyes. "Not all parents are willing to even consider letting their kids transition," she said, her expression suddenly bleak, "and some of those kids aren't doing so well."

I reach my hand back to Jacob's car seat and say, "Hey, buddy, can you squeeze your mama's hand, please?" He obliges. *Don't let go, Jacob,* I think. "If you're ever upset about anything, or just feeling . . . sad or angry, promise me you'll come to me or Daddy to talk?" "Okay, Mama," he says, giving me a quizzical look before leaning toward the window again, closing his eyes as the breeze plays with his short-short hair and the sun warms his smiling face.

Jennifer was right. It does get easier. It even gets easier to talk to our friends about "our transition." Some of them are immediately and vociferously supportive; others ask probing questions first. I can tell they're not so sure about what they're hearing, and I'm not sure I blame them. If I had just heard about a transgender preschooler for the first time, I'd have had a hard time wrapping my head around it. I'm glad that they are asking questions, though, because that gives me room to answer them. It's the silence that's difficult to deal with.

Inside our family, things are getting easier as well.

Jacob is the clear beneficiary. He continues to blossom, to grow in confidence and emotional resilience, and only rarely, very rarely, does the hood come down again. He has taken to denying an existence before he was called Jacob. "You did know," he ac-

cuses us. "You knew I was a boy when I was born!" We are allowing him this redaction. These are things I am confident we will be
able to discuss openly when he has had more time to heal from
the suffering he has endured.

Ella, too, is healing from the loss of her sister. She has taken
on the mantle of "little mother" in our house, which can lead to
a fair bit of bossiness. Jennifer has pointed out that Ella is trying
to gain some control over a situation that has been outside of her
power. Jacob and his older sister have become attached at the hip.
They hold hands when they leave the house and frequently hug
each other spontaneously. They are constant playmates. There
are still moments when the sadness and the memories overwhelm
Ella and she asks for some time alone with me and cries in my
lap. Sometimes we take out her "birthday book," a photo story I
made for her second birthday, and we read about a sister named
Em. Then the book gets tucked away behind her bookshelf for the
next time she needs it.

Jacob has asked that we take down any photos of himself from
an earlier era. If he comes across one, he denies any connection
with it. At first, he wanted me to destroy the pictures, but I asked
that they be kept in the attic. For my sake, he agreed, allowing me
to retain my role as the keeper of memories while he has moved
on, shedding his old skin as he grows into something wonderful.

In a few months, Lucia, two years old, will barely remember
she used to have two sisters. In a way this is a blessing, and in another way, this is immeasurably sad. I will ask her one day if she
remembers a girl named Em, and she will shake her head.

My mother writes me an e-mail a few weeks after she returns to
England, asking me how the therapy sessions are going. There are
a number of bullet points, things she would like to know. At the
end is a request for *what you would like to expect from me.* The
wording and the tone seem to indicate a continued ambivalence,
but it's a huge step forward, and for this I am grateful.

What I need, I tell her on the phone later, is for her to respect the use of Jacob's name and pronouns and to learn as much as she can about the subject of transgender children. I offer to send her articles, even books, but she shies away. "I'll read them next time I come to visit." "It's a marathon, not a sprint," Joe reminds me when I express my disappointment. We are in this for the long haul, and I need to be patient. My mother still leads two lives, one as a devout Orthodox Jewish wife and the other as a grandmother who loves her transgender grandchild.

My brother, Uriyah, who upon first meeting Em had declared our middle child a kindred spirit, has welcomed Jacob with open arms. They have a bond that is deeper than uncle and nephew. There is a way in which they understand each other, emotionally and temperamentally. When he hears about Jacob's transition, my brother books a flight from Israel for the fall. He will sweep into our house, casting his zany energy and childlike goodness into every corner.

The end of summer is as glorious as its beginning.

Ella is heading to kindergarten, the thought of which is bittersweet for me. Our town throws a celebration for the entire incoming kindergarten population, a carnival of sorts in a local park. As I'm wiping ices goo from Jacob's fingers, I feel a tap on my shoulder. It's Christine, a mom from Purpose School.

We chat for a minute and then she looks down at Jacob and says, "Em, are you in the Sun Room this year?"

This is the moment I've been dreading, the moment that was bound to happen, the one I thought I was prepared for. Now I feel a sense of panic, and on autopilot I say, all peppy: "Actually, it's Jacob now. And we're not going to the Purpose next year; he'll be at the ECC." Before I can get a grip on myself, I begin to cry. My face is still smiling broadly but the tears are spilling down my cheeks. Christine's mouth is slightly agape, and she looks concerned for me. It's not her fault I'm crying but I can't seem to hold back. I also don't want Jacob to see me crying; what would he think? I am not sad that he is my child. I am blessed.

So I give a wave of my hand and back away. Jacob asks if he can go to the ices cart for seconds and I gratefully say yes. Over the next few minutes I try my hardest to regain my composure, standing with Lucia in the face-painting line, but I cannot. Finally, I text Joe, half a football field away: *I can't stay. I'll explain later. I'm sending the kids to you.*

I find our car on a side street and curl up in the passenger seat, hugging my knees to my chest. That's where my family finds me later. Joe quietly buckles the kids in. "What's wrong with Mama?" Ella asks. "She's not feeling well," Joe says softly. "Feel better, Mama!" Jacob reaches over and pats the top of my head. "Thank you, sweet boy," I say. "I know I will."

And I do.

The next time grief creeps up on me, I go up to Jacob and give him a hug. I look in his eyes to see if the hood is still up, and it is. Every so often I ask him: "Is this still what you want?" "Yes," he says, and eventually, "Stop asking me."

It is August 24. Jacob and I walk hand in hand to his new school to visit the classroom where he will start prekindergarten next week. He's wearing his new gray-and-blue doggy shoes, the ones with the puppy face on the tops, and the red-and-white-striped shirt with his name emblazoned on the front: JACOB. He's taken to introducing himself, and then, just in case you *didn't get it,* he will spell it for you: J-a-c-o-b. He's grinning and swinging the box that his shoes came in, made to look like a miniature dog crate. We're almost late because he has to stop for treasures whenever he spots them. Today's haul so far: a penny, a few inches of electrical wire, and a bright yellow flower.

When we get to the classroom, we see the hooks lined up outside with each child's name on a laminated place card. We look for his name and when he finds it, JACOB, he points, excited. "Look,

Mama, it's my name!" Ms. Krystina and Ms. Lianne, his new teachers, are there to greet him. He ducks his head shyly, looking away at first, but then his eyes dart back with curiosity. He slowly lets go of my hand and begins to roam, examining each corner of the colorful, toy-filled room, and when he finds his name on a tag hanging from a lanyard and his very own cubby, he grabs my hand to show me, pleased as punch.

The first day of school has arrived. The kids wake up to the little chalkboards I have decorated for them, celebrating this milestone. Jacob's board has his name written in large chalk letters, along with *First day of Pre-K,* and the date, September 2, 2014. I've found and tacked on some treasures of my own: some coins, a few mini-carabiners, and a plastic yellow googly-eyes ring. He loves the board and prances around with it, so excited that I can barely get him to stand still for the picture. After dropping Ella off at kindergarten, Lucia and I walk Jacob to school. As we get close to the door of his classroom, he suddenly turns to me and says with a smile, "Okay, Mom, I can go by myself now."

My heart gives a squeeze. "One more minute," I ask of him, and so he gets his lanyard with the name tag and stands in the doorway, all cocky, as I snap a last picture and grab a last kiss. Then he turns and runs into the room, ready to start a new day.

"First days are hard," I tell Lucia, swinging her up into my arms. She doesn't ask me why I'm crying, which is a good thing. I wouldn't know where to begin.

Epilogue

Every mother can easily imagine losing a child. Mother-hood is always half loss anyway. The three-year-old is lost at five, the five-year-old at nine. We consort with ghosts, even as we sit and eat with, scold and kiss, their current corporeal forms.   — KAREN JOY FOWLER, *Black Glass*

IN THE EARLY HOURS OF MARCH 22, 2016, I WOKE UP TO discover that district schools had been delayed for two hours due to an overnight snowstorm. I promptly rolled over and fell back into a deep sleep.

I'm on a large lawn in front of an unfamiliar home; it's covered with bountiful piles of amber and orange leaves. A small fig-ure stands at a distance of twenty yards or so. It is Jacob, I see. When I blink and look again, I realize it's not Jacob but Em, dressed in her rose-pink puffer coat and metallic brown Mary Janes looking as I remember her at the age of two and a half, poised on the knife's edge of her journey.

As I watch, a powerful gust of wind picks up the pile of leaves and swirls them above her head in a golden cloud. She laughs in delight, dancing with her arms outstretched to grab them.

"Em!" I call, wanting her to see me and run into my arms. The dancing figure ignores me. *"Em!"* I yell louder. She doesn't turn to me. By now I am yelling as loud as I can: "Em! Em!" She continues her dance with the leaves, reaching down, grabbing handfuls, and tossing them in the air, jumping up to catch them as they descend. "Em." I begin to sob. "Em! I love you, Em! I love you."

I need her to hear me, to understand that I haven't abandoned her, that she isn't forgotten, that she had been and would always be loved. But no matter how loud I scream, she does not look up from her happy play. *Is she a ghost?* I wonder. *Am I?*

I woke up convulsed in grief.

The pall lingered the entire day and into the next, leaving me strangely exhausted. I tried to brush it off. My sadness felt like a betrayal of Jacob's happiness, of all we had fought and would continue to fight for. I had told this story dozens of times already; Em wasn't real, Jacob was — and always had been.

I shared my grief with an online support group of parents and caregivers of transgender kids. I admitted to the struggle I was having. I had forgotten that my brother had joined the group too. He wrote to me immediately in a private message: *I think that "she" did exist; at least, she was for that brief moment in time the brave little "girl" who was just discovering that "she" was Jacob and getting ready to fight for it. They both existed — you haven't lost anyone.*

My brother was right, I realized. If we erased Em, then we risked erasing the courageous and painful path of discovery that brought us our son. Em is the oracle and the road. She lives in my memory, while he lives in my arms, growing and becoming more magnificent by the day.

And that is all right. That is as it should be.

I don't need all the answers; I must learn to walk forward without them. Neither can I peer into the future, if I wished to. I will leave the door open for possibilities, even, perhaps, for some grace. I have him today, and today is the only day.

A Note on "A Letter to My Son Jacob on His 5th Birthday"

It is not your job to complete the work, but neither are you excused from it.   — *Pirkei Avot (Ethics of Our Fathers)*

DECEMBER 30, 2014, WAS ONE OF THOSE PERFECT WINter days. The kids and I had risen late, still basking in the post-holiday glow of a wonderful Christmas. After a morning of puttering about, I curled up on the couch and opened my laptop to scan the day's news.

TRANSGENDER TEEN KILLED IN TRAFFIC AFTER WRITING SUICIDE LETTER.

The headlines were everywhere, along with a photo of a gamine girl with large, haunted brown eyes. Her name was Leelah Alcorn; she was seventeen years old, had lived in Ohio, and had died there when she had stepped onto the highway and into the path of an oncoming truck. By the time I reached the middle of the article, I had retreated to my bedroom to hide the tears that ran down my face. *What compels a child to do this?* I asked myself. Attached to the article was a link to Leelah's suicide note. I soon understood.

I understood not only the harsh reality of a transgender child living with unaffirming parents but also the rare nature of the warm and safe little bubble that our family had been sheltering in. The story in and of itself was tragic enough, but it was the comments section to these articles that sounded an alarm for me.

Public reactions to the story of Leelah's suicide varied wildly. Many were horrified that her parents had taken the route of so-called conversion therapy, a coercive and shaming practice where Leelah had been told that being transgender was a sin, a selfish affront to God. Others thought that these actions were well within the purview of parental rights, some going so far as to say that Leelah's transgender identity was a mental disease that her parents had correctly tried to "cure." There seemed to be widespread confusion about what *transgender* actually meant.

And time and again I read this baffling assertion: *God does not make mistakes.* Somehow, while reveling in the infinite variations in every species that live on this remarkable planet, there were those who could not conceive of transgender people as a part of God's plan. Some called them evil, a sign of the decline of man or the end of days. Others, less theologically inclined, seemed to be making a chilling case for eugenics, implying that, somehow, the death of transgender people was *a good thing.*

I had had enough. I closed my laptop, wiped away my tears, and headed downstairs to play with the kids. As we sat around a board game, I stole glances at Jacob, lying on his stomach on the rug, wearing his pajamas, his fleece-encased feet waving back and forth in the air, the dinosaurs on them bobbing. I shook my head. *How?* How was it possible that these precious children could be considered evil or even deeply flawed? How could I make others see what I saw when I looked at Jacob?

Leelah Alcorn had concluded her suicide note with these words:

The only way I will rest in peace is if one day transgender people aren't treated the way I was, they're treated like humans, with valid feelings and human rights ... My death needs to mean something. My death needs to be counted in the number of transgender people who commit suicide this year. I want someone to look at that number and say, "that's fucked up" and fix it. Fix society. Please.

It *was* fucked up, and that day I began to wonder what we could do to fix it — could our experience provide the message that there was another way? I had thought about sharing our story earlier, knowing how important those few examples out there had been for us, but I had felt comfortable in my privacy and perhaps, I now realized, unjustifiably complacent.

I asked Jacob if I could write about our experiences as a family. I explained that there were children out there in the world like himself, children who were transgender but whose parents did not understand that they needed to be allowed to live as they truly were. "Should we tell them?" I asked. "Yes," he answered. I was proud that he was willing to think about others, but that did not remove the possibility that eventually, growing up, he might regret this decision and wish to remain hidden, or stealth, about his past. I held on to our story.

With each passing day, more stories came out in the news. I had new names and faces to put to the horrifying statistics on suicides, and I learned how unsafe many transgender people were at home and in their communities, how they were forced into hiding to keep their jobs, their families, even, at times, their lives. The feeling of urgency grew. What kind of world would Jacob inherit if no one spoke up? Was there any way that I could help others see people like Leelah and Jacob as being who they were *meant to be?*

By early February, with the words of Hillel the Elder, one of the Talmud's greatest sages, in my head, I sat down and began to write. He had defined what I now think of as the advocate's creed: "If I am not for myself, who will be for me? Yet if I am *only* for myself, then what am I? And if not now — when?"

On February 24, 2015, the morning of Jacob's fifth birthday, with tears of trepidation and much hope, I posted my longer-than-usual birthday letter to Jacob on Medium.com.

My hope has since grown stronger than my fears. I continue to believe in the goodness of people and that sharing our story may contribute to a world where children can live as they are and become the adults they were meant to be. We are all capable of seeing the worth in one another's lives.

Sometimes all we need is to be invited in.

Acknowledgments

And Rabbi Elazar said that Rabbi Hanina said: "Anyone who attributes words in the name of he who spoke them brings deliverance to the world" (Babylonian Talmud, Tractate Megillah).

The sages, we are told, derived this lesson from Queen Esther, for had she not credited her Uncle Mordecai for discovering a plot against the King of Persia, he would not have been in the position to save the Jewish people. I have always felt that this lesson—the importance of proper attribution—could well be applied to crediting others for their *deeds,* not only for their words.

To that end, it is with deep gratitude that I thank the individuals who brought this book to life:

To my literary agent David McCormick, thank you for reaching out to me in the belief that I had a story that needed telling, and thank you for supporting my vision for this book.

To Susan Canavan, thank you for being my champion at Houghton Mifflin Harcourt, and for the opportunity to bring this project into the world.

To Alysia Abbott, thank you for accepting a panicked novice into your Master Memoir class when I found myself with a book contract but no idea of how to write a book. Your guidance gave me confidence in myself as a writer and helped me find the unique structure of this memoir.

To Nicole Angeloro, my editor, most intuitive and compassionate guide, thank you for your light touch and for appreciating at every level what I was trying to convey. I have felt throughout that my words were in the hands of a friend.

Thank you to Tracy Roe, my copyeditor, not merely for working your magic, but for creating a fun and edifying experience of the process.

A huge thank you to the excellent and passionate production, marketing, and sales teams at HMH, including Lisa Glover, Liz Anderson, and Taryn Roeder.

Beyond the scope of this book, to all the advocates that have lifted me on your shoulders so that I could stand up for my son, to all those parents and caregivers that have shared this road with me, and especially to my chosen family on Human Rights Campaign's Parents for Transgender Equality Council: There is nowhere I would rather be than by your side. You are my heroes.

Last but never least, to my family and friends who cheered me on, provided space for me to embark on this adventure, and held me in your arms and hearts as I struggled to bring this story to life—I owe you the biggest debt of gratitude. This book is your effort, as well as mine. I hope I have made you proud.

A LETTER TO MY SON JACOB
ON HIS 5TH BIRTHDAY

It was a frigid New England February day, much like this one, when we were first introduced. Of course, I imagined that I knew something about you beforehand, by the way you moved and kicked and somersaulted in my belly — by your satisfied silences and painful protests. The only "real information" I had was that you appeared to be healthy, and that you were a girl.

I prepared your sister and our home for your advent: Another crib with attractive floral bedding, matching dresses, spring bonnets in duplicate, and coordinating bathing suits for the summer. Your dad protested all this unnecessary expenditure, but I slyly reasoned that birthdays a half year apart meant that hand-me-downs would be seasonably unsuited. And so, I dreamed, and I clicked, and adorable and trendy confections in pink and purple and mint and magenta arrived at our doorstep. It was folly, but it was fun.

When we finally met, you were momentarily silent. You took a pause to adjust to your surroundings before announcing your presence as I anxiously strained the only autonomously movable part of my body, my neck, to catch a glimpse of you around the blue curtain where the surgeon had extracted you from my womb. The surgery had been painful, the anesthetic insufficient, but all that was forgotten as every fiber of my being was focused on your unseeable presence. And then I heard you. You didn't whimper, you didn't cry, you didn't squall. You roared: "Here I am!" Soon after, as you lay swaddled near my head in a white towel with pink and blue stripes, I was able to gaze into your eyes through a happy haze and introduce myself in return. "Hello, princess," I said. "I'm your mama."

Your dad often recounts the moment he held you first. Your hearty, solid body, your pumping fists and legs and his surprised thought, This one is a *different* model, comparing you to your dainty sister. In the weeks after, we would share all the funny and not-so-funny moments with our friends: the attempted VBAC, the ensuing complications, and that hilarious moment when the anesthesiologist, from her poor vantage point at the head of the gurney, called out, "It's a boy!" Hilarious because you were not, most definitely *not, a boy.*

What you most definitely were was a spirited little thing. As you grew, you had a way of fearlessly barreling around and into things that earned you the nickname "Honey Badger." For mild plagiocephaly (flat head), you wore a bright pink football helmet for several months before your first birthday. We assigned your audacity to the fact that the helmet protected you from the consequences of most of your escapades.

• • •

You had a curiously deep voice and a blithely cheerful personality. As our second child, you benefited from the benign inattention of more relaxed parenting. However, despite its charms, your "knock-aboutedness" began to concern us as time went on. You lacked coordination, constantly falling off and into things, sometimes seeming to deliberately throw yourself into the couch or floor. We contacted our local Early Intervention specialists and after a lengthy assessment you received services for sensory perception disorder, a minor hiccup in an otherwise pristine medical record.

When your baby sister came along you were still in diapers. You welcomed her with generosity, with no significant jealousy or displacement. You three were so close, so affectionate to each other. Our family was complete. Three healthy, bright, beautiful girls; we had spun the wheel of fortune and won the jackpot. There were no clouds on the horizon and the sun shone in perpetuity. Of course, I exaggerate. There were tussles and tiffs, bumps and bruises, reflux and influenza, terrible twos and tormentuous threes. But for the most part, I was grateful beyond measure that our lives were so lovely, so ordinarily good. I enjoyed posting pictures of my darling daughters, now dressed in triplicate, to Facebook, and I reveled in the compliments we received.

As you crested the middle of your second year you developed a curious habit, a persistent routine. You started to change your clothes repeatedly, maybe ten to twelve times throughout the day. I reacted with both annoyance and mounting concern. Your pile of sartorial rejects meant exponentially more laundry. *Goodbye, matching dresses.* My concern was that your habit was tinged with compulsion. When you woke up crying at two a.m. one night, begging to be allowed to change into a new outfit, I called your pediatrician. Since you did not display other signs of compulsiveness, we associated your desire to change with your general sensory-seeking behavior. You were changing clothes in order to feel the fabrics rub against your skin. Children with a sensory deficit often seek sensations because they do not experience them to the full extent that the rest of us do in the ordinary course of our day.

This theory held water for only so long, for soon after you started preschool, at 2.9 years, you became attached to one *particular* garment — a short-sleeved cornflower-blue turtleneck sweater with a brown dog on the front that you wore for the next six months with few exceptions. You wore your Doggy Sweater day and, sometimes, if you won the battle, night. You wore it over your tutu to ballet class and over your holiday dress to see Santa at the mall. I ordered several more on eBay. Again, I cursed silently as I increased the frequency of my laundry to accommodate your needs. Since the weather was chilly we had a temporary reprieve from having to figure out how the Doggy Sweater would work on top of swimwear. I decided to fight that battle come spring. But by the time spring arrived, our struggles over the Doggy Sweater would seem trivial compared to something new and far more alarming.

In the interim between the advent of the Doggy Sweater and your third birthday, you set a stake in the ground and declared yourself a boy. At first, we bantered with the word "pretend." We explained, and you acknowledged, that you were *pretending* to be a boy. At preschool you tentatively assigned yourself to the male faction of the class and you were told that you were pretending and that pretending was fine as long as it didn't interfere with the workings of the school day. When *I* was told that *you* were told that you were pretending, I nodded and acquiesced. It made sense. This new thing was foreign, and it was troublesome, and, above all, it seemed unhealthy. *Another obsession. Another whim.*

Whim or not, our home soon became a battleground over gender with you constantly pulling me, your dad, and your older sister into unwilling skirmishes. You would glare at us with your huge defiant brown eyes and say, *"I am a boy,"* and I, a great believer in the principle of the inverse proportionality of parental disapproval to a child's sedition, gave little protest. I would sigh: "That's fine, sweetheart. You can be what you want to be in our home."

I kept your sister off your back when she protested your apparent disregard for basic biology (which we explained to you). We started to have discussions about the narrow-mindedness of gender expectations: pink and blue, dolls and trains. We assumed that you were stating a preference for things *un-girlie.* We couldn't comprehend that you could even conceive of what gender was when you had barely begun preschool. So we told you to go ahead and wear boy clothes, and that gray was a perfectly acceptable favorite color for a three-year-old girl, and that yes, if it was important to you, we would call you Jackson or Max or Jake or whatever the *nom du jour* was.

You never asked us to call you anything but Em, your birth name, in the public arena. But our soothing acceptance never seemed to be enough. You became watchful and guarded at school and in public. At home, there were many occasions that you let go, hitting, kicking, and punching, wailing and screaming: "Don't talk to me!" "Get away from me," and, frequently, "You ruin *everything!*" Your anger seemed atypical, in excess of the ordinary emotional vicissitudes of being three.

You had always been jolly and loving as an infant but now I was the only one you would kiss and hug — you frequently exploded if anyone else tried to show you affection. Sometimes even with me, if I casually brushed your hair with my hand or gave you an unsolicited hug, you would recoil and bark angrily at me. And that was another thing — your new, quite unsociable habit of pretending you were a dog when people addressed you. You would lope around in a circle, as if chasing an invisible tail, tongue hanging out, saying, "Aarf! Aarrrf!," leaving us to explain your odd behaviors. To be fair, we had many peaceful moments and it wasn't all bad. Sometimes you relaxed, and your beautiful happy nature shone through. Those moments were a blessing, a dream — and I cherished every one, bracing for the next upset.

I knew that being "*as* a boy" was important to you. I knew little of the word *transsexual.* I had first encountered it as a young adult, riveted to the dark thriller *Silence of the Lambs,* in which the antagonist, Buffalo Bill, skinned his victims in order to create for himself a "woman" body suit. I was aware that there was a newer term — *transgender* — and that, in my way of thinking at the time, younger people could be "afflicted" with this too. It was weird; it was beyond the pale: it was, to my current shame, slightly grotesque. I did not truly believe that it applied to my beautiful, round-faced, bright-eyed, innocent preschooler.

But then one day in the late fall of your third year I attended a routine parent-teacher conference. Your teacher expressed her concern in hesitant tones: "You know, Mrs. Lemay, has it ever occurred to you, is it *possible*, that Em may *actually believe* she is a boy?" You had just learned how to write your name, all jumbled letters and fat precious pen strokes. We were so proud of you. You, however, did not share our pride. Apparently, when required to write your name, you would comply, but then immediately cross it out. This obliteration of the marker of your given identity spoke volumes about how you perceived or, rather, refused to perceive yourself.

Reality, which had been hovering just out of conscious reach, struck. My stomach churned. I tasted the ash in my mouth (I never understood that expression before). Tears stung as they welled up in my eyes. I tried to stem the flow out of embarrassment, wiping my eyes and nose on my sleeve, standing in the middle of the bare auditorium, no box of tissues in sight. *Not my little girl. Not happening. Please wake up.*

I stumbled through the next days in a painful haze. We were a few weeks shy of winter break and I reached out to a friend of ours, a therapist who had worked with at-risk LGBTQ youth. As we stood doling out cheddar cheese crackers and pretzels to our raucous offspring on a playdate she confirmed my fears — we should consider that you might be transgender.

I pressed her to tell me what that *meant*. Not the dictionary definition, but what the *implications* were: to your future, to your physical and mental well-being, and to our family. I heard words like *outcomes* and *high-risk* and *medical intervention* and statistics like "over 40 percent attempted suicide," and my world started to unravel. She tried to temper these dark things with words of encouragement and moral support; however, it was impossible to process any further. The blood was rushing too strongly in my head as my heart was being carried downstream with the vestiges of my fantasy of a wonderful life for you.

I freely write about the negative emotions that the possibility of your transgender nature evoked with regret, but no shame. By now, you know how proud I am of you, how happy I am to be your mother, and how I perceive your unique nature as a precious if puzzling gift. At the time, though, it was a devastating blow.

I began to grieve, waking up in the early-morning hours biting my pillow to silence the sobs, my sheets bathed in the stink of bad dreams. I was losing you, my precious daughter. You were in the room next to me in peaceful childhood slumber, but you were most assuredly slipping from my grasp, hurtling into a void of social rejection, physical mutilation, and suicidal depression. I felt helpless. I began, as many parents do when faced with a child that has unique needs, to ask, "What is the treatment?" by which I meant: *What is the cure?*

I called the Gender Management Clinic at Boston Children's Hospital, and although you were too young for the program, they referred me to a therapist who had experience with transgender youth. She was not covered by our insurance at the time but was willing to speak with me at length on the phone. She told me that many children who present as gender-non-conforming (running the gamut from tomboy/effeminate to truly transgender) revert to their assigned, or born, gender upon reaching puberty. *Oh, phew.* What a relief. "Keep things fluid," she further advised. "Try not to box your daughter into making a choice either way. Just show support." All good advice and I was temporarily buoyed by the hopeful news. To my desperately seeking ears, this meant you might well be going through a phase. *How wonderful.*

And so we left things. You asked to cut your hair and we gave you a sweet pixie cut. *Keep it fluid.* It was all about compromise those days. Slowing your inexorable march toward all things boy. For your dance recital, your instructor graciously allowed you to wear a tux with a bright pink bow tie and cummerbund to match the sequined tutus your classmates wore. Your wardrobe was by this time mostly boy clothes. I say *mostly* because I snuck in girl clothes in dark colors . . . they had tiny embellishments, embroidered hearts and bows that reminded me that one day, you could be my little girl again. In my eyes, they also served to ward off the questions I imagined I would have to answer about your appearance to those who knew you as a girl.

For a while you tolerated this deceit, but you soon became quite canny at the subtleties of gendered clothing. You would reject the white Peter Pan collar in favor of the crisp button-down. A-line shirts and ruched sleeves disappeared from your drawers, along with velour and Lycra. Hanukkah and Christmas came and went, and you received superhero action figures and Matchbox cars from us and your wonderfully perceptive Grammy and purple pajamas and pink pencil sets from well-meaning loved ones who didn't understand the extent of your preferences. You jumped for joy with the one and wrathfully rejected the other. Even I still clung to the belief that if you could only see the gray areas between the pink and blue you might find yourself at home somewhere in between. Hence the Katniss Everdeen doll that made its way into your heap of Christmas loot. I still recall your look of utter disdain.

It was soon February again and we celebrated your fourth birthday. And you grew taller, wiser, and accomplished many things. Over the winter break I had tentatively broached the topic: Would you be happier with a boyish/unisex name at school? You categorically refused. Your answer gave me a covert thrill of hope. I dared to dream that you were not fully committed to being a boy and that you would be one of the preponderance of kids who "figured it out" because their parents didn't make a huge deal out of it. For use at home, you settled with us on a name that sounded similar to your given name in order to avoid the confusion of the daily merry-go-round of arbitrary boy names. We urged you to choose one, and you chose the name Mica.

It was enough — for a while.

But I knew in my mother's heart that you were not truly happy. Not like your sisters. Not like the unburdened joy that I thought you ought to have felt coming from a warm loving home with plenty of affection, positive experiences, and toys galore. There was an un-childlike, persistent sadness that lay about you like a pall in those years that should have been so magical.

You see, I believe that what had happened while I was wasting my energy hoping that you would make peace with your biology was that we had become unwitting contributors to your fracture into two different people: Mica and Em. Home and school. Boy and girl. Unguarded and guarded. Open and shut. Reality (yours) and role-play (ours).

On the home front things were most certainly getting "better"— or should I say "easier"? Your tantrums subsided as we managed to convince you that we were truly okay with you being a boy and that we believed that what you felt about your identity and your expression of it was your choice. Your sister had become a huge support in this regard. Not many five-year-olds could act with the grace and compassion that she did (and still does). She stopped teasing you about not being a "real boy" and accepted our mantra that "what you are in your heart and your mind is far more important than what you are in your body." The hard knot of your anger started to dissolve. We all basked in this momentary détente.

In the early spring of your fourth year we went on a glorious trip to Disney World where you were the only kid we saw in a Prince Charming costume. You glowed when strangers stopped and remarked, "Isn't he adorable!" and "What a handsome little man!" and we didn't correct people, because we knew how much you enjoyed being "mistaken" for a boy. The status quo was an okay place to be.

But back at school, activities, and in our community at large you remained markedly withdrawn. Our reports from your teachers were that, if prompted, you joined in group activities. You rarely, if ever, engaged your peers in free play. The day you hugged your teacher for the first time brought her to tears. I believe you occupied a special place in her heart and that she felt protective of you. I am so grateful for the good people in our lives.

Despite the fact that you were beginning to relax in the classroom, you continued to erect walls between yourself and others. The barking and loping persisted, and always there was the hood that would come over your eyes that said *shutting down now*. In my ignorance I even wondered at times whether you were touched by a mild form of autism, but it seemed incongruent that this behavior turned on and off as if by a switch.

It was that playdate at Papa Gino's that shuttled me right over the edge from *keeping it fluid* to *the time is now*. To be truthful, there were many small fissures forming in the Theory of Status Quo as I have now come to see it. There was your tearful sister begging me to force you into a dress so that "people will treat her nicer." There was the sweet little girl at a birthday party that asked me about you: "What is *that*? Is *that* a *boy* or is *that* a *girl*?" There were the burgeoning signs of dysphoria ("What's wrong with my body? Why did God make me like this? Is He stupid?").

But what finally broke me from my unhappy trance was nothing more complicated than a post-last-day-of-school pizza party where I got a chance to see you interact with your classmates outside of a structured setting. Everyone was there, the boys, the girls, and most of the moms. You sat down at the edge of a gaggle of girls and tucked into your slice. No one jostled you in friendly banter, no one yelled, "Come on, Em! Let's run to the end of the restaurant and back!" The happy little bodies were in constant locomotion, stepping around you and over you as you sat staring at your pizza. Then you looked up at a group of boys being disciplined by their frustrated moms for running amok: "Sit down, Jack! Behave, Grady!" And the expression on your face skewered me. It was a hunger that I had never seen before. You weren't confused. You knew where you belonged. You just didn't know how to get there. What if it was *I* who was responsible for showing you the way?

School was officially out for the year. You were signed up for the next year. Another year, deposit down, of living two lives. *Open/shut, boy/girl.* I watched you carefully during the next week while you enjoyed a camp run at your preschool, and I thought and I weighed, and I deliberated and I doubted, until a million possible futures nearly drove me to distraction. *What if?* Your dad and I talked long into the evenings after you had gone to bed and in the mornings before we emerged from ours. A video had gone viral in the weeks before. A slide show of a transgender boy, not much older than you, whose loving California family had supported his public transition. We wondered if seeing the pictures of this boy who was so obviously happy in his "new skin" could make you believe in the possibility of your own fulfillment.

It was Friday, in the evening after your last day of preschool camp when we called you upstairs into your dad's office. We told you we had something for you to see and so you sat, engulfed in your dad's big black swivel chair as he cued the video on his laptop. I translated the words into "kidspeak" as they began to flit across the screen, accompanied by wonderful, endearing pictures. You viewed intently and solemnly as young Ryland Whittington was transformed from a beautiful little girl with golden locks into a handsome smiling boy in a buzzcut and tuxedo. When the video ended you asked to watch it again. Then you sat staring at your hands. We asked you what you thought about the boy and you shrugged, stonefaced. The walls you had erected were made of hardier stuff than we'd expected. But the moment was now. All three of us in this room, your palpable pain, the resolution we needed to help you find.

So I got down on my knees and took your soft, still baby-like little hands in mine. I asked you to look at me, but when you lifted your beautiful gaze to mine, I was momentarily speechless. I rallied: "*I believe you,*" I said, and I didn't bother to wipe the tears with my sleeve this time. "*We believe you.* All we want is for you to be happy, but *you* need to help *us* understand what will make you happy." Your dad knelt down next to you too. "Do you want to be a boy all the time like that boy we showed you?" Your eyes filled immediately. "I can't," you responded with a quivering lip. "I *have* to be Em at school and Mica at home."

So we told you. We told you about the choices, any of which you could make — or not. We told you that these choices were yours. Among which, you could continue at your school as Em. Or you could go there next year with any new identity, and finally, more radical yet, we could find you somewhere to start anew, to simply be the boy you had insisted for so long that you were. You paused a long while. I didn't know if you could do it. I didn't know if you had the faith in us to tell us what you truly wanted. I didn't know if you could imagine a future where you were whole — one identity, body and mind. You broke the silence. "I want to go to a new school. I want to be a boy *always*. I want to be a boy named Jacob."

Jacob, my love. It's been nine months and change since that fateful Friday and so much has transpired to make us believe that the journey we are taking together is the one we need to be on. It's been tough, make no mistake, and solving your more immediate identity crisis did not resolve all the latent feelings of shame and sadness that you have suffered. But the powerful effect of your transformation was almost immediately felt by all who knew you and loved you.

Within days of beginning life anew as Jacob you began to stand up straight and look people in the eye. You stopped barking like a dog and running for cover. In allowing your transition, we were only hoping to help your spirit survive. We did not expect the seismic shift in your personality that we experienced. You cracked your first real joke within a week, took a fresh interest in learning your alphabet (ironic, since school was out), and so much more. You started to cuddle and kiss, laugh and sing — and the dam just broke. You talked and talked and talked as if someone had taken a muzzle off your mouth. You took up hobbies, collecting anything and everything you found that piqued your interest (mostly detritus: scraps, stones, and screws you picked up off the street, to my chagrin). That summer, the world opened up its treasures to you.

Your dad and I were astounded, delighted, and profoundly gratified. These positive experiences were crucial for us, because those early days were laden with fear. We were always double-, triple-, quadruple-guessing our decisions, approaching each "re-introduction" with trepidation. It all seemed so fragile. We fretted: Who would break your trust? Who would clip your wings? Who would sneer or goggle or laugh, sending you running back for cover? But you were strong, not fragile. You were brave, not weak.

Together we weathered the firsts. The first time you wrote your name, the first time I did — for you, a triumphant experience; for me, accompanied by a flood of tears. The first time I asked someone to call you Jacob and, finally, the first time that you did. Your first Christmas acknowledged as a boy. You confessed afterward that you had half expected Santa would forget and bring you Em's presents. *Oh, baby.* The first public announcement, followed by a deluge of love and support from beloved family and friends — their support carried us and continues to carry us. The first week of the new school (you were obsessed about the bathrooms for the longest time) and the first time we ran into someone from your old school (it was awkward; we survived).

Jacob, my love, it is *you* that have transitioned *us* to a life less ordinary and so much more meaningful than it ever would have been.

Thank you deeply for your sacred trust. The mystery that is you may never be amenable to a full resolution. I don't know what's beyond the next bend in the road, but I am no longer afraid.

I believe in the goodness of people. And I believe in your ability to dispel much of the ignorance and intolerance in those you may encounter. I look at how fine a human being you are becoming — far beyond my meager original intentions — and I know that the future is bright for you. I am no longer afraid.

And it is because I no longer fear the outcomes, the medical interventions, the bigotry, that I will not be filing this birthday letter in a box in our attic with those of earlier years. Rather, momentarily, I will set these words free — relinquishing my control over their trajectory and destination. Their intent is to provide comfort and strength to another mother or father with an aching heart. To provide this message: It doesn't get *better.* It gets *awesome.*

For I have seen and wish to share *remarkable things.* In your early days as Jacob, I saw the most authentic parts, in the deepest reaches of you, begin to unfold. I saw you take your first huge breaths. I saw the clouds above your head scatter and run. At first there was a silence, as you paused to take in the new world around you, and then you roared: *I am here!*

It was then that I realized that we had indeed met before but that truly I had not recognized you that first time. It was then that my grief began to depart as I knew in my soul that you had *always* been my son, Jacob.

And so *always,* my love,
Mom